Published by:

Lokesh Thani

SPORTS PUBLICATIONS

H.O. 4264/3, Ansari Road, Darya Ganj, New Delhi-110002
B.O. WP-474, Ist Floor, Shiv Market, Ashok Vihar, Delhi-52
Phones: 23290142, 27241050,
(R) 27562163, (M) 9868028838
E-mail: sportspublication1@rediffmail.com
Website: *www.sportsbookshouse.com*

.S.B.N. - 81-87818-68-9

RINTED IN INDIA 2004

er Typeset by:

IN MEDIA GRAPHICS

/40-A, Lawrence Road, (Keshav Puram),
Delhi-110035 Ph.: 27183573, (M) 9811430646

d by:

DEMATRAM PRESS

ur, Delhi

Rs. 4,200/- (In 5 Vol.)

ENCYCLOPAEDI
OF EDUCATION
TERMS

(In 5 Vol.)

Edited & Compiled by

Ekta Thani, Rohit Shar
Anoop Jain, Mohit Sharma, K
C.H. Judd, & L.B. Ear

Vol. V

SPORTS PUBL

4264/3, Ansari Road, Da
Ph.: 23290142, 272410

P
A
No
or
ph
wr
Las
JA
B-4
New
Printe
BAN
Mauj
Price:

VOL. V

PART 7

TEACHING CHILDREN TO STUDY

CONTENTS

PART 8

GENETIC PSYCHOLOGY

CONTENTS

I

THE NATURE OF LOGICAL STUDY

1. *The universal necessity for study*

THROUGH the whole course of our lives we are confronted with situations the successful mastery of which compels mental effort. Whether the tasks laid upon us are assigned in school or outside of school, and whether we wish to do so or not, we must struggle mentally. In the sense that it gives us frequent occasion to study, life itself may be called a school. In this school all are enrolled, from the youngest child to the wisest philosopher. Whittier indicated a few of the out-of-school lessons in his poem, "The Barefoot Boy": —

"Knowledge never learned of schools,
Of the wild bee's morning chase,
Of the wild-flower's time and place,
Flight of fowl and habitude
Of the tenants of the wood;
How the tortoise bears his shell,
How the woodchuck digs his cell,
And the ground-mole sinks his well;

TEACHING CHILDREN TO STUDY

How the robin feeds her young,
How the oriole's nest is hung;
Where the whitest lilies blow,
Where the freshest berries grow,
Where the ground-nut trails its vine,
Where the wood-grape's clusters shine;
Of the black wasp's cunning way,
Mason of his walls of clay,
And the architectural plans
Of gray hornet artisans!"

Some thousands of years ago a number of problems in the form of a series of questions were proposed which the scientists and philosophers have not yet worked out to a final conclusion. The series begins thus: "Where wast thou when I laid the foundations of the earth? declare, if thou hast understanding. Who hath laid the measures thereof, if thou knowest? or who hath stretched the line upon it?"[1]

The present age is full of problems, some of them inherited, and some peculiar to itself. We find people occupied in determining how to reach the north pole, how to navigate the air, how to prevent and cure diseases, how to earn a living, how to keep expenditures within the bounds of one's income, how to train and educate children, how to square conduct with ideals, and how to

[1] Job xxxviii.

solve innumerable other puzzling questions of varying importance.

2. *The inadequacy of instincts to solve problems*

Because human beings are not born with a full set of fixed instincts which control their activities in every circumstance when action is required, it is clear that people must often think about what they do. They must determine how they shall act and what associations of ideas they shall make. For example, there is no instinct which will carry us inevitably into our life-work, nor which, when we have chosen our careers, will determine the means by which we shall pursue them successfully. Neither does instinct settle the general question as to whether honesty or dishonesty is better on the whole, or which of the two is better in some particular case. We are all compelled to be students since we cannot dismiss our problems at will and lead that careless existence which is something less than real living.

3. *The need of learning how to study*

Among the subjects of study with which people might profitably occupy themselves, there is one of great importance which, as yet, has received little consideration, and that is the process of studying itself. Unless by nature we study in the right way, we must either be taught to do so, or else there will be waste of energy, loss of time, and sometimes either incorrect results, or no results at all. Investigation shows that neither children nor adults naturally study as they should. The right method must be learned in some way, if it is acquired at all. Individuals must either work out a method for themselves, more or less consciously, or they must be taught how to study by others who have already learned.

4. *The nature of study*

We are confronted, then, by these two conditions: (1) that all people have occasion to study, and (2) that people on the whole do not study as well as they should. If we attempt to meet the situation by teaching people how to study, we at once find that we must be acquainted with the nature of the process before we can teach it. We need to know the basis of it and the various steps involved in it before we can train others in its use. This is the problem which confronts parents and teachers, since they are the ones who must teach children how to study, and it is for parents and teachers that this book is mainly intended.

First of all, some definition of the term *study* is

necessary in order that misunderstanding may be avoided and that we may know our problem definitely. Studying in its highest sense is the process of assimilating knowledge, of reorganizing experience. As ordinarily employed, the term studying often means much less than this, and includes any mental activity directed towards the accomplishment of some end, whether that end be the memorizing of facts in a geography lesson, the learning of a story in reading, or the mastering of a list of words in spelling. In this common usage of the word it includes the mind's activity that is directed towards the acquisition of ideas, whether these ideas become an organic part of knowledge or not. Learning dates in history, and committing poems and definitions to memory do not always involve the assimilation of knowledge, yet teachers call the effort to accomplish these tasks by the same name that is applied to the mental efforts of a philosopher who is engaged upon some weighty problem. The two kinds of studying are quite different. The one is more mechanical than the other and results largely in accretion of facts. The other is organic and results in rearrangement and assimilation of ideas; in short, it involves thinking. It is this latter form of mental activity, which is generally acknowledged to be of a higher type than the first, that is the object of investigation and discussion in this book.

When teachers are asked what they think studying is, many of them say that studying means to imagine, to memorize, to apperceive, to think. In other words, they mean that studying is a psychological process. But these answers do not furnish much of a clue to the proper method of teaching people how to study because they do not show when or how one shall imagine, memorize, apperceive, or think. There must be some other explanation of the process than an enumeration of the psychological states that may or may not be involved, if we are to understand it fully and to be able to teach it intelligently. This explanation we shall now seek.

5. *The kind of thinking employed in studying*

It has been said that proper study involves thinking. The thinking which is employed in studying is reflective or purposive as distinguished from spontaneous thinking. In the latter sort, the ideas are not controlled by the thinker. They come and go at random. But in reflective or purposive thinking, there is a definite end in view and the ideas are selected and controlled so as to accomplish this end. When a person gives the rein to fancy and lets his thoughts wander where they will, his thinking is of the spontaneous kind; but when he sets himself to accomplish some task, to solve a problem, or to find the way out of some difficulty, he controls his thoughts and chooses or rejects the ideas which come into consciousness, taking as the basis of his choice the bearing which these ideas have upon the end he is trying to reach.

6. *The origin or source of the problem*

It is just this consciousness of some end in the form of a problem which causes the thinking and governs its course. In the determination of this problem lies the logical basis of study; hence it is important to know whence and how it is derived, and by whom it must be felt as a problem if it is to influence thought.

a. *Failure of habitual modes of thought and action*

Problems frequently arise because for some reason our habitual ways of acting or thinking cannot be employed. An entirely new situation, or some change in an old one, may break up our usual way of doing things, and compel us to seek for a plan of action that will meet the new conditions. A flood, a fire, a financial panic, the loss of some tool or utensil, a blockade of the street-car system, the stopping of a watch, the increased cost of foodstuffs, — any one of these may prove a serious problem and compel thought in order to master the new situation. Such apparent dilemmas arise frequently in connection with nature study, geography, arithmetic, and other school studies, as well as in connection with the formal routine of schoolroom procedure. For example, a child's idea of a desert is frequently found to be that it is a place where nothing can grow. When confronted with the statement of the fact that certain places, hitherto deserts, are now very productive, he is face to face with a difficulty which should furnish him with a valuable problem. The pupil who comes upon a verbal noun for the first time may find that it puzzles him to classify it properly as a part of speech. Similarly in arithmetic, there are problems varying sufficiently from those already mastered to cause the degree of thought needed to analyze and master them.

b. *The need of relating new knowledge to old*

Sometimes the problem originates in the attempt to relate some new fact to the knowledge already possessed, as in the case of the pupil and the verbal noun just referred to. The significance of the new must be seen before it is of use to the individual who acquires it. "What is the use of this object or idea?" "What is the purpose of this?" "What difference will this make in my ways of doing or thinking if I accept it?" All such questions look forward to purpose or end. Or, instead of looking forward to see the effects which the new ideas will produce, one may seek out the cause or explanation of them in previous knowledge. Washington was made commander-in-chief of the American army at the time of the Revolutionary War. That is the new fact learned. Why was he elected to that position? With the ordinary class, this question compels a review of Washington's character and career in order to find the reasons for his selection for so important a position. The warmer air in a room is found near the ceiling. Why? Frequently the explanation is to be found in ideas already possessed by the observers.

c. *Conflict of ideas*

Sometimes two sets of ideas or lines of action seem so contradictory that it is difficult to decide which is true and therefore the one to choose. In political campaigns, different speakers will advise for or against the election of a certain man, according to their political bias, and will present on one side strong arguments to show that he is in every way desirable, and on the other, will give what seems convincing evidence that he cannot safely be trusted with the political office in question. Which side is right?

Again, when one is trying to decide upon a plan of action, arguments present themselves both for and against almost any course proposed. From one point of view it is very desirable to follow a certain plan of conduct; while, viewed from another standpoint, this same plan seems unwise. "To be or not to be. That is the question." This conflict of ideas extends to the mastery of school subjects. When it is a matter of finding explanations for facts observed in science lessons, of selecting the right method of solving some problem in arithmetic, of determining the right way to dispose of some part of a sentence in grammatical analysis, of making the correct interpretation of the thought of some author in the study of literature, the opportunities for conflicts are numerous. There is frequent occasion for the explanation and reconciliation of apparent opposites.

d. *Curiosity as a source of problems*

A prolific source of problems, whether in school or out of it, is curiosity. We wonder *why*, or *how*, or *what*, and reach out in other directions for more knowledge. This curiosity may be of an idle, fleeting kind, which, left to itself, would result in little effort and progress. It may be of a primitive nature, not being based upon previous knowledge. A teacher appeals to primitive curiosity when he leads his class to desire to hear a story they have never heard before, or to see something new. He arouses expectation and desire which are directed towards unknown objects. Rightly valued and employed, however, curiosity may be made a valuable agent in education. Intelligent curiosity, which is based upon partial knowledge, which reaches out to some definite end, and which leads to some adequate method of attainment of that end, cannot be overestimated as a means of development and training. Consequently the suppression of curiosity just because it is curiosity, or the rejection of a method just because it appeals to curiosity, is short-sighted. The appeal to curiosity is justifiable, but it should lead to some intelligent end, and not remain upon the level of mere idle wonder. A teacher may have in view the teaching of an important lesson in some subject; she may lead the children to approach it by appealing to a curiosity initially connected with some superficial fact. The explanation of that fact leads into the subject step by step, until, when the lesson period is over, the teacher's aim is accomplished. A lesson on glaciers may begin with the observation of markings on rocks, or the discovery of boulders in the soil. The question arises, "How did they come to be there?" and in answering it the subject of glaciers is taught. A comparative study of cotton and wool might be introduced by the question as to why wool was used before cotton for making cloth. Similarly in other subjects, some fact may be brought to the attention which provokes the curiosity and tends to direct thought into desired channels.

e. *The necessity for activity*

Not only does the need of knowledge, apparently for its own sake, frequently give rise to problems, but also the need of knowledge for the sake of some activity which is to be based upon it may become the source of careful thought. What to do, how to do, how to improve the execution of some process, — these are problems frequently met, and their solution often includes the physical expression of the theory evolved. Drawing, painting, manual training, physical education, games, and all other subjects involving bodily activity provide problems of this kind. Drill for rapidity and accuracy in arithmetic or geography calls for the same sort of treatment; that is, knowledge of the process, and repeated and intelligent exercise in its use. In all these situations involving physical activity, thinking is necessary to determine the cause of the difficulty, to select the means to overcome it, and to judge of the efficiency of the latter when they are employed. They are therefore to be classed as thought-provoking situations, as sources of problems.

f. *Feeling as a source of problems*

The value of feeling as a spur to the discovery of problems should not be overlooked nor lightly estimated. As already shown, curiosity leads to the recognition of limitations both of knowledge and of skill, and so brings to consciousness a tension in experience which leads to study. The negative side of the importance of feeling has often been recognized by teachers in inducing pupils to work in school. They threaten various unpleasant consequences which will be visited upon those who do not complete their work in a certain manner, or before a specified time. The pupils, in order to avoid these consequences, bend their unwilling energies to their work and strive to master it. There are many instinctive feelings, both pleasant and unpleasant, which find their outlet in ways which demand either new knowledge or some change in the usual modes of activity. Some of these instincts are sympathy, sociability, friendship, pugnacity, emulation, love of praise, hatred, jealousy, envy, love of self, and love of physical activity. In addition to the instinctive feelings, there are both feelings and attitudes which are the result of cultivation. But whether instinctive or acquired, these emotive states influence both the origin and outcome of the thought-situation which constitutes the problem for study. Sympathy, friendship, envy, hatred, love of mental or physical occupation,—these states of mind, if strong enough, seek appropriate expression, and the question of ways and means arises. Or, if the problem does not arise in the feeling itself, but is accompanied by a strong feeling of some kind, the energy put forth to accomplish this end is influenced. If a boy is sure that something in grammar or arithmetic is worth having, and that it bears upon some felt need, whether of his own or of the society in which he is interested, he will put forth more intense and continuous effort than he otherwise would. When there is an accompaniment of pleasant feeling of some sort, the fatigue is felt less than when the problem is regarded as a useless task.

7. *The aim of study*

Whether the occasion for thought lies in the need of knowledge or of activity, or in the necessity for expressing some emotive state, the aim is to readjust experience so that tension or friction shall disappear and harmony prevail. Each specific situation presents its own peculiar incentive to thought and furnishes the occasion for its exercise. It is clear that the thinking thus occasioned cannot be of the spontaneous kind, but must be selective, purposive in its nature. Its course, too, is not complete until the validity of its results has been tested in some way. Conclusions and theories must be tried by further experience before their validity can be affirmed positively. When, however, their use has become habitual so that they have reached the mechanical stage of application, they present no further aim to thought, and the problem is regarded as solved; that is, the studying is completed.

8. *Thinking, memorizing, and habit-forming*

In this connection, the relation between thinking and memorizing, and thinking and habit-formation should be noted. In thinking, ideas are associated according to their meaning, and when the process is ended, memorizing is at least partially accomplished, and that, too, in its best form. Reviewing the associations thus established completes the process. This is rational memorizing as distinguished from that which is purely mechanical. In habit-forming, thinking may be very prominent during the first stages. The form of activity to be learned, the way of responding to a certain situation must sometimes be chosen as the result of reflection, and progress in efficiency must be watched with care until the mind is freed from conscious oversight of the process. Learning long division is a typical form of habit based upon thinking. Each step is thought through carefully, and then thoughtful repetition brings mechanical accuracy.

9. *The relation of the problem to the person who is to study*

It is self-evident that in normal conditions the tension, the lack of harmony, or want of completeness must be within the experience of the person or persons who are to do the thinking, since the thinking arises from personal motives. A thing is of interest and worth doing, and demands to be done because in some way it affects our own welfare and the equilibrium of our ideas. Professor James, in discussing interest, says: "You will understand this abstract statement easily if I take the most frequent of concrete examples — the interest which things borrow from their connection with our own personal welfare. The most naïvely interesting object to a man is his own personal self and its fortunes. We accordingly see that the moment a thing becomes connected with the fortunes of the self, it forthwith becomes an interesting thing. Lend the child his books, pencils, and other apparatus; then give them to him, make them his own, and notice the new light with which they instantly shine in his eyes. He takes a new kind of care of them altogether. In natural life all the drudgery of a man's business or profession, intolerable in itself, is shot through with engrossing significance because he knows it to be associated with his personal fortunes."[1] If the problem is to have interest, and is to be a motive power to the child, it must grow out of his own experience, some situation in relation to himself, otherwise no genuine thinking will result.

For a teacher in the elementary schools to assign a lesson without first preparing the class so that the pupils go to their work with a definite problem in view, and that problem one which touches them vitally, one which they have some interest in accomplishing, is to invite mechanical memorizing, and that, as has been said, is not study in the higher sense because it is not the assimilation of knowledge. When the teacher gives the problem to the class, which is usually the case when there is any aim present at all, the pupils may have a motive for thoughtful work and they may not. It depends upon the extent to which they recognize the problem as valid for them, as involving their own needs, as possessing personal interest, as presenting a situation which they accept as theirs. Thoughtful study will depend upon their appropriation of the problem as given by the teacher. But if the teacher can so

[1] James, *Talks to Teachers*, pp. 94, 95.

direct the experience of his pupils that this problem arises in their own consciousness of need, then it is felt to be theirs and the situation is most favorable for thinking.

10. *The need of definiteness in the aim*

Another point of importance to note in regard to the problem is the fact that it should be as clearly defined as possible before its solution is undertaken. To be aware that there is a crisis or tension in experience is one thing; to have analyzed the situation so as to see just where the difficulties lie is quite another; and to determine possible modes of accomplishing the solution is still another. It is as if a person, who had seen a long pendulum set swinging in a north and south direction, should discover after several hours that the record shows a change in direction, and being puzzled, should ask, not "Why does it swing?" because he saw it set in motion, but "Why, having been started to swing in one direction, does it now swing in another?" Probably several answers suggest themselves, some to be rejected at once as manifestly contrary to fact and consequently impossible. Only those hypotheses are accepted tentatively for investigation which show some possibility of furnishing an adequate solution.

TEACHING CHILDREN TO STUDY

It may be necessary to look into the nature of the problem itself before a solution is sought. Analysis is employed to discover its meaning and its implications; and reflection, reading, investigation may be required to make clear what is to be done, and the ways by which the solution is to be attempted. This process of defining the problem and formulating hypotheses for its solution may require a very short time, or it may occupy an extended period. Children's guesses as to what things are, or why things are so and not otherwise, are simply childish hypotheses intended to meet natural situations. The trouble with their studying is that they frequently end their mental efforts with the mere formulation of their problems, rather than accept such formulations as starting points on the way to positive knowledge. The clear understanding of the problem furnishes the criterion for the acceptance or rejection of material, and for its organization. The keener the individual's sense of need, and the more intense his desire to acquire a certain body of knowledge, the clearer his statement of the problem will probably be, and the more definite his demand for what he wants.

11. *Recognition of the problem the first factor in logical study*

This recognition of a problem is a factor in proper study, that is, in study in the sense in which we are here considering it; and since it precedes the other steps, it may be called the first factor in study. The problem must originate within the experience of the students, or be appropriated by them in order to arouse thought, and it must be defined clearly in order to furnish a definite guide to thought.

General Summary

The points presented thus far are as follows: (1) The necessity for study is universal, as is also the need of being taught to study properly. (2) Studying, in its higher meaning, is mental activity directed towards the assimilation of ideas, the reorganization of experience. (3) Proper study involves purposive thinking, since it is thinking that is directed toward some end. (4) Back of the psychological steps involved in studying is the logical basis of the process. This is the tension in experience which constitutes the aim or purpose of thinking, and furnishes the criterion for the acceptance or rejection of ideas in the attempt to readjust experience. (5) The recognition of a problem is the first factor in proper study. (6) This problem must be felt as such by those who are to study, or else the motive and guide for thought are lacking. (7) In order that the thinking may be accurate, the problem must be clearly defined in the mind of the person who is to do the thinking. Its requirements must be plainly perceived, and some hypothesis formed as a tentative explanation. This hypothesis determines the direction which the solution of the problem will take. It should conform to known facts. It should have some reasonable basis.

NOTE.— For a fuller discussion of the ideas in regard to the thought-situation presented in this chapter, see *Studies in Logical Theory*, by Professor John Dewey.

THE NATURE OF INDUCTIVE STUDY

II

THE NATURE OF INDUCTIVE STUDY

1. *The distinction between inductive and deductive study*

THE difference between inductive and deductive study is the same as the difference which exists between induction and deduction whenever they are employed. When a person studies deductively he seeks to solve his difficulties or satisfy troublesome situations by employing principles, rules, or some other form of generalized knowledge which he already possesses. In inductive study, on the contrary, the generalization, whether it be definition, rule, or principle, must be discovered by the student before he can apply it to the solution of the problem upon which he is engaged. This latter form of study always originates in a relatively concrete situation and tends towards the formation of some general idea or concept which will explain the problem that set the thinking process in motion, so to speak. As will be shown in the following chapter, deductive study may begin either with the data or with some generalization. Inductive study may begin with data or with an untried hypothesis. It cannot begin with a logical generalization or concept, since these are the result of the inductive process itself and therefore cannot be the starting point.

2. *Collecting data a factor in inductive study*

When in the course of experience such a problem as has been described in the preceding chapter becomes a part of consciousness, it controls the nature of the mental process which succeeds it, unless it is inhibited from so doing. One of the most prominent aspects of this process is the gathering of material bearing upon the problem in hand. This collecting of data is a most important factor in study, for through its agency we are furnished the means whereby we may prove, amend, or reject the hypotheses formulated for the solution of the problem, and arrive at more definite theories.

The material brought together for these purposes may be drawn from several sources. It may be a part of previous experience that is recalled. Information may be gained from others by inquiry or through reading. It may be gained through the processes of experimentation and observation.

a. *Memory a source of data*

The data culled by memory out of past experience possess varying degrees of value. Even though the ideas relating to the new problem were originally gained by means of direct observation, they may be incomplete because the present problem was not in existence at the time the observations were made, and so exercised no influence upon them. In consequence, the ideas lack fullness and clearness and are not to be trusted entirely. Loss of time and the presence of other mental states tend to weaken ideas, however complete and clear they may have been originally. In looking over their old letters or diaries, people sometimes find that their memories of past events have changed radically from the record made at the time the events occurred. Furthermore, the very attempt to recall past experiences in the light of a present problem favors the activity of the imagination, so that ideas are not recalled exactly as they were. Changes are made, sometimes quite unintentionally and unconsciously, so that it is difficult to say where recollection ends and imagination begins. In spite, however, of all these drawbacks to memory as a source of data, the past must be searched frequently to discover what contribution it can make to present crises in experience; but it is sometimes necessary to scrutinize the ideas thus obtained to see whether they are correct and complete. The following instance will show what is meant by incomplete observations and the interference of the imagination. When asked what becomes of the blossom of the dandelion, the students in several classes tried to recall their observations of that flower. All remembered the flower in bloom. Some remembered that the flower closes after blooming, but some had never noticed that fact, and some had forgotten it. All remembered the fluffy white head that appeared later. Not more than one or two had noticed what becomes of the blossom. In every class, several ventured the reply that the yellow flower turns into the fluffy white ball, — an imaginative reply built upon incomplete observation.

b. *Group-experience a source of data*

When memory fails to furnish the data necessary to solve the problem in hand, the individual may try to make up the lack by referring to his classmates, to his teacher, if he be a student in school, to the members of his family, or to any others who he thinks may be in possession of the ideas he needs. The value of resorting to group experience to supplement or correct individual experience should be recognized by the teacher, and pupils should be encouraged to seek information bearing upon their problems from one another, from parents, or from others who may be able to supply it.

In addition to one's own knowledge and the knowledge of the social group, the knowledge that is stored in books constitutes an important source of data. In many schools it is almost the only source utilized, the experience and knowledge of the pupils and of the society in which they live being quite or almost disregarded. The books should not be neglected, but teachers ought to consider the question whether they should always be the first resort in looking for data, or whether they should sometimes be left in the background until other sources have been utilized.

c. *Experimentation and observation as sources of data*

In addition to the means already given for obtaining ideas relevant to the problem to be solved, the field of experimentation and observation furnishes abundant data of the greatest value. Observations made *for a definite purpose* are more complete and accurate than mere casual, purposeless perceptions. The same may be said of experiments. There is a vast difference existing between study *about* nature and study *of* nature; between study *about* machinery and study *of* machinery; between study *about* the function of adverbs and study *of the use* of adverbs as they occur in literature or in spoken language. Experimentation and observation may not always be practicable, but the fact that the field work in geography, agriculture, nature study, and arithmetic is increasing shows that more can be done than has been done. The difficulty has been that teachers have not recognized the value of direct observation, or have hesitated to make the trial of conducting experimental or observation lessons. In solving problems, the experimenting or observing may be done by one pupil or by a group. Individual assignments and group assignments are both valuable, and the pupils can work out their results and report to the class. Opportunities for such assignments occur frequently in connection with the subjects studied in school. In geography, facts about clouds, winds, evaporation, condensation, and precipitation can readily be observed. In arithmetic, the actual measures are frequently used by pupils. In higher classes, tax receipts, household bills, insurance policies, checks, and notes are sometimes found, but should be used to a much greater extent than is now the case, since the pupils can gain the facts about them from direct observation. The pupils themselves can obtain much of the material needed, and for their own sakes they should be encouraged to secure and study it. The wise limits of the use of observation and experimentation as sources of data bearing upon problems to be solved by pupils have not yet been reached, and the teachers of children have a problem of their own in studying the questions of when and how they should be resorted to by pupils who are trying to study independently.

d. *The teacher as a source of information*

In connection with the subject of gathering data several questions are heard frequently. A common one is, Shall the pupils always be expected to find the materials or information needed, or shall the teacher sometimes tell? When the cost in time and effort would outweigh the benefit to the pupils either in the knowledge or experience gained, or when the sources of information are too difficult for the children to master with a reasonable amount of effort, the teacher should give the information to his class. There is a time to tell and a time to refrain from telling, and the teacher must distinguish between the two.

e. *Lectures versus books as sources of data*

Another question heard sometimes is in regard to the relative merits of lectures and text-books for students who are advanced enough to listen to lectures. Students sometimes expect and desire the instructor to pour out the subject to them in lecture form, and object to being sent to books or other sources to acquire it through their own research. If studying means the realization of a problem and reflection upon it, then books offer a better opportunity for study than do lectures. While one stops to reflect upon some point which a speaker has made, he misses the succeeding portion of the lecture. The case is different with a book. One's attention may be challenged by some problem, and during all of the succeeding study the text waits for the student and he is not losing the following thoughts. When he is ready to go on, the subject matter is there. An instructor must sometimes resort to lectures to present material obtainable in no other way or for the reasons already given above in regard to telling things to children, but on the whole these are exceptional cases. For pupils in the elementary and high schools especially, the lecture should be the exception and by no means the rule.

The procedure is better from the point of view of the mental activity of the class, when, instead of the uninterrupted lecture, opportunity is given at times for inquiry and discussion by the students. Then the lecture, like the book, halts until doubtful points are made clear, wrong ideas are corrected, and the material offered becomes part of the student's data with its value duly recognized.

f. *The use of original sources by pupils*

Since the use of classics has superseded the old school reader with its fragmentary selections, and since it has been found that pupils can read and enjoy entire literary productions, the idea has been advanced that pupils can profitably make use of source material in the study of history, instead of depending entirely upon the accounts given in school histories. It is doubtless true that objects and places of historical interest, letters, diaries, reports, and other official documents, as well as the literature of the period under investigation, may be used much more extensively than they now are, and that the data derived from such sources may have much greater value than those derived from the school texts. Pupils ought to know from what sources historians derive their materials and how histories are prepared. They should also have practice in finding data in original sources and in selecting and interpreting them when found. The matter may easily be carried to the other extreme, however, and too great a burden put upon pupils both as regards the amount of time required and the difficulty of the materials to be used. Experienced historians are doubtless perplexed at times in determining the significance of historical materials; therefore too much in the way of sifting evidence and drawing conclusions should not be exacted of immature pupils. Carefully prepared texts adapted to the ability of the class will long have their place in education for the reason that they put data within the reach of the pupils in an economical form; but study of original sources should be encouraged within those bounds of time and ability which experience determines to be proper. Probably very few teachers will carry their use to an extreme; the error is more likely to be on the side of neglecting them.

g. *The fallacy of relying habitually upon one source of data*

All the resources at our command should be drawn upon in the effort to solve our problems, and in general, it may be said that too great a reliance upon any one source is unwise. The person who knows nothing but books and the person who relies entirely upon his own observations are both depriving themselves of material that is valuable ; so also does the person who is content with what he already knows as the basis for the solution of problems which arise in his life. There is a one-sidedness in such an attitude which defeats the very purpose of thought, that is, the discovery of truth.

h. *The rejection of irrelevant data*

It frequently happens that in this gathering of data, many ideas enter consciousness which are not relevant to the problem and which, therefore, must be rejected ; but having clearly defined the problem in the beginning, the sorting process is simplified. We cannot prevent the obtrusion of these irrelevant ideas, and it is consequently all the more necessary to learn to discriminate between that which bears upon the problem and that which does not, and to accept or reject accordingly. For example, if a person plans a trip to Europe, the details of other trips are recalled or read, or they may be suggested by friends. Many of these ideas will doubtless be valueless, because they have no bearing upon the problems of the proposed trip, while some may be very helpful. Unless the prospective traveler can sift out the latter and neglect the rest, he will probably do some foolish things, and neglect certain wise preparations for his journey.

i. *The necessity of having data representative*

A consideration of very great importance in regard to data is that they must be gathered from such a number and variety of individual instances as to be sufficiently representative, and hence reliable. For example, data in regard to the physical measurements of Europeans would be very unreliable if obtained from the Anglo-Saxon nations alone, even though many individuals in those nations were measured. And similarly, measurements to be representative of the English should include all classes of English and not merely a selected group. Likewise, to base all study of the phenomena of the adolescent period upon observations limited to high school students would be manifestly unscientific, since high school students are a selected group. Only a small per cent of pupils entering the first grade ever enter high school. There is a weeding-out process all along the elementary school course, so that by the time the high school is reached, those who have survived are a chosen few. Studies based upon them alone would not be truly representative of all young people of the same age. It is thus important to remember, in considering the reliability of data, that they must represent enough individuals and classes to make conclusions based upon them valid.

Summary: The collecting of data is a factor in logical study. Significant facts may be brought into consciousness by recall, by conversation with others, by reading, by experimenting, or by observation. It is unwise to depend upon any one course exclusively. These ideas, however gained, must be judged on the basis of their relevancy to the problem, and accepted or rejected accordingly.

3. *The organization of ideas a factor in inductive study*

A very important element in inductive study is the grouping of related ideas. It is a natural process for ideas to become associated in groups, but in purposive thinking this process must be consciously aided. The ideas accepted because of their bearing upon the problem are examined to discover the nature of their relations to one another. Certain elements of similarity cause certain ideas to form a group, as when concepts are formed. Other ideas are attracted to one another because of the similarity of the relationship which they bear to some other idea. The idea of the navigation laws and the idea of the tax on tea are very dissimilar in nature; but because they both bear a functional relationship to the idea of the Revolutionary War, they are frequently associated in people's minds. Then there is the causal relationship among ideas, when the value of one idea depends upon the value of some preceding idea or series of ideas. For example, the idea of weather-of-a-certain-kind becomes associated with the idea of wind-blowing-from-a-certain-direction. Also, in studying parts of speech, the idea of pronoun becomes associated with the idea of noun because of their logical relationship. These relationships of similarity, of function, of cause and effect, and of place in a logical series, all of which are of importance in the solution of the problem on hand, should be sought out and established. The natural tendency to associate must be supplemented by conscious effort. Furthermore, as a matter of convenience and clearness in dealing with ideas, it is frequently helpful, especially with a long or difficult problem involving much material, to prepare a classification showing the main topics arranged in order, with the subordinate points properly grouped under them. In most of the situations which present us with some problem, no such formal classification is necessary, but undoubtedly much incoherence and lack of logical treatment would be overcome by the more careful arrangement of material employed in attempting to work out some hypothesis.

4. *The results of the selection and organization of data*

As a result of the selection and organization of data, the hypothesis, which in the beginning was merely a more or less intelligent guess, is much more positive in its nature and has become a theory. Starting with an hypothesis based merely upon the facts immediately connected with the problem, there has been a wide search for data, a careful elimination of the irrelevant, and an organization of that which has been found to bear significantly upon the solution of the problem. During this process, the original hypothesis may have been altered, rejected, or confirmed as a whole or only to a certain extent. For example, the pupils who in the beginning of a recitation hazarded a guess as to what a verb is, ought to be able to correct any error in the guess or to show wherein they were correct in their statements. Without these two steps, collecting and organizing, the hypothesis would have remained a mere guess. Both hypothesis and theory must be looked upon as tentative conclusions and must be put to the final test of application before being accepted as principles.

5. *Scientific doubt a factor in inductive study*

In the paragraph on the selection of data, it was said that data relevant to the solution of the problem should be accepted. This statement must be modified somewhat. The data must be not only relevant, but reliable. Whatever is accepted should be accurate. It frequently happens that material is presented in the working out of a situation which would apparently meet every difficulty, but it lacks the most necessary characteristic,— that of accuracy. If the problem to be solved is of any importance to the person who engages in its solution, it is obviously of considerable importance to that person that he accept none but reliable data. He must, then, scrutinize with care that which he accepts, and his attitude in general must be that of doubt. The greater the significance of the problem the more important doubt, scientific doubt, becomes as a factor in study, since freedom from error depends largely upon its existence and exercise. Because much of the information which is obtained from people, whether through their books or their spoken utterances, is based upon incorrect ideas obtained from others, upon faulty experiments, imperfect observations, or false reasoning, and because it is sometimes willful misrepresentation of facts to accomplish some ulterior motive, those who avail themselves of such sources without investigating the truth of the information imparted are frequently led into error. Ordinary gossip and unprincipled newspapers which are published for political purposes are extreme instances of unreliable sources of information. But even books which are written thoughtfully, with every intention of being accurate, contain statements which are biased or untrue. The path of learning is strewn with discarded ideas, theories, hypotheses, which fuller knowledge has shown to be false. The attitude of scientific doubt which opposes blind acceptance of information makes for advance in true knowledge. It should be cultivated so as to counteract the tendency of people in general, especially of young people and of others inexperienced in proving hypotheses and in working out carefully the solution of problems, to accept without question the statements found in books, papers, and magazines, even though they may have learned to exercise some discrimination in regard to what they hear. There are reasons for this attitude of receptivity, but they are not sufficient to warrant the continuance of unquestioning belief, since that frequently leads to inaccurate solutions of problems, and distorted views of facts.

Our judgment as to the validity of data offered by any author is influenced, or should be influenced, by his sources of information. In scientific studies, direct observation and experimentation are valued as insuring accuracy. In historical subjects, the use of written evidence, or original sources, is a basis for acceptance of statements. In either case, if the author has gained his information through hearsay, there is greater doubt of his reliability as an authority than if he had employed research to obtain his ideas. It is impossible to test every statement made by the people to whom we go for information, and we must therefore either reject all statements which we cannot verify, or place sufficient confidence in the men consulted to accept their presentations. There is a place for the experts in various lines of knowledge; and when men are known to have worked in a scientific spirit within their respective fields of research, that is adequate reason why their results should be accepted as authoritative, for the time being at least. There is no loss of self-respect to the student in such acceptance. As for verifying data, there is still sufficient opportunity for that, since not all people are experts, and not all the problems are yet solved.

The reliability of data can be tested in different ways. It may be necessary to consult the original sources, and the training in this work, spoken of in connection with the collecting of data, serves a valuable purpose in enabling the student to verify evidence when its reliability is in doubt. Close observation is sometimes all that is necessary; or reflection, comparison, and, in some cases, experimentation may at times be employed. We may recall the results of our own experience and use them as a test for the new; or we may compare one man's statements with those of another in whose methods of working we have confidence, for in weighing evidence it is not so much the men as their methods of working which are to be accepted as authoritative. But, after all is said and done, some doubt is still in place.

6. *The tentative nature of hypotheses and theories*

It is very important in studying to recognize the fact that both hypotheses and theories are tentative in their nature, although they may differ greatly in degree of probability. An hypothesis is a guess. It may be more or less scientific, but it is still a guess. A theory, on the other hand, is an hypothesis which has been carried through the stages of investigation, and perhaps experimentation, and which has been modified or confirmed by the process. It is based upon the study of data, and consequently possesses a greater degree of certainty.

Theories may vary in probability. Where data are lacking, or where there is grave doubt as to their validity, the formation of judgment or theory may be quite suspended for the time being. When evidence is ample in amount and variety and is of such a nature as to warrant it, a very positive, definite theory may be formed. Between these two extremes are theories of varying degrees of certainty. Some theories or judgments, therefore, are more tentative in nature than others, but all theories must be looked upon as tentative until verified by experience. When thus verified, they become principles, and serve as positive bases for decisions in future thinking.

Whenever evidence is doubtful, and yet is accepted because of lack of opportunity for proving it, or for any other reason, the conclusions based upon such data should be regarded as hypothetical rather than theoretical, until doubts of the validity of the data can be removed. Sometimes the material used as the basis for judgment is accurate, but it is not sufficient because it does not meet every requirement of the problem. Conclusions based upon incomplete data should also be held to be lacking in positiveness. While such judgments have value in that they furnish temporary explanations, their incompleteness should be recognized, so that the mind of the student may be left open for further progress. Not to recognize them as partial, as tentative, is to become fixed and dogmatic and to close the door to investigation and development. It is equally detrimental to character and learning to accept judgments based upon doubtful or inadequate evidence as final in their nature and to make no further efforts towards positive theories.

Summary: As a precaution by which the way to accuracy of results should be hedged, scientific doubt, or the consideration of the accuracy and reliability of data, must be valued as a factor in study. The data selected in the process of studying because of some bearing upon the problem must be known to be reliable before there can be assurance of validity in the conclusion. This is true of all data, regardless of their source or the method by which they are obtained. But even most reliable data are still properly subject to doubt. Both hypotheses and theories should be regarded as tentative in their nature, and as such subject to further investigation and proof.

7. *Verification, or the application of theory, a factor in study*

Since it was the need of readjustment of some phase of experience which furnished the problem for thought, the verification of the theory formulated must consist in its application to the specific situation which gave rise to the thought-process, or to similar situations. The process of logical study is not completed until the theory has been expressed in some form so as to test its validity; therefore expression, or the application of theory, must be regarded as an element in study.

Application of theory is the only means by which we can be sure that the tension in experience has been removed and the problem solved. Conclusions which cannot stand this test must, of course, be revised or thrown aside, and those which meet the requirements in a satisfactory manner may be accepted. Furthermore, the application of theory, if repeated, tends towards facility in its use, and makes it more thoroughly a part of the person who thus employs it.

As was stated in an earlier paragraph, the application of theory may be carried out very carefully, close attention being given both to process and results. If repeated frequently enough without too great a lapse of time between the applications, the process reaches the mechanical stage and becomes a habit which requires little or no conscious effort for its execution. The occurrence of any favorable opportunity for its use then calls it into activity unless it is inhibited for some new and special reason.

The testing of theories may take the form of using the conclusions as bases for further thinking; it may consist of some act of construction, the execution of some design embodying the ideas worked out in the thinking process; or it may manifest itself in oral or written expression, in some social activity, or in some other way. A person does certain things because of the conclusions reached; or by an act of will he refrains from doing because his thinking has led him to decide that it is best not to act. Both definite choice and intelligent action are based upon the mental product; they test the value of that product, and serve as a corrective for careless or inaccurate thinking.

In general, the more genuine the problem has been to the individual who has been studying, the more vital will be the conclusion reached, and the keener the desire to put the results into practice as soon as possible for the sake of verification. In life outside of school, the opportunity for application is sometimes delayed, but if the judgments are strong and clear, they will survive delay and will even force an occasion for use. In school, conditions can frequently be so arranged that pupils may apply the results of study immediately; but even there delay is sometimes inevitable. This possibility of postponement is a strong argument in favor of making circumstances as favorable as possible for the formation of clear, vigorous judgments.

Summary: In review of this topic, it may be said that application in some form constitutes the test of theory and is therefore a part of the study process. It is indispensable as a means of verifying, correcting, and fixing conclusions, and of giving facility in their use. Application frequently follows the formulation of theory immediately, though it must sometimes await an opportunity. This possibility of delay increases the necessity of strength and clearness in judgments.

8. *The place of memorizing in inductive study*

It is sometimes advisable to remember things in a certain wording or order, and for that reason memorizing forms an important element in study. Whatever conscious memorizing is done to give permanence to thought, naturally follows the completion, or at least the partial completion of the thinking process involved in the working out of a situation. The very act of establishing relationships of meaning among ideas tends to make the ideas thus associated easy of recall, so that by the time a certain problem has been thought through carefully, the ideas involved are already partially memorized in their proper order. Thinking the steps over repeatedly, reviewing the relations already established, completes the memorizing process. Thus memorizing is seen to be a very thoughtful procedure. Its misuse arises in the attempt to substitute it for thought instead of basing it upon thought, and in making it the sole, or at least the main factor in study.

All memorizing takes place through the forming of associations of some kind. These associations may be of a very mechanical and arbitrary nature, as when we learn words in columns, or commit sentences to memory with no idea of their meaning. Such associations are not the result of thought. Mechanical or arbitrary memorizing has its place in school work, since words must be spelled, the principal parts of verbs learned, and other matter of similar nature so fixed that it may be recalled readily when needed. This memorizing involves concentration of attention, the perception of the correct order, and then repetition to fix the idea in the perceived order.

The memorizing which is a factor in the higher form of studying is based upon associations of meaning among the ideas involved in the study. In this case committing to memory is based upon analysis. Similar or contrasting ideas are associated, as are also groups of ideas relating to some one subject; also ideas bearing the relation of cause and effect, and ideas in a logical series. Thus, if a history lesson is to be memorized, it is better to memorize the important facts or topics which have been thought out and associated than it is to learn to recite the words glibly without having had any glimpse into the significance of the ideas expressed. In learning a poem, memorizing is usually well advanced when the thought of the poem has been mastered. In geography the causal relations, and in mathematics the logical order, may form the basis of the memorizing process.

There is a double clue to the recall of matter thus associated. One may recall a mere fact, as, for example, that there is much rainfall in Ireland; or, one may have forgotten what the climate is, but may be able to repeat the reasoning process which resulted in the statement about the amount of rainfall in Ireland, and so may again arrive at the fact. Some people, having reached a conclusion, may remember it absolutely; while it may always be necessary for others to recall the reasoning process in order to recall the conclusion reached. We find thus three kinds of memorizing: first, the memorizing of a purely arbitrary order; second, the memorizing of conclusions or statements based upon reasoning; and third, the memorizing of the chain of reasoning rather than of the results of the reasoning, so that in recalling, the reasoning process must always be repeated in order to bring to mind the statements the recall of which is desired.

Summary: In general, it may be said that while mechanical memorizing has a certain place in school work, it should be limited to its own legitimate sphere. Thoughtful memorizing is of a higher type and should be employed much more extensively than it now is. It is accomplished by placing emphasis upon associations of meaning rather than upon associations of place. When employed consciously it follows the other steps in proper study.

9. *The preservation of self in and through study*

The studying which has been described in the preceding pages affords an opportunity for self-preservation and self-development which mechanical study can never yield. While preservation and development of the individuality are not a separate factor in study, they should be present in study and should be advanced to some extent, at least, through its agency.

Human beings vary greatly in native endowment. This variation manifests itself in differences of interests, of capacities for working, and in ways of working. Any method of study which disregards individuals, disregards also these fundamental differences. It subordinates the human being to the subject-matter, and aims for the acquisition of facts rather than for the assimilation of knowledge. In proper study, the individuality of the student has a chance to assert itself. One may respect his own ideas if he has tested them and has found that they satisfy the requirements. He need not yield ready acceptance to all that he hears or reads or thinks, but may reject what is false or irrelevant. He need not lose his identity or his respect for himself even though he does accept the ideas of others, provided the acceptance follows judgment of value. He need be no one's tool or blind follower, but may learn to esteem ideas because of their worth rather than because of their source. He needs to learn the distinction between beliefs and convictions, but having the latter, he may have courage in the face of any amount of opposition. To be alone in one's views is not necessarily to be in error, while to fall in with popular views is to place one's self very frequently in the wrong. Even though a number of people should start to solve the same problem and should employ in general the factors of study here presented, their procedure would vary from stage to stage because of differences which would manifest themselves at every step.

A very important element in the development and preservation of self is the exercise of initiative; the higher form of study affords excellent opportunities for the manifestation of this activity. The recognition of a problem, the selection and discrimination of data, the organization of ideas, the deferring of judgment, the formulation of theory or hypothesis, the consideration of the truth or falsity of statements, and the final testing of theory involve its use. The highest ideals formulated by educational theory include the right training of whatever initiative man has been endowed with; hence so excellent an opportunity for its proper use as is furnished by logical study should not be neglected.

Summary: In studying, it is an important consideration to preserve and develop one's personality, to exercise initiative, and not to subordinate one's own ideas to those of others without due consideration; otherwise one becomes a mental nonentity; a "passive recipient," and the whole process of study loses its value as a means of training and as a means of arriving at truth.

NATURE OF INDUCTIVE STUDY

General Summary

The points made thus far in this chapter are, in brief, as follows: (1) A second factor in study is the gathering of data bearing upon the problem. This material may be gathered from many sources, but only that which bears a relation to the problem should be accepted. (2) The organization of material into groups of related ideas is a third factor of study. It tends to take place naturally, but should be carried on consciously with close attention given to the relationships established. As the result of the second and third steps we are able to formulate a theory which is intended to satisfy the problem. (3) A fourth factor in study is the exercise of scientific doubt, or judging as to the soundness of statements. Whenever significant facts bearing upon the problem are presented to consciousness, their validity should be determined in order that the theory based upon such evidence may have value. All hypotheses and theories must be considered as tentative judgments until verified by experience. The value of such judgments is that application or further investigation is encouraged, and the tendency to form positive judgments upon a slight or faulty basis is discouraged. (4) In order to verify the conclusions reached in the process of logical thinking, a fifth factor in study is needed. This is application, or the execution of theory. Through the use of this factor of study theories are rejected, corrected, or accepted according as they meet the conditions of the original problem which gave rise to the thought situation, or of similar problems. Through use, also, the theory is fixed as an element of knowledge and the expression becomes habitual. (5) To fix knowledge in a certain form memorizing is necessary, and this process, accordingly, makes a sixth factor in study. Thoughtful memorizing is accomplished in part during the course of the thinking process. It is completed by consciously attending to the relationships to be fixed in mind and by reviewing them in their logical order. (6) Throughout the process of inductive study, there is opportunity for the preservation and development of the individuality of the student. This is as it should be, since training in process is fully as much needed in life as the accumulation of facts, though the facts are not to be despised. Inductive study calls for individual effort and individual judgment and affords opportunity for the exercise of initiative. Training in its use is training in the use of native power and ability to the best advantage. Like results need not be expected, therefore, in all cases, since minds differ in native endowment, in the nature of the store of knowledge already acquired, in the ways of judging data, and in the modes of making application.

THE NATURE OF DEDUCTIVE STUDY

III

THE NATURE OF DEDUCTIVE STUDY

1. *Necessity of understanding the problem*

In the deductive process of studying there is the same need of recognition and analysis of the problem as in the inductive study. Without a clear understanding of the situation, there is no criterion for the selection of the theory or principle which is to furnish the solution, since its relevancy is not apparent until the problem has been made plain.

2. *Deductive study which begins with the data*

In making use of theories, principles, laws, definitions, or other forms of general knowledge already existing in the minds of the students, two kinds of problems arise. In one kind, the facts, or data, are present and call, not for the formulation of a new theory, but for the use of one which is known. Examples of this form of thinking are seen in recognition, interpretation, identification, and in other uses of general knowledge. Effort in such cases is directed towards identifying the facts or data present in consciousness with some group of facts for which a satisfactory theory already exists. Through this identification we read into the fact the significance or meaning of the principle which is applied to it. The mathematician who sees that the facts given in his problem involve a certain principle or rule; the scientist who identifies some plant or animal as belonging to some group he already knows; and the pupil who recognizes some part of speech as a noun and consequently attributes to it the properties of nouns, — all these are employing principles, theories, or classifications which they have found already existing in consciousness as the result of previous thinking.

A very frequent opportunity for deductive study of the kind just named is found in the diagnosis of diseases. The physician is sometimes confronted with symptoms which are so pronounced and so characteristic that he recognizes them at once as indicating a certain disease. At other times, the symptoms are more obscure, or exhibit some peculiarity, so that the physician must delay judgment until he has been able to obtain more data by watching the development of the symptoms. The chemist is constantly employing this deductive process in his analysis of compounds. He makes his examination to ascertain the reactions manifested by a certain specimen, and then classifies it according to the facts he has been able to discover, because, according to the science of chemistry, the reactions manifested by the specimens he has tested are characteristic of certain substances already known and named, and the specimen, therefore, must belong to this class.

3. *Deductive study which begins with general knowledge*

In the process of study just described, the thought may be said to move backward from the specific facts to the principle or general truth underlying them. In the second form of deductive study, the movement is from the principle to the data. It is because of a knowledge of general truths that one is able to prophesy, to calculate and foretell results of activities which have not yet occurred. The architect who plans a house or the engineer who plans a bridge must keep many laws in mind as he determines the particulars of his structure. The amount of pressure exerted, the materials which will best resist it, the most advantageous arrangement of this material, — all these and many other details are based upon rules or laws which must be observed if the results are to be satisfactory. We sometimes hear of attempts being made to forecast the political career of the United States, the predictions being based upon conclusions drawn from the study of nations which have gone through the various stages of development and decline. For example, we are told that a prolonged period of national prosperity results in moral decline, and that the moral decline is followed by political decay. When business is highly prosperous, certain social conditions are pointed out as evidences of a decline of the moral tone of the nation, and the warning note is sounded that such conditions are the forerunners of national ruin.

In the study of geography, this form of deductive study may be employed very often. For example, if the conditions governing the production of rice are known, any country may be studied to see if such conditions exist in it, and the conclusion as to whether rice can or cannot be grown there can be based upon such an investigation. Similarly, the conditions favorable to manufacture and commerce may be treated with reference to any city or country and the proper conclusions drawn as the result of the application of general truths to particular instances.

4. *General knowledge prerequisite to deductive study*

When any new subject is taken up by a student, he must in some way gain a knowledge of the general laws or truths belonging to that branch of learning before he can resort to deductive study. He cannot intelligently employ principles which he does not possess, and as we are dealing here with thoughtful study, we shall limit the discussion to the intelligent use of formulated knowledge. In pursuing such a subject as physics, a person cannot apply the law of falling bodies, the law of equality of action and reaction, or the general conclusions in regard to pulleys and levers until in some way he has gained possession of them. Any subject must be treated inductively until a body of principles is acquired for deductive use. Because of this fact, each subject, however ancient it may be, and however long its truths may have been formulated, is new for each individual learner. Its truths are fresh discoveries for him, and in making these discoveries he is repeating history. He may be able to arrive at his conclusions without the use of illustrative material or experiments, but he may be greatly aided, and the time required much reduced, by the use of such material or processes.

5. *Using generalizations in related fields*

When subjects are carefully related, or when one subject is a form of application of the principles belonging to another, the principles derived in one subject may be carried over into the related one and employed there. Thus the laws of physics are employed in various applied arts, such as the different kinds of engineering, architecture, and hydraulics, and it is not necessary for a student to rediscover them in order to use them. Having learned them in physics, he can employ them wherever necessary. The same is true in regard to applying the general knowledge of chemistry in a subject like domestic science, where the constituents of foods must be known, also the effects of the various food elements. Furthermore, the preparation and preservation of various kinds of foods directly involve the application of the principles of chemistry.

6. *The study of typical forms*

This idea of carrying over principles or conclusions from one field to another finds its application in the so-called "type study" of biology, geography, and other subjects. In geography a typical river system, mountain system, agricultural district, commercial or manufacturing city is studied intensively, and the facts which the teacher knows to be characteristic of the various classes represented are emphasized so that the pupils get clear ideas of them. When other mountains, rivers, agricultural areas, or cities are studied, by analogy the pupils apply to them the conclusion which they reached through the intensive study of the type form. The study of types is an attempt on the part of the instructor to use a shortened form of the inductive-deductive method, and it will prove successful only to the extent to which the pupils are able to grasp and apply the features which are general.

7. *The use of analogy in moral training*

Analogy is frequently employed in studying those subjects which have to do with the moral nature of man. In this field experimentation may be dangerous either physically or morally. The burnt child dreads the fire, but to expose him to the risk of burning in order that he may acquire the dread may be to expose him to too great a danger. One would hardly encourage a pupil to be dishonest in order that the advantages of honesty may be discovered ; or cause him to lie to teach him the evils of untruthfulness. From history, from the surrounding social life, from fiction, and from imagined characters or actions, materials for study can be obtained which will enable pupils to see the truths which they ought to know. It may be possible to obtain data by observation, or they may be brought out in discussion. The inductive process occupies a relatively smaller place in those fields which pertain to the humanities than in the natural sciences. In ethics, in sociology, in religion, there is but little resort to experimentation, and wisely so because of the great risk attending such procedure in these lines, and because both past and present afford abundant materials which can be made the basis of analogy. This form of study is safer and more economical in various ways, and is therefore to be preferred to the experimental method.

8. *Doubt as a source of problems*

Doubt in some form gives frequent occasion for the examination of creeds and principles. Every realm of belief, whether ethical, religious, political, or scientific, is assailed by doubt at some time or other, and men are called upon either to defend their own beliefs, or to demonstrate that the doctrines of others are false. The socialist maintains that it would be best for society if government should own and operate the agencies for the production and distribution of commodities. His statement is called into question, and he tries to prove that he is right. He may also assail his opponent's contention that individual ownership is best for society. Thus we have the two sides of doubt, — proving the truth of statements and proving their falsity. Many a man, when called upon for proofs, discovers that what he has been holding as true has been accepted upon the authority of others, and has not been the result of his own thinking and observation. In other words, he has cherished a belief rather than a conviction. A challenge in the form of doubt brings investigation, and may result in the confirmation of the belief or in its rejection or amendment.

The student must see his problem, in whichever form it comes, and must see what is required of him, whether it be the application or testing of a principle already at hand, or the discovery of the theory which will furnish the proper solution. Intelligent procedure depends upon the analysis and definition of the problem, hence the necessity of these.

9. *The need of collecting data*

In whatever form the problem requiring deductive study may present itself, it will usually, if not always, require the collecting of data. In case a concrete situation is given, and the principle which will explain it is sought, it frequently occurs that much more needs to be known about the situation than appears at first, before a right solution can be found. When a man is brought to trial for having taken the life of some fellow man, it is not enough for the members of the jury to know merely the fact that he has caused the death of some person. They must know many details of the circumstances attending the commission of the act before they can determine fairly the degree of the prisoner's guilt, or, indeed, whether he is guilty of murder at all. The deed may have been entirely accidental; or the man who is on trial before the jury may have acted in self-defense when he committed the act; or his deed may have been deliberate and willful murder, with no extenuating circumstances. It would not be safe to classify the act and determine the punishment without having learned enough about the case to decide intelligently. This investigation means gathering and weighing evidence or data.

The need of collecting data is still more evident when the studying process begins with rules, laws, or principles, or some other form of generalized knowledge, and seeks to discover their application. The scientist who, knowing the conditions necessary for the culture of the date palm, wishes to find out if it will thrive in the United States, must try to find a place where the necessary favoring conditions are all present, and where no harmful element is found to offset their influence. The final proof of the correctness of his reasoning is the actual growth of date palms in the region selected. If the scientist has taken into his account all of the necessary factors, he will select a favorable place and his plants will thrive; but if he has overlooked some important element, as plenty of moisture for the roots, he may plant his trees where there is an insufficient water supply, and his venture will fail.

In the matter of doubt, when one's own beliefs

are assailed, or when one attacks the beliefs or statements of another, there is much searching for data which shall serve to confirm one's own view or to confound that of the opponent. Evidence is much sought after in all such cases where one does not rest upon mere dogmatic assertion of authority, as did the learned doctors, who, instead of experimenting to discover if oil will freeze, sought to find out by referring to the writings of Aristotle.

10. *The sources of data*

The same means of collecting data may be employed in deductive study as in inductive, and it is therefore not necessary to enlarge upon them here, as they have already been explained. Briefly stated, they are observation, experimentation, memory, imagination, reading, and consultation with others. All of these may be resorted to in solving problems by the process of deductive study. It will frequently be necessary to collect data, but the sources employed will vary with the nature of the problem involved. Unless one knows the problem and is familiar with the sources of materials available for the students who are attempting to solve it, it is difficult to lay down specific directions for particular cases. Sometimes experimentation must be employed to demonstrate some principle; sometimes books must be searched for principles, or for facts illustrating them; sometimes the information desired is best gained from classmates, teachers, or people outside of school. The nature of the problem will control largely or entirely the method of collecting data, and as problems vary, so also will the sources employed vary.

11. *The organization of ideas a factor in deductive study*

Grouping together ideas which relate to one part of a subject or topic, and then arranging such groups in the order of dependence, whether logical or psychological, gives clearness to the whole subject, and is a great convenience in working with ideas, and in memorizing matter. The lawyer or debater frequently arranges his arguments in the way first described. He first makes his general statement, and then his various points in explaining and sustaining it. He is thus enabled to give an orderly presentation of his material, and in such a way that the audience may get the proposition and the main points in the argument. Sermons are often arranged according to this same plan. The minister announces a text which is a statement in general terms, and then takes up the argument and application under several heads. A careful listener can get these main points, and from them can afterward retrace the course of the lecture, argument, or sermon.

Similar organization is sometimes possible and helpful in deductive study, which makes use of investigation, experimentation, reading, or other sources. A problem may be so simple as not to require it, but there are times when it is necessary and helpful, and therefore pupils should have practice in using it.

12. *Judging the soundness of statements or the adequacy of a theory a necessary factor in deductive study*

In deductive as in inductive study there is occasion for the examination of data to determine their accuracy. Whenever statements are employed as a means of arriving at a conclusion, or of demonstrating one already reached, there is occasion for judging their soundness. One will not always doubt the truth of the evidence submitted, yet there are times when doubt should be present, and when statements should be carefully sifted to determine their reliability.

In deductive study, the theory, also, must undergo criticism, as we must judge of its applicability, its adequacy to the solution of the problem. A theory or principle may be relevant but not adequate, and it is therefore necessary to discriminate between that which is sufficient to furnish the desired solution and that which is not.

13. *Suspension of judgment an element in deductive study*

Sometimes a final judgment as to the theory or principle must be deferred, either because the problem itself has not been completely analyzed, or because no adequate theory has been formulated, or because we are not able to find the right theory. We must then either accept a judgment or classification tentatively, or we must try to remove the difficulty which has prevented the definite acceptance of a solution as adequate and final. This may be done by further study of the conditions of the problem itself, by an inductive study of the theory, or by further search for a theory which has already been formulated.

14. *The testing of theory in deductive study*

The test by which the adequacy of a theory is determined is its application to the situation which caused the search for the theory. As long as theories are never applied to problems, it matters little which ones are selected; but little progress is made by this plan. The more genuine and vital the problem, the greater the need of the application of whatever theory is selected after careful examination. Thus the chemist or physician who attempts to produce a serum for tetanus or rabies, proceeds upon certain principles believed to have been established through the discovery of other serums. Having obtained the serums according to principle, he usually applies them first to some animals to test their efficacy. The bridge-builder or the boat-builder who seeks to meet a new or peculiar situation, not only searches for his theory or principle, but frequently tests it in the manufacture of a model before using it in the actual situation. The final test, however, is its use in the connection for which it was intended.

15. *Memorizing in connection with deductive study*

Memorizing based upon thought-associations, or associations of meanings, is present in deductive study also. It may not always be as prominent or as necessary as in inductive study, since frequently the results of previous memorizing are employed and thus the process is tested. In the new work, the relation of the data giving rise to the problem to the theory which solves it may call for memorizing to fix the relation for future use. Teachers often neglect this part of the school work. The pupils learn to reason out situations in arithmetic or geography, and often let the matter rest there. There are many results which should be kept permanently, and therefore the associations should be made strong enough to endure. After all the reasoning, there must be a residuum of things known exactly and permanently. Memorizing, then, cannot safely be omitted.

16. *Self-expression and self-development through deductive study*

Whenever there is a genuine problem present which is felt as such by the student, and whenever the factors of logical study are employed freely by him, there is opportunity for the expression and development of self. It requires initiative in deductive study as well as in inductive to discover the problem, see its implications and conditions, and find and test the solution. Where, however, the process is purely formal, and is carried on under the direction and dictation of another, the higher thinking powers of the student remain inactive, and consequently undeveloped. Such formal use of theory is seen in the application of rules, principles, or definitions in mathematics, grammar, or physics, when the pupils have little idea of the meaning of the problems and possibly none at all of the rules, definitions, and principles.

Carefully conducted experiments have shown that pupils in the elementary schools are capable of using all of the factors of logical study. Observations have shown that they are given little opportunity to use them. The teacher is the most active element in the schoolroom, and she usually controls much or all of the work. She herself knows very little about thoughtful study, and consequently she cannot give much intelligent training in its use. The result of such a situation is that the child is controlled instead of being trained and directed. He depends upon the teacher to a large extent and is afraid to exercise initiative for fear of consequences; or else he avoids it because it involves too much energy, or because he distrusts his own efforts. Any one who is a frequent visitor in the schoolroom will testify that the pupils either are given little opportunity to exercise initiative, or else that there is a lack of training in its use. Like other activities, it needs training, and thoughtful study affords an excellent opportunity for such training.

General Summary

In conclusion we may say that the factors present in inductive study are present in deductive study also, though they may be modified to suit the changed purpose of the study, which is to apply principles rather than to formulate theory.

THE RELATION OF RATIONAL STUDY TO TEXT-BOOK STUDY

IV

THE RELATION OF RATIONAL STUDY TO TEXT-BOOK STUDY

In the preceding chapters, the steps or factors in logical study, both inductive and deductive, have been described and illustrated. The discussion has been general in its nature, as it was thought best to show the broad significance of study before confining the attention to the form it takes under certain limitations.

Schoolroom conditions and traditional procedure are the limitations which hedge in the pupils in the years devoted to so-called study. In the ordinary schoolroom we find a group of pupils of nearly the same age, pursuing the same subjects from the same books, and with freedom of physical activity at least greatly restricted. The question is pertinent here as to whether the factors present in purely logical study are possible in the study of the text-book. Some reflection upon the nature of text-book work shows that to a large extent these factors may be employed, though in a modified form.

1. *Consciousness of the author's problem or purpose the first factor in text-book study*

First of all, in systematic text-book study as in other study, there is the necessity of some problem. In ordinary experience aside from books, the problem is found in some life-situation, but in the book the author provides it, and the student must find and appropriate it. An author may have written a chapter of psychology to show the nature, kinds, and uses of interest; of geography to show how the mountains of Europe affect the climate and drainage of that continent; or of history to show how New England came to be settled by the Puritans. The problem was present in the author's mind and was worked out by him in some section of his book. The student must rediscover it, and appropriate it as his own in order that he may benefit by his study. His questions to himself must be: "What was the author's purpose in writing this?" "What is the main thought of this section?" "What underlying idea runs all through this chapter, connecting the various parts?" "What important question is answered in this paragraph or chapter?" "What would be a good heading for this paragraph?" Through some such self-questioning and self-directing of thought, the author's purpose or problem is revealed, whether in geography, history, grammar, arithmetic, or some other subject.

It will frequently be the case that the teacher will bring the class to a consciousness of the problem during the lesson assignment; it may be with the help of the book, it may be without the book. Then with curiosity whetted, the class studies the book for further information in regard to the problem and its solution. As pupils grow older and more capable of independent work, they should assume more independence in finding the problem from the text itself. Less presentation by the teacher should be necessary.

2. *Gathering data a factor in text-book study*

When the author's aim has been grasped, the gathering of data is necessary in text-book study, just as it is in any situation where there is a problem to solve. The author supplies much of the material that is to be used when a text is studied, and the student must look upon the book as data presented with the idea of solving the author's problem. The student is not limited to the author's text, however, but may draw upon his own experience and upon his imagination. He may read books, papers, and magazines, and may talk with people who are informed in regard to the subject he is studying. He may perform experiments and make observations. In any or all of these ways he may supplement the author's text and add largely to the material bearing upon his problem. The criterion for acceptance here, as in other study, is the relevancy of the facts to the problem. That which is irrelevant should be rejected, and only the relevant accepted. If, for example, the problem is, "How the mineral products of the Western states have influenced the development of those states," then students engaged upon such a problem may neglect all the statements made by the author which do not bear upon it, but they must sift out and accept that which contributes to its solution.

It may be urged by some that this gathering of data will consume more time than the class has at its disposal. However, rejecting irrelevant matter saves time; and the examining of other sources than the book can be divided among the members of the class so that the labor is divided. The interest arising from the presence of a problem will also quicken the efforts of the pupils and so save time.

3. *The organization of ideas in text-book study*

The process of organizing ideas differs in text-book study from the organizing that is done when the student must seek and accept data which have not already been organized. Text-books present a certain form of organization, and the student must discover it in order to see fully the author's treatment of his problem. This includes finding the main points in the chapter or paragraph involved in the problem, and in grouping the related minor points about these main points. This organization of the text may be extended or otherwise changed by the use of supplementary material which the student has gathered and accepted as bearing upon the author's problem. An example of organization of text-book material is the following: Examination of a section in a text-book in United States history shows the author's problem to be the explanation of how slavery was introduced into the United States. Further study shows a number of details which group themselves into a few points: —

How slavery was introduced into the United States.
1. Reasons for its introduction.
2. The introduction of negroes as slaves.

a. Time.
b. Place.
c. Agency.

3. The introduction of indentured servants.
a. Reason for practice.
b. Character of these servants.
c. The end of white slavery in America.

Such organization not only shows the author's mode of treatment of his subject, but it also enables the student to handle his material more conveniently. It brings out the main points clearly, and about these can be grouped the needed details. The irrelevant and the unimportant are weeded out. As a result of organization, the author's theory as to the solution of his problem should have been grasped by the person who is studying. The act of making such an outline involves a partial memorizing. The teacher will probably find that it does not require as long a time to memorize such an outline as it does to try to learn the words of the text verbatim in the old way, and the value of the result is greater.

4. *The necessity of deferred judgment in the study of books*

The same caution which is necessary in logical study in general, in regard to accepting hypotheses and theories as provisional rather than final conclusions, is necessary also in the study of books. The same conservatism, also, in forming such theories is necessary. Forming hasty judgments and jumping at conclusions are of frequent enough occurrence in dealing with literature, history, and other such subjects, to show the need of greater discretion in this direction. It frequently happens that judgments of persons, or actions, or of events, are formed before the situation has been sufficiently worked out by the author to make the formulation of theory possible. To anticipate the course of history so as to introduce the results of a movement at the place where its beginning is described is not always feasible or advisable, and final judgment of its significance should be deferred until adequate knowledge has been acquired. Any other judgments must be regarded as mere hypotheses, and pupils should learn to regard them as guides and not as proved conclusions. Final judgment of character in literature or history must await the development of events sufficiently to warrant it. The results of some treaties and laws are so far-reaching that immediate judgments as to their value would probably be erroneous. Geography, also, frequently calls for the use of caution in drawing conclusions. To judge of climate on the grounds of latitude alone, and to think that because the people of the Western states are far removed from the Atlantic seaboard, they are therefore uncultured and live in a primitive way, are manifestly rash acts of judgment, yet such judgments are not uncommon. Further data would doubtless cause the correction of one hypothesis and the abandonment of the other.

If children are permitted to do so, they frequently ask their teachers for reasons and explanations, showing that they are aware of lack of fullness in their books and that they desire further data. Here again it happens that the forming of a positive theory must await the right opportunity for the acquisition of knowledge. In the end, the ideas gathered may not be sufficient to warrant the formulation of theory, and if any judgment is formed it must be an hypothesis. But the elements of tentativeness in both hypotheses and theories must not be lost sight of. The need of final verification must always be kept in mind.

5. *The consideration of the soundness of statements a factor in the study of a book*

The attitude of scientific doubt which manifests itself in the consideration of the soundness of statements and the validity of data of any kind is quite as essential a factor in text-book study as in any other. If it was necessary to scrutinize statements with a critical eye when the text-book was but one of several sources from which facts were sought, it is the more necessary to exercise care when the book becomes the main source of data bearing upon the problem. Histories, grammars, geographies, and other texts have been known to contain inaccurate material, and even the truth is at times so startling as to cause a challenge in the mind of the readers. For example, a certain text in grammar gives the following definition of a phrase: "A phrase is any combination of words that does not include both subject and predicate."[1] Then any group of words selected at random might form a phrase, if only no subject and predicate are included. This second definition makes the weakness of the first one more clear: "A phrase is a group of related words without subject and predicate,

[1] Welsh, *Lessons in English*, p. 34.

and having the use of a single word."[1] The following statement in regard to the Russian peasants is taken from a geography text-book published before the recent Russo-Japanese War and still in use: "It was not until 1863 that serfdom was abolished. Hence it is no wonder that the masses are without education; but great progress is now being made."[2] A certain text-book in United States history, in treating of the opening events of the Civil War, says: "But the attack on Fort Sumter changed the whole situation. Doubt was at an end on both sides. Virginia, North Carolina, Tennessee, and Arkansas, forced now to take one side or the other, soon joined the Confederacy."[3] The question might well be asked, "What was the situation in the Border states where both sides were represented? Was all doubt ended there by the attack on Fort Sumter?" Furthermore, the statements, "We are to remember that, though the war was caused by slavery, it was not at first about slavery, but about secession,"[4] and "The Southerners were naturally more military than the Northern

[1] Webster, *Elements of English Grammar*, p. 39.

[2] *The Werner Grammar School Geography*, Part i, p. 244.

[3] Eggleston, *Household History of the United States*, p. 310.

[4] Eggleston, *Household History of the United States*, p. 311.

people,"[1] are somewhat startling to the pupils who have been taught up to this time that slavery was the cause of the war and have heard little or nothing of secession, and who have believed the Northern soldiers to have been in every way equal to the soldiers of the South. Such statements should challenge pupils to question and investigate their worth. The author's accounts or explanations may be compared with one's own experience. His use of sources and his method of treating problems need to be considered to determine whether he works cautiously or is hasty in his judgments. It is often worth while to ask the questions, "What is the writer's authority for the statements he makes?" "Does he base his conclusions upon observations, upon written evidence, or is he relying upon hearsay?" These questions are frequently in order in the study of history, geography, and the natural sciences. Other books and sources of information may be consulted as a means of verification or correction. Caution is especially necessary if magazine articles and newspapers are used as texts in studying certain subjects or phases of subjects.

It is not intended that pupils shall question

[1] Eggleston, *Household History of the United States*, p. 312.

everything they read or hear. Usually they will not need to have doubts as to the reliability of the statements made. But the attitude of ready acceptance of everything needs to be replaced by the attitude of mind which questions that which seems out of harmony with previous experience, which is startling in its nature, which seems to lack sufficient evidence, or which seems too general in its scope. Such instances, and possibly others, furnish occasion for thought and investigation as to the validity of the material offered. In this respect, text-book study does not differ from any other study in which data are presented to throw light upon some situation. Judgment as to the soundness of statements is usually necessary, though due credence should be given to the results of the labors of experts in the several fields of knowledge.

6. *The need of verification or the application of theory in the study of the text-book*

The use of verification as a factor in studying books is frequently modified by the fact that the author makes his own application of the theory he has advanced. But because the books are text-books they are limited as to the amount of space that can be devoted to any part of a subject;

consequently, the space which is given to verifying theories is usually small, and the amount and variety of material presented for giving facility in their application are often inadequate. There is much that can and should be done to apply the theories, presented in the books and rediscovered by the pupils, to life-situations in which pupils participate. Real occasions for the use of arithmetical ideas and correct grammatical constructions are possible, and lend a vitality to the principles presented in the text-book as the examples given by the author of the book cannot. All of the forms of expression described under this topic in the consideration of logical study are applicable in text-book study, whether it be oral or written expression, constructive work, social activity, some application to the affairs of ordinary life, or even the use of the theory as the basis for further thought. To test the matter, let the reader who has followed the discussion of proper study to this point read *Silas Marner*, some play of Shakespeare, a chapter in some history or other book which contains thought material, and make use of the various steps of study in his reading. Let him note the effects of such effort upon his idea of the right way to study. After such a test, he will be better able to state whether he considers the plan feasible and whether the results are worth the effort. One need only recognize the value of application as a factor in higher study and look for opportunities for employing it, and frequently some appropriate form will be found. As was said in a previous chapter, the time for using the theory may be delayed until a favorable opportunity arrives, but often the verification may be made as soon as the theory is clearly understood. Strength and clearness of the ideas are very necessary in order that these may function when there is an opportunity for them to do so. It must not be overlooked that strong feeling associated with an idea aids its recall and adds to its effectiveness when recalled. A purely intellectual idea of a lie is not hard to gain, but if the lie can be shown to be stupid, cowardly, and harmful, there is a greater probability of its being avoided because of the feelings associated with the idea.

7. *Memorizing as a factor in study*

With ideas selected and associated through the use of the factors of study already discussed, memorizing of the logical type has been provided for to some extent. Its further use in the study of material selected from text-books does not differ from the memorizing described under logical study. Its use is both possible and advisable in such a connection. But mechanical memorizing, so commonly employed, is to be avoided. In thoughtful study, either the results of reasoning should be memorized, or the chain of reasoning which led to the results. For example, after having discovered the rule for changing common fractions to decimal fractions, the pupils may memorize the rule, or the steps by which it was developed.

8. *Some phases of deductive study of books*

To any one who is at all acquainted with text-books, it must be clear that there is frequent occasion for deductive study in connection with them. The solution of problems in mathematics, parsing and sentential analysis in grammar, the explanation of geographical phenomena, the interpretation of history, the consideration either of form or of thought in literature, the classifications of science, — all involve the calling up of principles, rules, theories, or other general forms of knowledge, and the application of them to concrete instances. There is the same need for discovery of problem, and for analysis of data as in any other study. There is the same need for the exercise of discrimination in the selection of the rule or principle which is to be applied, or of the class to which the individual is to be assigned. The problems may vary in the number of steps of logical study involved, but some of the steps will be present always, while others may be present at times. There will always be data to be examined, the problem to be recognized, and some form of general knowledge to be applied to the data. It may not always be necessary to collect outside data, to judge of the validity of the statements given, to organize the material, to suspend judgment, or to memorize. The steps involved will vary with the nature of the problem. When the proof of a proposition or the application of a principle or rule is required, facts or data must be collected and examined with reference to their bearing upon the statement which is to be tested. Such examples are found all through geometry: *e.g.* "The sum of the angles of any triangle is equal to two right angles." In a similar way the axioms in mathematics are tested: *e.g.* "Things equal to the same things are equal to each other;" and "If equals be added to equals, the results are equal." Some of the questions found after each chapter in Fiske's "History of the United States" call for the same kind of activity: *e.g.*

"Should all things that ought not to be tolerated be forbidden by law?" "Was it right for the New Englanders to disobey the navigation laws?" "Is general disobedience of law and authority ever justifiable?" "Why have so many people come to America to live, and so few left it to live elsewhere?" In some of the examples given, proof of some general statement is called for. In others, concrete facts are stated, and underlying principles which will explain them are required. In both kinds of problems, generalized knowledge already in possession of the pupils is employed, and hence the study is deductive.

The criticism has been made that this form of logical study has been over-emphasized in school, and that pupils have been expected to apply general ideas which they do not clearly understand. Since both inductive and deductive study are possible in school work, it may be said in general that when pupils are found to lack the general knowledge needed for the solution of problems, the inductive form of study should be employed; but that when the pupils possess the principles needed for explanation or interpretation, the deductive form of study should be used. The two methods may thus be used in the same study period in connection with the same lesson, or they may not thus occur. It depends upon the nature of the lesson and the mental equipment of the pupils how frequently and closely they are associated.

9. *The relation of proper text-book study to initiative and self-development*

Although the use of books does not afford the same opportunity for the use of one's own powers, nor provide the same motives and interests as the study which arises from life-situations, where the problems are felt to be of moment, yet it does furnish a means for self-development and self-expression if it is rightly used. It is for the purpose of furthering this right use that the explanations of this chapter have been given. If one would be helped by the use of books, he must master them and not be mastered by them; that is, he must weigh, judge, and test before he accepts statements, or else he will lose his own individuality. It requires the exercise of initiative to discover the problems in books, just as it does to discover them in logical study aside from books. It requires it, also, to select data, accept, reject, and organize them, and grasp the author's theory. One of the highest expressions of the self will be found in the testing of statements and in the recognition of judgments as tentative because of faulty or inadequate data. And so, also, in the form of application which the student employs, there is opportunity for the development of personality, provided the student be free to exercise choice as to its form.

If text-book study be limited to rote learning or to deductive study, the opportunities for the exercise of initiative and self-expression are greatly limited. Since the school's recognized function is to further the wise development of these powers of the pupils, it should not neglect so valuable an agency as the higher form of study offers. If study could be directed in genuine life-situations where problems of real importance to pupils abound, the opportunities for self-expression and development would be most favorable. But text-book study is not devoid of possibilities in this direction and these possibilities should be recognized and utilized.

10. *Are all of the factors employed in all study?*

Before leaving this discussion of the use of systematic study in connection with school work, the question should be considered as to whether all of the factors of higher study are necessary in all study. The answer must be a decided negative. First of all, as was pointed out in the first chapter, a great deal of school work does not deal with the assimilation of knowledge, but with the mastery of technique ; for example, spelling, mechanical work in arithmetic, and the formal side of reading. There the mechanical side prevails and the readjustment of ideas based upon their thought-relations is not involved. In the second place, much of the subject-matter which does involve the relationship of ideas based upon meaning is of such a nature as to present little of value in the way of problems. It is intended to entertain, or to cultivate taste and sentiment rather than to furnish food for thought. Some school histories, books about nature, and a good deal of the reading matter and literature put before pupils belong to this class. They present few logical problems of value and call for little purposive thinking. Whether they should do so to a greater extent than is now the case is a question worthy of consideration, as is also the question as to whether the logical possibilities, slight though they are, should not be more fully realized. Even in subjects or subject-matter which call for systematic study, there are great differences in the nature and importance of problems presented from time to time. Not all problems are worth the time and effort involved in the use of all the factors of study; and some problems may not require the use of all these factors in order to be solved satisfactorily. Frequently minor problems present themselves during the study of larger ones. It is sometimes necessary to ignore them entirely or to postpone their consideration until some other time. If their solution is indispensable to the main problem in hand, then time and attention must be given to them as to other problems.

It may be said, further, that some problems may involve several or all of the factors of systematic study and yet be solved quickly, while other problems may require a long time for solution, being taken up for consideration from time to time as circumstances determine. For some reason the gathering of data may be deferred, and meanwhile the problem may rest unsolved; or delay may be due to some other cause. In general it may be said that the length of time spent in studying problems varies. Several may be disposed of in one study period, or one may extend through a long period, being considered from time to time as opportunity offers.

General Summary

The proper study of text-books does not differ from logical study, but is identical with it. In studying books, the student must discover the author's problem, and must see what data are given which bear upon it. There is the same need of gathering data, and of testing and organizing them that is present when the problem arises from some experience aside from the book. It is clear that books are not always able to offer the final word in the solution of problems, and that the conclusions hazarded by authors cannot always be accepted without verification. In such cases, judgment must be deferred. There is just as much need of testing theories derived from the study of books as there is of testing any other conclusions in order to give certainty and facility. The study of books calls for memorizing, though the memorizing employed should be based upon associations of meaning and not upon mere mechanical relationships. In deductive study, caution must be exercised that pupils understand the principles which they are to apply. Such text-book study as has been here described is highly favorable to the development of the personality, since it calls for the exercise of initiative and of all one's powers, instead of being based solely upon rote memory. It has been shown, also, that while all of the factors of proper study may be employed in the study of a text-book lesson, it is not always necessary for all of them to be present. The problem may not require it, or the pupils' ability may be such that they can safely omit one or more of the factors.

DO CHILDREN POSSESS THE ABILITY TO STUDY LOGICALLY?

V

DO CHILDREN POSSESS THE ABILITY TO STUDY LOGICALLY?

1. *The importance of knowing whether children can study*

HAVING seen the nature of logical study and having followed the application of its various steps to the mastery of a lesson in a book, it is of great importance to know whether children are capable of studying in the manner described. Can children see the author's problem, or find the underlying thought running through a lesson? Can they collect material bearing upon this problem? Can they find the important points in a chapter, or paragraph, or other section, offering a problem? Can they question statements, and see discrepancies in the material presented? Can they, in general, employ the various factors of logical study? If mechanical study is the only kind of which children in the elementary schools are capable, then the whole discussion of study down to this point is irrelevant so far as they are concerned.

2. *Factors influencing the preparation of the experiments to determine the ability of pupils to study*

The attempt to find an adequate answer to the question in the preceding paragraph involved the consideration of many serious difficulties. The grades, the number of children, the location of the schools, the subjects to be used in testing, the nature of the exercises, and the manner of conducting them, — all these and various other points had to be determined before the tests could be given. The situation was made even more complicated by the desire to train part of the classes in systematic study after the first tests had been given, and then to give all pupils, both trained and untrained, a second series similar to the first, with the purpose of finding out what differences were to be observed in the results obtained from the two classes of pupils.

3. *The subject and classes chosen for the tests*

The subject of geography was chosen for the tests, both because it furnishes abundant opportunities for proper study, and also because it is a subject which is quite sure to be taught in all of the higher grades of the elementary schools. History is not taught so generally as geography, and for this reason was not selected for the experiments. The ideal procedure would have been to train the pupils in the method of study in connection with all of their school subjects, and to test them in all of these; but while the teacher might have trained them in all branches offering opportunities for logical study, the testing would have been too arduous and too time-consuming, especially since more than a thousand pupils were tested.

The tests were given to pupils of the sixth and seventh grades only. Pupils in these grades are supposed to be able to express themselves sufficiently well in writing to be able to work upon the material given. The eighth grade was not chosen because of the possibility of wishing to give similar tests during the following year, in which case the eighth-grade pupils would not have been available because they would have left the elementary school.

In order to make the results as general as possible, the tests were given to as many classes as could be obtained for the purpose. More than twelve hundred pupils wrote upon the first series, which was given early in the year 1907. When the second test was given three months later, several classes dropped out, and the number was reduced to about eleven hundred. In each pair of tests, only those results were considered which were obtained from pupils present in both of them. Between the time when the first series of tests was given and the time when the second one was written, part of the classes were trained in the use of the factors of study, while the others were left without any change in their mode of working. The second series of tests, accordingly, made it possible not only to compare each class's record with its former one, but also to compare the results obtained from the trained classes with those obtained from those not trained.

4. *The nature of the tests*

The first test in each series was probably the most difficult. It consisted of a short selection from one of the geography text-books and was accompanied by the following requirement: "Here is a lesson from a book such as you use in class. Do whatever you think you ought to do in studying this lesson thoroughly, and then tell (write down) the different things you have done in studying it. Do not write anything else." It was hoped that the results would show whether any pupils were employing the factors of logical study, and to what extent they were employing them.

In another test, the pupils were given a question with this direction: "Do not answer this question, but write down everything you think you ought to do in finding the answer to it." For the first series in the sixth grade, the question was, "Why is Pittsburg such an important commercial and manufacturing city?" For the second series, it was the following: "Tobacco used to be grown almost entirely in the Southern States, but now it is grown extensively in the Northern States as well. Why has this change come about?" In the first series for the seventh grade the question was, "Why do terrible famines occur in India every few years?" In the second series, the pupils were asked, "If you were a voter and a governor was to be elected in your State, how would you decide which of the candidates to vote for?"

This test, like the first one, instead of making some definite requirement of the pupils, emphasized the subjective side of the problem. In the first test the pupils were to tell what they had done; in this one they were to tell what they would do. The object was the same, that is, to discover to what extent the pupils were employing the factors of logical study.

The last test in each series called directly for systematic study of a lesson. It consisted of a slip containing subject-matter from a text-book, and an accompanying slip containing the directions and requirements, both slips being given to the pupils at the same time. The pupils were to find the answers to the following questions, numbering them as the questions are numbered: —

1. What is the subject of this lesson?

2. Write a list of the principal topics in it.

3. What do you think is the most important thing in this lesson?

4. What are your reasons for thinking this so important?

5. What other facts do you know about any of these topics?

6. What questions would you ask in regard to anything in this lesson that is not clear to you or that you would like to know more about?

This test was placed at the end of the series, so that it might not serve as a clue in the writing of any of the other exercises.

5. *The ability of pupils to find what a lesson is about*

The results of the tests indicate that while these pupils do not find the subject of the lesson to any great extent when studying without definite directions, they are capable to a considerable extent of finding it when they are required to do so.

6. *The ability of pupils to organize subject-matter*

In judging of the adequacy of a list of principal topics, two questions were kept in mind: Do the topics cover the entire lesson? Do they include the main points only, or are they too detailed? Some pupils gave topics which were very good as far as they went, but they left out some important section of the lesson. For example, in the last test of the second series, a number of children omitted to include a topic which would cover the last paragraph, the paragraph which tells about the homes of the different races, and how the homes of the races are separated from one another. On the other hand, some pupils prepared a topic for nearly every sentence in the lesson. Such lists as these could not be reckoned as adequate because they were either too meagre, or because they were too detailed in nature. However, even such lists show some degree of ability, and taken into consideration with those considered adequate, they show that these children are able, in varying degrees of efficiency, to analyze a lesson and find the essential facts in it.

7. *The ability of pupils to exercise doubt*

On the whole, the pupils accepted the subject-matter placed before them without questioning its accuracy. The tests do not reveal any power the children in these classes may possess of seeing discrepancies between what they read and what they know. Whether they really possess this power and would exercise it if permitted or required to do so is a point left undecided by these exercises.

8. *The ability to supplement the text of the lesson*

The evidence in regard to the ability of pupils to supplement the text, that is, to seek data from other sources than the book, is stronger than it is regarding the factors already considered. The supplementing is shown by the fact that the pupils drew upon memory for additional data, used their imaginations to picture scenes, resorted to books and maps, and asked questions relevant to the lesson, but not answered in it. They named, also, various ways by which they would increase their knowledge of the lesson if they had opportunity; *e. g.*, read books, or question people who know. About thirty per cent of the pupils gave additional facts relevant to the lesson, and about one third asked questions calling for more knowledge about it. Many questions were so indefinite that their real purpose was obscure, but many excellent questions were asked. The evidence is very strong that pupils can collect data from outside sources intelligently and profitably.

9. *The ability to see problems relating to the lesson*

The power of the pupils to sense the author's problem is revealed in a curious way. In writing the first test, a number of pupils began to write a list of the important topics in the lesson, and gradually changed their statements to questions, indicating that they had confused the statements of facts with the questions which called for them. They were feeling the author's questions or problems which had brought about the statements in the text.

In some papers, statements or topics only were given. In others, there were questions only; but a good many were of the mixed type shown above.

The questions asked in the first and last tests

of each series indicate strongly that pupils can feel the author's problem, and can see problems growing out of the lesson presented, that is, supplementary problems.

10. *The ability to group related ideas*

The tests showed almost nothing about the power pupils may have to organize subject-matter. However, a series of experiments conducted by the writer with a fourth-grade class, and observations of other classes, show conclusively that pupils can be trained to see the large points in a lesson, and to group the related ideas about these large centres.

11. *The formulation of hypotheses by pupils*

An unexpected result of the tests was the manifestation of the ability of the pupils to form hypotheses as a basis for solving the problem presented to them. More than a score of children in each of the two grades volunteered explanations which were quite relevant. This was especially noticeable in the sixth-grade test about tobacco growing in the North, and in the seventh-grade test about famines in India.

Some of the explanations given by the sixth grade are as follows: 1. Change in climate either in the South or in the North. 2. South needs land for cotton. 3. Better facilities for manufacture and transportation in the North. 4. Cheaper to grow tobacco in the North than to have it shipped from the South. 5. Increased demand for tobacco. 6. Changes in economic conditions in the South due to the Civil War. 7. People of the North have learned how to cultivate tobacco. 8. Possibly a better quality can be grown in the North than in the South.

In regard to the frequent famines in India, the seventh-grade pupils hazarded the hypotheses that they might be due to climatic conditions, to the nature of the surface, to poor soil, to unfavorable winds, to inability to obtain sufficient water for irrigation, to occasional floods, to some insect which destroyed the crops, to oppressive government like that of Turkey, to density of population, to lack of knowledge of farming, to indolence, to lack of foresight or thrift, or to lack of adequate means for transportation and communication.

Not all the theories advanced were as relevant or sensible as those just given; but the fact that so many were given is indicative of the ability of children in these grades to form hypotheses which are worth considering as possible explanations of the problems demanding solution.

General Summary

On the whole, the different kinds of tests in geography given pupils in the sixth and seventh grades show that these pupils can employ the various factors of higher or logical study to a considerable extent. They were evidently not conscious of the steps in systematic study; yet supplementing their account of what they had done or would do in study by the results produced when they were called upon to employ the various factors, a sufficiently large number gave evidence of their use to warrant the conclusion that these pupils can find the subject or leading thought of a lesson; they can organize the material presented; they can supplement the text-book intelligently; they can ask intelligent questions involving valuable problems; and they can to some extent formulate sensible hypotheses for the solution of problems. The ability to work in characteristic ways is shown by the sources employed for information, by the theories advanced, by the questions asked, and, to a lesser degree, in various other ways.

ARE CHILDREN TAUGHT TO STUDY LOGICALLY?

VI

ARE CHILDREN TAUGHT TO STUDY LOGICALLY?

1. *The waste of effort shown by the tests*

In the preceding chapter it was shown that a sufficiently large number of pupils in the grades tested employed the steps of logical study to warrant the conclusion that it is within the power of pupils of at least the fifth and sixth grades to make use of them. Aside, however, from the indefiniteness of the language employed, which often quite concealed the pupils' meaning, the tests reveal the fact that there is great waste in studying. In the first test of the first series, fourteen per cent described their procedure in studying in indefinite terms, saying they would "think," "study," "try to understand." About thirty-eight per cent of the pupils thought the thing to do was to write a more or less literal version of the text, and about twenty-nine per cent memorized the text to some extent. Nearly one fifth of the whole number showed, either by doing nothing at all or doing something not required, that they did not know what to do. These figures show that a good deal of effort was undirected, and that much was misdirected. The pupils wavered between indefiniteness and mechanical study. They did not clearly know the right things to do, and there was a great scattering of effort in various fruitless kinds of work.

The second test in the series shows a very high per cent of those whose ideas were so indefinitely expressed that the meaning could not be determined. It shows, also, great expenditure of effort in unnecessary ways. While about one third of the pupils showed by their answers that they could take adequate measures to solve the problem given, thus indicating that it is possible for pupils of the age of these to do such work, the question is, What about the two thirds whose work was not adequate? Some solutions were distinctly inadequate, from about one fourth to one third, and the rest of the papers were so indefinite that no judgment could be formed as to their worth in this particular.

The third test reveals a still greater degree of inefficiency than either of the other two. In the last test of the first series, more than 73.6 per cent of the pupils failed to find the main thought in an ordinary geography lesson; in the corresponding test of the second series, more than 86.2 per cent failed to find it. More than two thirds in each of these two tests failed to make an adequate list of the principal topics, though the matter presented was simple enough for some pupils to make excellent lists. The greatest difficulty experienced by the pupils was in connection with the requirements to find the most important thing in the lesson, and to give reasons for thinking it so important. An appreciable per cent chose a minor point in the lesson, and several chose something not in the lesson at all. Many named more than one thing as being the most important thing in the lesson, some even including practically every point of the lesson. Such answers had to be classified as indefinite. Many gave a topic which was so general, so unlimited, that their answers, too, were marked indefinite. The reasoning gave the poorest results in these tests. It was based frequently upon some personal consideration. A thing was considered most important because it was interesting to the writer; because he had never known it before; because he had known it before; because he might need it in his geography lesson; because he might need to talk about it some day. Or, having named several items as being most important, a pupil would then advance reasons for the importance of one of them.

The lack of clearness in expression and the misdirection of mental activity are shown in the responses to the fifth and sixth requirements of the last test. In response to the question, "What other facts do you know about any of these topics?" more than fifty per cent of the answers in each test were irrelevant, were taken from the text which was being studied, or bore no relation to the requirement.

2. *Reasons why the factors of logical study are not employed more generally*

If enough pupils use the various factors of proper study to show that it is possible for children of their age to employ them, the questions arise, Why do not many more of the pupils employ them? Why are they not in common use? In trying to solve this problem, a study was made of the present schoolroom situation by means of visits to some seventy classes, and by a *questionnaire* given to one hundred and sixty-five teachers, with the object of trying to find what their ideas in regard to study are, and what they try to have their pupils do when they teach them to study. As far as could be avoided, no clue was given to the teachers writing this *questionnaire* which could in any way influence their answers. The aim was to discover the things which stood out prominently enough in consciousness to secure expression when the process of study was being described or illustrated. Had direct questions been asked about the various factors of study, probably many of the teachers would have felt the influence of suggestion in shaping their replies.

The *questionnaire* as a whole reveals that these teachers themselves are lacking the proper conception of the process of higher study; that they tend to exalt memorizing; and that they do not as a class accord recognition to any factor or factors as being essential to study. In several instances, the factors which they have recognized to a considerable extent were employed largely by the pupils in their studies; and the factors which the teachers have overlooked in their reports were used but little by the pupils in their tests.

3. *A second means of investigating present procedure in teaching children to study*

With the purpose of investigating still further the extent to which pupils are being taught to study in the higher sense of the word, seventy recitations were observed in various cities of the United States. During the year 1905–06, a *questionnaire* was sent out to a number of principals of schools. This *questionnaire* was to be filled out by the principals after certain recitations had been observed. While information was desired mainly in regard to how the teacher treated the thought-content of the lesson in the assignment, what he expected the pupils to do with it in preparing the lesson, and how he disposed of it during the recitation period, other items were added, not only to supplement the chief purpose, but also that they might prevent the main points from being so prominent that the report upon them would be more or less biased.

At the time that this *questionnaire* was sent out, the writer was doing some experimental work with a fourth-grade class in reading; consequently, the principals were asked to observe reading classes in the intermediate department, including fourth, fifth, and sixth grades. Reports were received from Duluth, Minn., Madison, Wis., Passaic, N. J., and Baltimore, Md. The writer visited a number of schools, both public and private, in New York City, and several classes in the public schools of Passaic, N. J. The subjects in which recitations were observed were reading, history, arithmetic, geography, and language.

The data obtained were tabulated according to subjects, and while there is much that is valuable in a recitation which is not susceptible of tabulation, for example, the spirit of the teacher and the class-room atmosphere, still it is worth while to note some of the things done or left undone in the way of training pupils to work independently and logically.

4. *General summary of the questionnaires, and observations*

Careful examination of the results of the observations and both *questionnaires* compelled the conclusion that, although pupils possess ability to employ the various factors of proper study, the teachers lack a clear conception of what such study is. The teachers who wrote the *questionnaires* do not themselves employ these factors to any great extent; and the teachers observed in the class-rooms are not training their pupils to use them. The teacher is the centre and moving power in nearly all of the work, and the requirements laid upon the pupils involve mechanical effort to a large degree. The aim of the work as a whole seems to be the mechanical acquisition of subject-matter.

The development of the power to work independently, intelligently, and economically is almost entirely ignored. The teachers do not know of what such study consists and consequently give little thought to its cultivation. They would probably do so if they had definite ideas as to its nature, for they are frequently heard to lament the fact that their pupils do not know how to study or to think. Unfortunately, the books on method give little or nothing in regard to method of study. They deal almost exclusively with the teaching side of the school-room situation, and do not say anything at all about training pupils to study, or else what they do contain is stated in such general terms that it benefits the teacher very little.

CAN CHILDREN BE TAUGHT TO STUDY LOGICALLY?

VII

CAN CHILDREN BE TAUGHT TO STUDY LOGICALLY?

1. *The attempt to train pupils in the use of the factors of logical study*

In Chapter V the statement was made that part of the classes tested in both the sixth and seventh grades were trained in the use of the factors of higher study between the first and second series of tests, the idea being to discover what difference such training would produce in the results of the second series. It must be stated frankly that the conditions governing this attempted training were far from ideal. Two of the five classes trained in the sixth grade and three of the four classes trained in the seventh grade were in schools of practice where the pupils were not under the care of one teacher continuously; but were taught by pupil teachers or special teachers part of the time. Under such circumstances, the influence and training of even a strong teacher would not have full opportunity to produce their effect, and not all of these teachers were strong, either in their mental grasp or their teaching ability. At least two were very weak.

Then, too, with but one exception, not one of the teachers of these classes had attended the lectures in which Professor F. M. McMurry of Columbia University had advanced the theory of systematic study; so that they lacked both the lectures and the accompanying discussions of them by experienced teachers. They were taught the theory of study at second hand by those who had attended this class, and an interval of three months was a short period for them to learn the theory and then apply it to classes with sufficient success to produce marked results.

To add to the difficulty, there was almost no literature on the subject to put into their hands to help them in understanding the theory and its requirements, and there were no schools practicing the theory which could be observed and used as guides. A copy of a paper read by Professor F. M. McMurry before the Department of Superintendence of the National Educational Association in Louisville, Ky., in March, 1906, on the subject, "Some Suggestions for the Improvement of the Study Period," was sent to each teacher who undertook the training work. In addition, there was sent a copy of the theoretical discussion of the steps in systematic study which was part of an essay on "The Study of the Reading Lesson in the Fourth Grade," prepared by the writer of this book.

Under the compulsion of circumstances the work of training was undertaken even with such adverse conditions, and the courage and good will of the school teachers and school principals who aided in the task are gratefully recognized.

If the training of the pupils was successful, the percentage of pupils in the trained classes who used the factors of logical study in writing the second series ought to be greater than the percentage who used them in the first series; and the number of trained pupils who wrote indefinite, general, or irrelevant answers should be lower in the second series than in the first. An examination of the results shows that the changes are not always in the direction of greater proficiency for the trained classes, though even under adverse conditions they excelled in a number of particulars.

Of the answers which are sufficiently definite to show what the pupils did in studying, those which approach nearest to higher study are in regard to finding the subject, finding the important points, verifying the statements, and supplementing the lesson.

2. *Summary of the comparisons of the trained and the untrained groups*

The three tests show that on the whole the trained sixth grades made a better record in the second series than the untrained sixth grades. The trained seventh grades excelled the other seventh grades in finding the subject and in selecting the main points of the lesson, both in the first and in the last tests of the series, but their record as a whole was not as strong as that of the trained sixth grades. It is doubtful whether, save in the two particulars mentioned, which are both very important, their record was any better than that of the untrained seventh grades.

3. *An experiment in teaching pupils to study a reading lesson*

Confirmatory evidence of the ability of pupils in the elementary school to study may be seen in the results obtained from a reading class in the fourth grade in the Speyer School, the practice school of Teachers College. A series of sixteen lessons was given by the writer to this class in the spring of 1906, to determine whether the pupils of the fourth grade possess the ability to employ the factors of logical study, and whether they can be taught to use them independently and habitually. The lesson periods were from twenty-five to thirty minutes long, and there was no study period. The text used for reading was a version of the *Odyssey* edited by Mrs. Lida B. McMurry.

This series of lessons showed plainly that pupils in the fourth grade are capable of finding problems for themselves, of organizing the lesson, of asking intelligent questions, of forming sensible hypotheses, of exercising judgment as to the statements made by the author, of mastering formal difficulties for themselves, and, in various ways, of exercising initiative wisely and profitably. It showed, too, that when pupils work in such a way they work with zeal and accomplish much more than is done when they must spend time upon useless details and mechanical methods of working.

General summary of the tests and experiments

The fourth grade was selected for these tests because it is usually the lowest grade in the intermediate department of the elementary schools, and it was thought that whatever abilities such pupils possess might reasonably be looked for to at least as great a degree in all of the intermediate and grammar grades. The results of this series of lessons, coupled with the results of the tests in geography given to the sixth and seventh grades, indicate strongly that pupils in the elementary schools in grades including the fourth, as well as higher classes, are able, not only to employ the factors of logical study, but also that by means of systematic effort they can be made to improve in their employment of them.

SUGGESTIONS FOR TRAINING CHILDREN TO STUDY

VIII

SUGGESTIONS FOR TRAINING CHILDREN TO STUDY

I. *The teacher's attitude toward the subjects to be taught*

TEACHERS have asked whether, under the conditions in which they must do their work, it is possible to train pupils to study thoughtfully. They must prepare their classes to face examinations set by the school authorities, and subject-matter means just so much material which must be learned by the pupils by the quickest possible process in order to cover the field before examination time. As a consequence subjects are not regarded as means by which pupils may be instructed and trained, but as so many things to be disposed of in the shortest time. But suppose we assume that pupils trained to study can not only master the subjects in less time, but can do so with much more profit to themselves, then what should be the teacher's attitude toward the subject-matter of his grade? Clearly the material should assume a new importance. Not only may it be mastered against the day of examinations, but it becomes a means of valuable training in ways of working which constitute a real preparation for life. In preparing for class-work, the teacher should not merely study the lesson for his own command of the facts. For the sake of the class he must try to discover the possibilities afforded by the lesson for training the pupils in thoughtful ways of working. Which steps can the pupils employ readily in the case of a given lesson? With which will they need help? Which must they employ? Which may be safely omitted? These questions are a few of the many which will surely suggest themselves to a teacher who undertakes to give his class systematic training in the higher form of studying. Like most new modes of working, it may in the beginning require a great deal of time to determine the possibilities of the material, but practice will bring facility. The teacher will be able to see quickly whether the lesson calls for inductive or deductive study; whether the problem is or is not quite apparent; whether the book offers sufficient data, or whether it must be supplemented; what organization is possible or advisable; whether the lesson contemplated should end in a positive theory or in a suspended judgment; whether memorizing is necessary; and what forms of verification are profitable and possible.

2. *The teacher's attitude toward the class*

Having done as much of this preliminary work as is necessary, the teacher needs to keep his mind open and flexible, so that he shall not dominate absolutely the efforts of the class. It often happens that the teacher gets his mind so fixed upon his own plan or his own idea that he is totally blind to anything of value in the plans or ideas suggested by the pupils. If the pupils are to be trained, their plans and ideas must be the starting point. They constitute the stock in trade, the raw material with which the work must be done. Guided at first by the teacher, and gradually more and more by their own developing experience, the pupils must learn to judge of the value of their own work, their own recitations, their own theories. To be helpful in this respect, the teacher must be on such terms with his pupils that his presence does not stand in the way of free mental activity. A teacher who frightens his class, who is over-serious, or who is sarcastic, will not be able to make much progress in training pupils to study, since his attitude retards rather than accelerates thinking on the part of the class. Fairness, frankness, the spirit of coöperation, a brisk procedure which brings a sense of accomplishment, — these are helpful to pupils, and experience shows that pupils respond to such qualities in their instructors.

3. *The need of training in many directions*

In undertaking to teach children to study, it must be kept clearly in mind that they will not learn the process so as to apply it generally unless they learn it in connection with many kinds of work involving thought. To narrow the training to the reading, arithmetic, geography, or any other one subject will not necessarily produce trained students except in the subject employed. The training must be general if the application is to be general.

4. *Consciousness of factors not necessary with very young children*

Another point to be kept in mind in training the very young children is that it is quite as unnecessary and just as time-consuming to make them conscious of the reasons for the various steps in studying as to make them conscious of the reasons for the various processes which they learn to employ in arithmetic, or for the various correct forms of speech which they are taught to use. They learn to do many things unconsciously in the early days, the reasons for which are wisely postponed until the days of better understanding. The reasons are not always necessary to the mastery of the process, and even though the pupils might be made to understand them, the expenditure of time and energy required with little children is out of proportion to the results obtained. They can learn with much greater ease a few years later, and therefore the rational side of many processes can safely be neglected until that time.

5. *Learning to find the problem*

Little children will learn how to study by being trained into right habits of studying by the teacher. In their early oral work in literature, reading, or nature study, the process of training may begin, and as the children gain in power and maturity, more and more may be expected of them. To decide upon the name of a story they have heard requires reflection upon the story as a whole, and judgment as to the most striking characteristics. To find a better title to the reading lesson than the author has given, to find a more interesting title, or at least to find a different one that is suitable, will require similar effort, and makes a good beginning in mastering thought.

In addition to finding the subject of a lesson and finding its large divisions, young children can be trained to see what question or questions the author has answered in a paragraph or section. Teacher and pupils may work together at this until the latter get the idea, and then a lesson may be assigned to give practice in their new way of working. Children naturally ask questions calling for more information, more facts or more reasons, and need guidance in making choice of such questions for class use. Questions related to the lesson but not answered in the book, or questions growing out of the thought given in the text, should be encouraged, and pupils should be trained to discriminate between those which are valuable and those which are not. They also need to learn how to express the questions well. A seventh grade which had less than a month of this work grew quite discriminating as to the nature and form of questions suggested by the members of the class. These pupils objected to questions as being too long, as lacking clearness, as telling the answer, as being too simple, as being clumsy or poorly worded, and so on. They were giving themselves some excellent training in the art of questioning, and were mastering their texts, since they had to judge of the correctness of the answers given to the questions which they asked. Grades much lower in rank can do something in this direction.

Children can also be trained to analyze a situation or problem and discover what the thing is which is to be known or done, and what the facts are which they can employ in solving the problem. Take an example in arithmetic like the following: A little girl bought two quarts of milk at four cents a pint. How much did the milk cost? When such problems are first begun in class, the teacher asks all the questions, as "What is it that is to be found out?" "What does the problem tell you?" "How can you use what you know so as to find out the answer?" and any other questions that are necessary. But unless the teacher helps the child to help himself, he is likely to remain a helpless dependent. He should learn to make his own analysis. He may even need to write down in one column what he knows and in another what he does not know, and then try to find some clue which leads to the solution. In sentential analysis, in parsing, in arithmetic and other branches of mathematics, in geography, just such opportunities for self-questioning, for analysis of the problem, present themselves, and unless they are utilized, we shall continue to have pupils in higher grades and higher schools who wait for the instructor to ask all the questions and direct all thought. It is necessary for the teacher to do all or most of the questioning with little children, but pupils of the fourth and fifth grades have demonstrated that they are able to assume much of this responsibility themselves. They need oversight, direction, help in various ways, but it should be help which leads to greater power in breaking up situations or problems and finding right solutions, not help which perpetuates dependence.

6. *The function of the lesson assignment*

In this connection, the lesson assignment assumes new importance. It is not merely a time when the pages containing the new lesson are indicated. It is the teacher's opportunity to prepare the class for right study. If the pupils need help in finding the aim, the lesson assignment should pave the way for its discovery. This function of the assignment holds true for all the steps manifestly involved in the mastery of a lesson by a class during a study period. This assignment may occupy a separate period, or it may be made in connection with some lesson out of which the new lesson develops, and with which it is closely related. Opportunity for the assignment of related lessons occurs frequently and should not be overlooked.

7. *Learning to supplement the text*

A form of supplementing the text which little children can begin to use, is the employment of other books upon which they make reports to the class. Or, indeed, the other material may be drawn from any one of many sources; from books, people, observation, or experimentation. But some supplementary assignment, however simple and easy, is given to the class, or to some individuals in the class, and is to be prepared and reported upon in a future recitation. The child becomes responsible for something definite, and his work assumes a new value in his eyes. Whether he is interested in the task for its own sake or does it through a sense of compulsion, he will still be the gainer. The point is that he learns to use outside sources, to cull the material relating to the topic, to arrange it in order, and to give it to the class. As he masters the use of the topical outline, this supplementary work becomes increasingly valuable, for then the pupils' reports are more orderly and reliable. These individual assignments enable a teacher to save much time for his class, since instead of having all of the class look up all of a subject, he can divide the work, and so get it done more thoroughly and with less expenditure of time by the class as a whole. A certain eighth grade prepares many of its history and geography lessons in the manner above described. When a boy is called upon to recite, he writes his subject and a brief outline upon the blackboard, and then recites to the class, following the order of his topics. The other members may or may not question him. If he has made some important omission, the teacher questions him. He may bring books containing maps or illustrations for the class to examine, and does not hesitate to draw a sketch in a simple way if it is necessary. This work has its beginnings in the lowest primary grades, where the children are made responsible for something which they can easily find out and which they must bring for the benefit of all the class.

8. *Judging the value of material*

In connection with the work in supplementing, comes the idea of training pupils to judge whether the information they find or present is true. Little children tell some very surprising things sometimes, and we often overlook them because we say the narrators have not yet learned to draw an exact line between the real and the imaginary. But when actual facts are called for and these marvelous contributions are offered, the child should be met with the question, "Do you know that to be true or are you making believe?" Even older people have sometimes to reflect that they are dealing with theories and not with facts. Then, too, children frequently read so hastily and so imperfectly that they get the facts of the book quite distorted. They need to be trained to an accurate rendering. In regard to hearsay evidence, they can learn to be discriminating, and to reject the wildly improbable. In many ways which will come to the careful teacher as he looks for opportunity, the pupils in the lower grades can be led to realize that the material which they present must be selected with discrimination, and that it must be true. Reading must be carefully done, observations must be exactly taken, and things heard must be sifted before reports are made. Gradually, as more responsibility is put upon the pupils for the selection of the sources of data, the children ought to be made discriminating in their judgment of these sources. They should consider why one newspaper should be consulted rather than another; why one historian or geographer should be preferred to others; and why certain people's reports are more to be relied upon than others. If they have been alert and critical in regard to the work done in class from day to day, this new expression of their judgment should not be arduous. Criticism of sources will often come naturally, as, for example, the criticism of newspapers and periodicals of sensational type; of writers whose statements are founded on slight evidences and permeated by an unfriendly spirit. These are only suggestions as to the possibility of training children in the critical judgment of materials. Doubtless the teacher will find many ways of directing and training his classes in proper attitudes toward data and conclusions. Under the criticism which he is led to make of himself, in addition to that offered by his mates, a pupil will gradually learn to refrain from wild guessing, even if he makes no advance on the positive side of sound thinking.

9. *Learning to organize data*

While preparing some story for oral reproduction or for dramatization, the pupils can decide which part must be told or played first, which next, and so on. In the third and fourth grades, this exercise leads to the formation of an outline for a topical recitation or to serve as a guide in composition. In all such work the teacher should guide the children toward being critical of their own titles, topics, and outlines, commending that which is good and pointing out that which is bad with a statement of the reasons for the judgment. The teacher must not demand perfection in these first attempts, but should accept the pupils' efforts without too much correction on his part. As their critical judgment develops, better results can be demanded.

These exercises, begun with material already presented before the class, prepare directly for individual study of books. As the pupils learn the various steps, they should be given opportunity to use them independently with suitable material, and should be tested in class that the progress they are making in their use may be seen. These topical outlines should be prepared independently by older pupils in preparation for class recitation, as a basis for composition, as a convenient means of note-taking, and for any other purpose where a concise and orderly survey of the content of a given piece of subject-matter is necessary. In the higher grades, the use of the written outline may be superseded by the purely mental outline. Not all pupils may be able to make and hold a topical analysis without notes, but how much they can really do is not known because we have not trained them to use the power they possess.

10. *Training pupils to work quickly*

Pupils not only need to master the contents of their books systematically and thoroughly, but they need to master them quickly. There are many students, in school and out, who spend hours poring over subjects which they might grasp in minutes rather than hours if only they had learned the habit of working quickly. Teachers can train pupils into rapidity even with the first oral work in studying, just as they train them into quick recognition of combinations of letters or figures in reading or arithmetic. When the study of books is begun, economy of time can still be insisted upon, and if a class, or individuals in a class, work too slowly, special exercises for increasing rapidity may be employed as in other subjects. Competition of row against row in the time required to prepare a good outline, to find the subject, to find the first large point, and the like, will accelerate effort. The time which is necessary for the whole class to find the main idea of a paragraph can be noted. Pupils can be encouraged to keep a daily record of the time required to prepare the lesson in the subject which consumes too much time, and to see how much they can lower the time record and still make thorough preparation. The main thing is to rouse their interest and coöperation in the effort to learn to study both quickly and well. Slowness is frequently a habit, and should be replaced by a rate of performance which secures good results in less time. The teacher's thought and ingenuity will help if only he recognizes the situation and determines to improve it. Much of the trouble comes, with adults, at least, from thinking that every word must be inspected. They have not learned to sweep through a paragraph to find the salient thought which it offers and to disregard the rest. Consequently, they waste time and wear themselves out uselessly. Habit holds them slavishly. Those who are taught to study when young may escape such slavery.

11. *The value of the puzzle problem*

An important help in training pupils in analysis and in the use of the various steps of study is the "puzzle problem." Such a problem appeals to the natural interests of children. It inspires to combat, so to speak, and arouses the desire to conquer. The answer is not especially important, however interesting it may be as a sign of victory. It is the intricacies of the process which engage the attention, and challenge one's best efforts. There must be very careful analysis in order to get the exact situation, and means and end must be carefully compared. Such problems used to abound in the old mental arithmetic, and in the miscellaneous problems found here and there in the written arithmetics. The newer books have "puzzle problems" in more practical form, so that the answers have more value; but when in the old books the dog pursued the hare, or the frog crept out of the well, or the proportions of the head, tail, and body of the fish were concerned, the answer had absolutely no value, and all interest centred in the process.

Ordinarily, the practical, every-day problems are best for a class, and should constitute the main part of all applied work. The catch problems, and the less practical "puzzle problems," serve as a stimulus, and can be used occasionally to give zest to the regular work.

12. *The position of the answer: its effect upon study*

In this connection, it is not inappropriate to speak of the position of the answer in the book, or in a lesson assigned on the blackboard. If the answer follows the question, an impossible situation is created for the pupils. The pupils are expected to realize the need of the answer and then to find it, — and there it is before their eyes! Why realize its need, and why find it when they already know it? It would be better to have it at the back of the book or in a separate book. Often it is best not to have it accessible at all and to have all pupils prove their work by employing the results they obtain. A class which has easy access to answers is usually a class which is not strong in its reasoning. Such pupils are not at all sure of themselves. They frequently juggle with figures until they get an answer that agrees with the one in the book, but they cannot explain their procedure, nor give reasons for the steps taken. Conditions which lead to such intellectual helplessness and dishonesty should be avoided as much as possible.

13. *The number of steps employed in solving any problem*

When the theory of the five formal steps of instruction was first introduced into this country, a number of teachers gained the idea that all of the steps must be employed in all teaching. The result was that the teaching became mechanical and formal, the teachers were greatly and unnecessarily overworked, and there was not enough gain to the pupils to counterbalance the expenditure of energy. If teachers attempt to force pupils to use all of the steps of thoughtful study in the solution of every problem, there will be a similar breaking down of the whole idea. The work will become hopelessly formal and will presently be abandoned. Common sense must prevail; and the nature of the problem, the ability of the pupils, and the materials available for use in solving the problem must influence the steps involved.

It has been shown in earlier chapters that it is necessary to all thoughtful study that there be a problem in the mind of the student. This step, then, the realization of a problem, must be present whether the study be inductive or deductive. Data of some sort must be present, from whatever source obtained, but the amount necessary, as well as the sources employed, will vary. Sometimes very little organization will be required, while at others there will be need of very careful and comprehensive organization. In solving some problems, the element of doubt may not enter at all as a factor, while at other times there may be need of close scrutiny of both hypothesis and data. Some problems are so simple, and the material attainable is so convincing, that a final judgment may be given quickly; but this is not always possible. It may be necessary to defer for a time a definite conclusion; indeed, final answers are sometimes never possible to the student who first discovers the problem. The theory of world formation is still an hypothesis, though it is long since men first began to reflect upon the making of worlds.

Memorizing, too, will vary. It may not be required at all; the order of the steps thought out may be memorized; the conclusions may be learned in the pupils' own wording; or memorizing may be necessary as in learning poems, rules, definitions, and other forms. It should be based upon understanding, and then carried out with vigor. Close attention and energy devoted to the formal side, after the ideas have been mastered, will make the process relatively easy.

As to verification, there should be enough of it, in some form, to satisfy the problem. In algebra and other forms of mathematics, this verification is carried out by employing the answer found and seeing if it satisfies the conditions laid down in the examples given. In the case of certain social theories, one may point to actual situations as a verification or may follow out imaginary results. *Enough to satisfy the problem* makes a good working rule for verification. In the past, our sins in this respect have been those of omission rather than those of commission. We are more likely to require too little than too much verifying, and to fail in improving valuable opportunities for training in testing results. The consequence is that pupils are left satisfied with very immature theories, and with little or no conception of the necessity and value of proof.

14. *The order in which the factors of study are employed*

Either reflection or experience will show a teacher that the factors of proper study will not always be employed in the same order. For example, doubt may be present at almost any stage in the solution of a problem; and some memorizing may be necessary when a part of the work has been accomplished in order to hold the results already achieved. In working out some long or involved rule or definition by the inductive method, it is often best to work out one part at a time and fix it firmly in the mind before proceeding to another section of the problem. Furthermore, the collecting of data is not limited to a certain place in study. The student may need to search for facts to enable him to define his problem clearly, or to help him formulate a theory for the solution of the problem, or to test the theory when it has been formulated. Hard and fast rules as to the order of the steps in thoughtful study can hardly be laid down. Recognition of the problem has been called the first step, but even this first step may be accompanied by doubt, by the collecting of data, and possibly by some of the others.

Whenever data are employed, the necessity for the exercise of doubt and for organization may arise; and whenever theories are formulated, there may be occasion for decision as to whether the conclusions are final or merely tentative. Naturally, verification must follow the forming of conclusions or theories. The path can only be marked out broadly for the use of the steps, and the conditions present when some individual problem is under consideration will influence the variations from the path.

To illustrate the variation in procedure, we may think of the problems connected with fishing as they are studied by the pupils who live in the fishing towns on the New England coast and as they would have to be studied by children living inland. The latter would probably have to gather much information about fishermen and fishing before they could even realize the nature of the problems; while the pupils living in the midst of the trade can more easily appreciate them, since they know the situation at first hand. These children of the coast, too, can gather their data from observation and consequently need not suspect their sources of information of being unreliable, as the other class of children might be obliged to do. They are also in a better position to verify conclusions. The whole situation is more favorable for them than for pupils remote from the sea. But when the problem relates to life on the plains or in the mountains, then the situation above described is exactly reversed, and the order of the steps of study would be materially changed for both sets of pupils; also, the extent to which some of the steps would be employed.

15. *External aids to study*

There are several external aids to study which pupils should master as they have need of them. One of these is the use of the dictionary. Children should know how to find a word, pronounce it, and select the one meaning which is applicable to the situation in which the word is used. To use the dictionary and pronouncing vocabularies properly, the pupils must know how to interpret the accent marks and also the common diacritical marks. Where several meanings are given, they must learn to choose the appropriate one. If they are looking for the meanings of words to satisfy a conscious need, they will be more likely to choose the correct definition, or the suitable synonym.

A second aid is the table of contents of a book. Pupils looking for material usually need to be trained to use the table of contents, or even to discover its existence. They need practice in finding the appropriate chapter, and then the part of the chapter relevant to the subject which is under consideration. Training in the use of an alphabetical index is also necessary. It is time well spent to teach the use of these various aids, and, when experience shows it to be necessary, to give special drill in the use of the dictionary, pronouncing vocabulary, table of contents, and index.

The encyclopædia offers a new difficulty because of its exhaustive treatment of various topics. Pupils need to learn how to find the volume needed, the topic in the volume, and the part of the article desired. The treatment of the material when found has already been described, as that is study of content.

When the pupils are old enough to use libraries where Poole's or other annual indexes of current literature are found, a new aid to study must be mastered, and either the teacher or some library assistant should give the necessary instruction. The use of the card catalogue of authors and titles may be learned in the same lesson. All these aids to study are a part of literary life. We frequently assume that knowledge of their use is universal, and consequently give the rising generation no help in processes which in themselves are not natural but must be learned. Training in these external aids greatly extends the power of pupils to acquire new material for themselves, and enables them to work much more rapidly.

TRAINING CHILDREN TO STUDY

16. *Hindrances to training pupils to study*

a. *Individual differences in ability*

Doubtless many teachers will think that in their particular conditions nothing can be done towards teaching their pupils to study because the obstacles are too great. They may urge as one objection that their pupils vary greatly in ability, and that therefore they cannot hope to give effective training in systematic study. It is not clear why inequality of ability should be a hindrance to training in proper study any more than it is a hindrance to any kind of teaching or training. No class of children have equal abilities in any one line, and yet teachers attempt to train classes in many directions. The objection urged applies equally to all work, and need not prevent training in study, since it does not prevent training in other lines.

Proper study gives the bright pupils a fitting opportunity to use their powers, since they may exercise initiative, search widely for materials, experiment, make reports, and in various ways employ their activities. They derive a benefit from being bright which mere memorizing never bestows. The slower, duller pupils will lose nothing by using their powers intelligently. At the worst, they can only fall back upon memorizing, a process to which they have been accustomed.

b. *The limitations of the teacher*

The teacher will find his own limitations to lie in mastering the theory of study, in applying it to his own study, and in teaching others to employ it. But these same hindrances have existed in connection with every advance in method and also in connection with every new subject introduced into the curriculum. They are transient. Not all teachers can learn to train pupils with the same degree of success, but with study and with thoughtful trial, progress can be made. There is no royal road in this special kind of work, any more than there is in others; but the obstacles can be overcome, to a great degree at least, by intelligent, persistent effort. Practice will make it much easier to lead the pupils to see problems and to become more self-helpful in solving them. Furthermore, as the children grow in the use of right methods of study, the teacher's work should become easier and more pleasing. The child will do his share of work and the teacher will be supervising interesting thought, not drilling on barren words.

c. *The tendency to overestimate small points*

One tendency which teachers will need to guard against will be the tendency of the pupils to attach too much importance to small points, to quibble over little things, and to spend too much time upon non-essentials. Because of their immaturity and lack of experience, children lack perspective and so are willing to spend time upon unimportant subjects. Their judgment needs developing. Consequently they need to consider such questions as these: Does the point you are considering bear upon the subject we are discussing? Is it important enough to justify our spending much time upon it? It may be necessary at times for the teacher to sweep the whole discussion aside with the statement that it is not valuable, and to direct the class to the consideration of other data or problems. An experienced teacher, in speaking of the difficulties lying in the way of permitting children to exercise initiative, said that he thought the initiative would have to be directed. He is doubtless right. Somewhere between absolute direction at one extreme, and absolute freedom of initiative at the other, the wiser course will be found.

d. *The lack of logical arrangement of subject-matter in books*

The arrangement of material in text-books will sometimes be found to constitute a barrier to proper study because the subject-matter is not well organized. Paragraphs are so confused that the author of the book as well as any one else would have great difficulty in writing paragraph headings. There is no logical order but rather a rambling, disconnected mass of statements. It is difficult to use such texts as supplementary material, and still more difficult to use them as sources of problems, since the authors themselves were apparently not aware of any. This lack of organization offers a genuine difficulty to pupils. If texts are selected which are well arranged, some of the difficulty will be overcome. It may, however, sometimes be necessary to use inferior texts because they are the best to be obtained.

When the subject-matter is poorly arranged, the teacher ought to do more teaching and to rely less upon the book. The latter becomes more of a reference book, a source for data bearing upon the problems developed in class. The pupils will be better able to sift out relevant material from a somewhat incoherent text than to discover problems when the author himself was not keenly conscious of them. Both teacher and pupils are at a disadvantage in using such books, but they exist as sources for information both in school and out, and the best must be made of them.

17. *Effect of proper study upon schoolroom procedure*

Any course of procedure which influences greatly the spirit of a school must affect the discipline of that school to a marked degree. Studying for the purpose of satisfying needs, of solving problems, must result in a different attitude towards subject-matter on the part of both teacher and pupils. It involves coöperation and a spirit of good fellowship between teacher and class. Out of these spiritual and mental attitudes must come a kind of schoolroom procedure which is very different from the rigid, repressive discipline which allows no initiative to pupils, and which centres all in the teacher. With the interest of the class aroused, the teacher has less occasion to resort to compulsion or to penalties in order to have lessons prepared. Nor should discipline be so difficult when pupils are working for purposes growing out of their own interests. Pupils will need to have freedom to consult maps, charts, and books of reference if they are to collect data bearing upon their problems. They may need to learn to do this in a proper way and at proper times, so as to cause as little disturbance as possible to class exercises. Some pupils need to realize that it is often best to find what their own text-books have to say on a subject before they go to the reference shelves for other books. But on the whole, with a working spirit, there will be an atmosphere of work, and that need not be unruly. It is for the teacher to see that energy is not dissipated and that the freedom of a busy class does not degenerate into a state of disorder which makes fruitful effort impossible to those who wish to study.

It has been shown in preceding chapters that the class exercises cannot consist solely of a series of questions propounded by teachers and answered by pupils, or of mere memory recitations of text. There will of necessity be questioning by the pupils themselves, the suggestion and discussion of theory, the weighing of statements made by different members of the class, and, in short, participation in a variety of ways by the class. The pupils should be expected to exercise initiative in discovering and solving problems relating to the school, whether they be problems pertaining to lessons or to discipline. They require encouragement and training in the wise development of such initiative. It is an important duty of the teacher to meet this requirement. Pupils should be held responsible for the recitations of their mates. They should demand that such recitations be made in tones loud enough to be heard. They should challenge incorrect and irrelevant statements, instead of leaving all criticism to the teacher, who, to be sure, usually assumes it at the beginning of the term and never delegates it. Responsibility should be placed upon the pupils more and more as they develop in ability. Children are not unwilling to exercise activity in the ways mentioned. The difficulty in many cases is that they are not expected or permitted to do so.

A large share of the teacher's responsibility is responsibility which belongs rightfully to the class. This point has already been touched upon in a preceding paragraph, but will bear repetition. The teacher who asks all the questions, finds all the large points, makes all the summaries and outlines, decides whether the problem is solved or not, is doing the work which pupils should do. Children in an average fourth grade can perform many of the activities just mentioned. A fifth grade can do still more, and higher grades will be found even more capable.

The field is open for experimentation in these and other lines in teaching children to study. The conclusions and suggestions here presented are based upon observations made in a large number of classes, and some good results have been witnessed. Experience has shown that even a little effort put forth brings a rich reward, though as yet the whole movement is in its beginning. Some teachers of only average ability have tried to train very ordinary classes into habits of systematic study, and have seen most encouraging results within a few weeks; so that no teacher should refuse to attempt to train his class because he thinks that only a chosen few can study successfully. The need of such training is urgent, and those teachers who will grapple boldly with the problems involved in it, who will discover the best ways of working with pupils, the difficulties to be avoided or overcome, and who will put the results of their efforts before the teaching world in some accessible form will be rendering valuable service. For the most part, however, each teacher will have to work out his own devices, based upon the fundamental principles.

In conclusion, one caution is urged upon teachers, and that is that they avoid making this training too formal. One teacher thought the best way to train her class was to teach it to recite the steps of logical study in order. She quite missed the point of the whole idea. If the children learn what the steps are from their frequent use of them, no harm is done; but simply to memorize them makes the whole theory a lifeless form.

It is difficult to write suggestions, because as soon as written they appear very rigid and lacking in adaptability. Let it be remembered that the teacher must read the spirit into what has been said, and that he must not lose touch with it as he teaches. If only he will do that, he will be able to work out much more for himself than the writer has been able to suggest.

General Summary

(1) The teacher who undertakes to teach his pupils to study must regard the subject-matter of instruction as a means of training in right habits as well as a means of acquiring knowledge. (2) He must establish friendly relations with the pupils, and must coöperate with them. (3) The training cannot be confined to one subject if it is to be general in its application. It must be associated with all possible situations. (4) Little

children should be trained to study without consciousness of the method. Right habits are the first consideration with them. As pupils grow older, they may be made conscious of the factors of proper study, so that they may better understand how to direct their own efforts. (5) In the earlier stages of training pupils to study, the teacher will need to work with the class, and he will throw the pupils upon their own resources as their ability to use the factors of study develops. (6) This training will include all of the phases of study at some time, but not all of the factors will necessarily be employed in every lesson. (7) The order in which the factors of study are employed is not fixed. (8) In training pupils to study, the use of such external aids as the dictionary, the encyclopædia, pronouncing gazetteers, indexes, tables of contents, and card catalogues must be included in the process. (9) While various obstacles oppose themselves to the successful issue of training pupils to study properly, very few of them are peculiar to this branch of training, and none are insurmountable. (10) The teacher must accustom the pupils to assume responsibility, to exercise initiative, to participate in the work of the class and school, to ask questions, and to be critical of their own efforts and those of their classmates. The teacher must to some extent eliminate himself. He must contribute less, and must demand greater contributions from the class. He must perform less of the work, and must train the pupils in thoughtful ways of working.

NOTE. — The following books contain helpful ideas on method of study: —

F. M. MCMURRY, *How to Study and Teaching How to Study.*

F. M. MCMURRY, "Some Suggestions for the Improvement of the Study Period," *Proceedings of the N. E. A.* 1906.

JOHN DEWEY, *School and Society; Moral Principles in Education.*

W. C. BAGLEY, *The Educative Process*, chap. xxi.

E. L. THORNDIKE, *Principles of Teaching*, chaps. ix, x.

WILLIAM JAMES, *Talks to Teachers.*

OUTLINE

(for study and discussion, consisting of chapter, main and sub-headings as given in body of work)

I. THE NATURE OF LOGICAL STUDY

OUTLINE

II. THE NATURE OF INDUCTIVE STUDY

III. THE NATURE OF DEDUCTIVE STUDY

OUTLINE

OUTLINE

OUTLINE

PART 8

GENETIC PSYCHOLOGY

I have made bold to say these things at the very outset in order that we may begin our discussions with a clear recognition of their spirit and aims. For I should not be here with these statements about the dangers and difficulties of our professional lives if I did not believe with all certainty that it is possible to overcome this harmful over-worry and this confusion which doubles the burden of work. It is possible for teachers to save themselves from mental stagnation, to advance day by day, and thus keep pace with our rapidly progressing educational life. The condition, however, which must be fulfilled in order to attain these desirable ends is that teachers shall consider and apply to themselves some of the common principles of education.

Did you never wonder why, in this age when we are studying so eagerly all the factors of the educational situation, no one has ever undertaken an exhaustive study of the teacher? We have a history of educational systems; we study present-day institutions and their organization; we study children with great care and with much enthusiasm; we take up psychology and sociology; but we do not seem to have waked up to the fact that bad order in our classes is sometimes a problem in teacher-study instead of child-study, that the introduction of a new subject into our schools is not always a question in sociology, but is more often a question of securing the cooperation of a body of teachers who, all unknown to themselves, are buried under a mass of traditional ideas.

Now do not have visions of a mass of dry material to be studied in this new science of teacher-study which I have brought to your attention, for I am not going to suggest that we send out elaborate *questionnaires* as our first step. I confess that when I look over some of the titles of child-study investigations, such as "Children's lies," "Effects of weather on children," "What children do out of school," etc., I have sometimes thought that it would be only fair for some juvenile victim of these child-study revelations to compare notes with his fellows on those modes of obscuring facts which are at times employed by teachers, and which parallel ethically what in children are called lies. And if the weather affects children, and if what children do outside of school affects their work in school, then why might not some of these same relations be assumed to have significance for the older and yet human individuals who conduct the affairs of the class-room? Some day the science of teacher-study may become mature enough and broad enough in its scope to venture on some of these investigations, which we now hardly dare to urge too seriously. For the present our range must be more limited. And yet I believe that within this narrower range the study can be made suggestive, if we will but look at ourselves fairly and frankly, and, having seen ourselves, not turn away and straightway forget what manner of men and women we are, but diligently and daily take up the task of educating ourselves as earnestly as we take up the task of educating others.

There is another reason why it is right to urge upon you the importance of this study which we have called teacher-study. It is only through an intelligent interest in one's own development that one can gain a true understanding of the needs of the developing child.

Let me explain a little more fully what I mean. We

have learned as one of the great lessons of our child-study that children are not small adults. There are essential differences in nature between children and grown-ups, which make it necessary for us to treat children in a way appropriate to their special needs. Now, the general fact that children are different from ourselves is one which can be more or less fully grasped without any profound study. But the teacher must go further than merely to grasp the general fact. The teacher must be able to understand in detail, first, his own mental characteristics, and secondly, the specific characteristics in which the child differs from himself. This is no easy task, for it is proverbial that by nature we interpret the thoughts of others in the light of our own experiences. If you think thus and so when you hear a certain sound, then you expect, unless your training has shown you the truth, every one else to do the same under the same conditions. It requires some careful study, both of oneself and of others, to realize that thought processes in the presence of the same object may be very different in different individuals. It requires a good deal of the most careful kind of self-study as well as child-study for the teacher to realize anything about how the child before him really thinks and feels.

Some hints as to the way in which children think and feel can be gathered from the few rather vague recollections that come to us of our own childhood's habits and experiences. Indeed, some one will do a great service for child-study if he will gather recollections of this sort more extensively than they have ever been gathered and put them into systematic order. But recollections can give us only hints, and if these were the only connecting links between adult mental life and the child's mental life, our knowledge of the child's difficulties in mental growth would be indeed meager. Fortunately there is another bond of connection. Each of us has undeveloped faculties, dormant possibilities, which make us in certain particulars close friends of the child. If, recognizing this, we turn ourselves into both teachers and pupils at once, and watch our own dormant possibilities as they grow and develop, the advantage will be twofold. We shall improve as pupils, and as teachers we shall learn some of the lessons of our art of instruction by seeing how the learner and the teacher may cooperate and how they have difficulty in understanding each other.

Mark you, I do not say that adult education in these undeveloped functions is the exact duplicate of that which should take place in the case of the child. What I do say is, that if you will discover some undeveloped faculty in your own mind and then observe its changes as you pass through the process of education, you will have one of the best experiences on which to base your child-study. For example, I once had a class of teachers who agreed to spend some time and practise in trying to improve their writing. We selected a very narrow line of study. Each of us tried to make the slope of his letters uniform, and to observe closely what the stages of development were. There are very few adults who have given much attention to the development of a uniform slope of their letters. We found this, accordingly, a proper subject to study. The effort to improve gave us, individually and collectively, I am sure, more insight into the attitude which children take in their efforts to learn to write, than could have been acquired from indefinite quantities of child-study unaided by teacher-study. And so I say we have a right to urge the importance of teacher-study as a necessary preliminary to child-study. The child's mind is indeed different from our own; if we would realize this fully, we must study the changes through which the learner passes, by direct, first-hand observation in ourselves. We must realize that mental progress never ends, and that at all stages it exhibits certain similarities and follows certain common principles, and we must seek out these principles of development where alone we can come into direct contact with them—namely, in our own experiences.

One does not need to go through any elaborate process of self-training in order to understand the meaning of development. He can find phases of his own experience which indicate that he is indeed a step beyond the child in mental life, but by no means yet at the limit of possible progress. Take as one of the best illustrations of this general fact, the adult recognition of distances and sizes. You see a man coming down the street two blocks away, and you recognize his true size with a fair degree of accuracy. This shows itself in the fact that your visual recognition of him does not have to be changed in any noticeable degree as he comes nearer. For short distances, such as two blocks, the facts which we all know as the facts of perspective do not make it difficult for us to recognize visual size. The result is, that in spite of the fact that the optical image of that man is much smaller at a distance of two blocks than it is at a distance of ten or twenty feet; in spite of the fact that you would have to draw the man much smaller if you wanted to represent him as two blocks away than if you wanted to represent him near at hand—in spite of these facts, you see him even at the greater distance in his normal dimensions. Put into other words, this means that you have so fully mastered the significance of this class of experiences that you get a fully developed, accurate form of knowledge and experience without difficulty, whether the man is near at hand or two blocks away—that is, whether your visual image is large or relatively small. But now increase that two blocks to a mile, or, better still, climb up to the top of a high building and look down at the man. How does he look now? As large as usual? Of course not. Look at him as you will, he looks small. Even your knowledge of the fact that he is of the usual size does not help you. Even the dictum of some learned teacher could not make that man look as large as usual. The trouble is that our adult consciousness is not used to dealing with men at ranges of a mile, nor is it used to dealing with men a hundred feet below us. The man at a distance of two blocks looked natural because he stood quite within the range of our ordinary training in the recognition of visual size. For short distances on level ground we have a developed faculty of recognition, but for long distances, and for comparatively short distances upward and downward, we have only very limited training. Some one may be led to ask, At what range does adult recognition of size cease to be accurate and fully developed? We can not answer this question in a general way. Different individuals differ very greatly. The determining factor is the amount of experience. And to make this clear we may at once appeal to some illustrations, which will at the same time serve to show the value of this teacher-study for the comprehension of the child's mind.

I remember when I was a little boy riding across a high railroad bridge with my father. Down on the flat land at the river level were some laborers. I was much interested in them, they were such little men. I could have held one of them in my hand. I decided to share my delight with my father, and induced him to look out and see my pygmies. Like all children, I believed, of course, in the infallibility of my father and of my own eyes. My beliefs received something of a shock that day when he told me that my pygmies were just ordinary men, and turned back to his reading. I dare say I charitably attributed his remark to the rather superficial glance he had given the men; at any rate, I remember believing in the testimony of my eyes in that case, and silently protesting against what was, from my point of view, a most unaccountable lack of interest in a curious race of men. Need I add the explanation of this experience? A little greater elevation, a little less experience in the interpretation of visual sizes, and man and boy might have had experiences more alike. As it was, those men were inside the range of my father's interpretation of perspective, while they were outside of mine.

Years after I was a party to a similar comparison of adult and child experience; this time, however, I was the adult. We were riding along together, and looking out over the broad pasture land, a little girl of six and I, when we saw some horses grazing quietly a quarter of a mile or so away. There was no difficulty in recognizing the horses as animals of full, ordinary size. And I was surprised into looking a second and even a third time by the little girl's cries of joy at seeing "those colts," as she insisted on calling them. Finally, I realized that the horses were to her untrained eyes colts. I even induced her to discuss the matter with me until I told her that they were really horses, and then the look of incredulous pity for my grown-up ignorance gave me one of the best insights I have ever had into the truth of the principle that children and adults live in different worlds. I also had a clearer understanding of the child's mind at that moment from my understanding of the fact that if the quarter of a mile had grown into two miles, I, too, might have been in doubt as to whether the horses were horses or colts.

If these illustrations have served to arouse in your minds some idea of how the problem of recognition of size may be made productive as a special study for teachers, we are now in a position to take up in somewhat more systematic fashion certain problems of teacher-study, which may be briefly indicated in the question, How do teachers, and indeed all adults, see and recognize form and size? The recognition of form is apparently a very simple function; and yet as our study progresses I believe we shall find that mental life as it appears in this function, is a most complex and highly developed form of activity.

Suppose we start with the simplest possible figure—a straight line—and see what are some of the conditions of recognizing its length. To begin with, let me draw a line on the blackboard and ask you to draw on paper at your seats a line of equal length. The result will invariably be (I have tried it time and time again with my classes) that your line on paper will be very much shorter than the one on the board, even if you foresee the result and try to aid your faulty recognition of length by adding somewhat to the line you would naturally draw. The fact is that the lines are so completely swallowed up by their surroundings that one can not see them apart from these surroundings. Estimated in terms of the blackboard, the line which I draw is short; if the same line were on paper it would not have the same relations to the surroundings, and consequently it would not seem short. If we start with this natural tendency to estimate lines in connection with their surroundings and give ourselves a little practise in the comparison of different lines, we shall find that we soon become expert in estimating blackboard lines in terms of paper. This does not mean that we merely learn how to correct our natural error. We actually learn to look at the blackboard lines and the lines on paper in a more highly developed and accurate fashion. The best parallels I can think of are those which come in our ordinary experiences of fashions. You remember those large sleeves that the women used to wear. They looked natural enough once. The whole standard of our estimation of sleeves was, if you will allow the phrase, on a large, blackboard scale. Now we have a different scale, and some of our old photographs give us a curious impression of the absurd largeness of our earlier standard. We have changed in our mode of looking at the sizes of sleeves. That change has taken place so subtly and so gradually that we overlook the change. But that change has taken place, not as a mere superficial correction of our way of looking at things; it is rather a radical and fundamental form of mental growth.

Come back now to our lines on blackboard and paper. Two facts are clear: the first is that ordinary adult experience is not developed fully in the translation of blackboard lines into lengths on paper; and the second fact is that we may gradually develop so that direct and accurate translation from blackboard to paper will be possible. And when this development has taken place, our mental life will be really different, just as our estimation of sleeves is different now from what it used to be.

One might find any number of examples of the same general fact that we have illustrated with our blackboard line, by comparing indoor objects with outdoor objects. Did you ever cut down a very small Christmas-tree and take it into the house and realize the difference in apparent size? Or have you tried to find a book in which to press autumn leaves, or noticed how small a chair looks when it stands out on the lawn? The lesson from all these illustrations is the same. We learn to recognize objects in their special environments, and if we are forced to look at them in new environments, we need more mental development. Do you wonder that children who have learned a certain fact in one simple connection need more mental development before they can make wider applications?

Let us, however, carry our study forward by turning to certain figures which the psychologists have drawn in their investigations of these matters of visual estimation of size. These figures are so simple that one does not make a very great mistake in the estimation of their size. But the figures are valuable material for our study, because, though the error is small, the conditions which give rise to the error are fairly simple and easy to comprehend. In Fig. 1, for example, there are two drawings which are in reality exactly alike in form and in size. The lower one seems, however, to be the larger of the two. The reason for this wrong estimation of size, or illusion as it is called, is not difficult to discover. The two curved lines that bound either of the drawings are different in length and in degree of curvature. When, now, one begins to compare the sizes of the two enclosed areas he naturally gives his greatest attention to the neighboring parts of the drawings. This is what we ordinarily do in comparing areas, and it is usually a successful method. But in this case the neighboring parts of the drawings furnish unsafe guides. The short curve, which is the lower boundary of one drawing, gives the impression that the whole area of that drawing is small, while the long sweeping curve which forms the neighboring boundary of the other drawing, gives the impression of bounding a larger surface. It makes no difference that the images in our eyes from these two surfaces are alike, the estimation goes astray in spite of the real identity of size and form. The interpretation is due to the relation

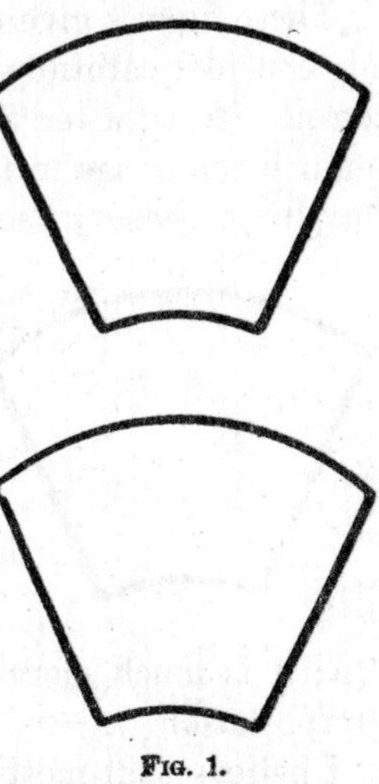

FIG. 1.

in which the drawings stand, rather than to the direct impressions themselves. If one wishes to emphasize this fact of the importance of the relative position of the figures, all one needs to do is to set the two drawings in a new relation, as is done in the second figure, when they will appear to be of the same size, as, indeed, they really are.

These figures give us an important lesson, if we will only consider carefully their teachings. Visual recognition of size is, after all, a complex process. It is not so much the image in the eye—that is, it is not so much the purely sensory fact which determines the recognition; it is much more the factor which we have called interpretation.

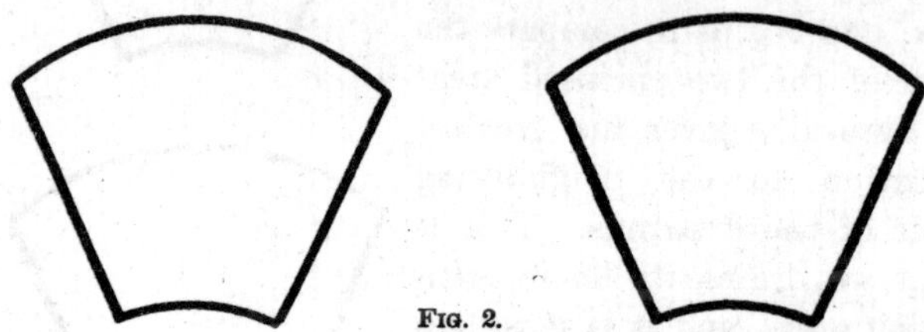

Fig. 2.

I believe that most of us have a crude notion about the way in which we get our knowledge of the sizes of things, a notion hardly more advanced than that of the ancients. Let me give you the account written by the Latin poet Lucretius, of how we come to see shapes and sizes. "I say then," wrote Lucretius, "that pictures of things and thin shapes are emitted from things off their surface . . . as a kind of film, or name it if you like a rind, because such image bears an appearance and form like to the thing, whatever it is, from whose body it is shed and wanders forth. This you may learn, however dull of apprehension, from what follows. First of all, since among things open to sight many emit bodies, some in a state of loose diffusion, like smoke . . . some of a closer and denser texture, like the gossamer coats which at times cicades doff in summer . . . and the vestures which the slippery serpent puts off among the thorns."[1] These thin outer films, Lucretius tells us, fly through the air in all directions and some of them enter the eye. With an exact copy of the object in the eye, Lucretius felt that his problem was solved. The mind sees what is in the eye, and the matter is disposed of. Of course we have advanced beyond Lucretius enough to know that there is no outside rind or film taken off the objects which we see; but I venture the opinion that most of us are quite as satisfied as was Lucretius, if we can once explain how the image gets into the eye. The light is focused in the eye as in a camera, we say, and here there is an exact photograph. How many of us have considered carefully the next, and the next step? As a matter of fact, and our illustrations up to this point have amply verified the assertion, the mere reproduction of equal lines and surfaces within the eye, is no guarantee at all that these lines and surfaces will be seen as equal. Seeing is a process of mental interpretation. It makes all the difference in the world what are the surroundings of the object. It is always a question of whether the mind has learned to take in its impressions in a fully developed or only in a partially de-

[1] Quoted from the English translation by H. A. J. Munro.

veloped way. Seeing is, even in its simplest cases, a matter of interpretation rather than of mere passive impression.

Do you not see the value of this conclusion for all phases of educational practise? When the teacher once realizes that seeing is not merely getting images in his eyes, but a matter of interpretation, do you think he will ever be guilty again of believing that children see things because these things are held up before their eyes? Our teacher-study shows us that in order to be seen, things must be held up before our minds as well as before our eyes.

Let us take up some other figures which will impress upon us still more deeply the lesson that seeing is a matter of mental interpretation. Fig. 3 represents two equal horizontal lines, with short additional lines forming arrow-heads at their extremities. The arrow-heads are turned in opposite directions in the two figures, and the effect is apparent in the underestimation of the upper figure and the overestimation of the lower figure. This figure can be modified by substituting for the arrow-heads complete or partial circles. One of the most interesting cases of this type of the illusion can be secured by asking some one to place four coins in such positions that the inner edges of one pair shall be the same distance apart as the outer edges of the other pair. Fig. 4 represents the way in which the coins should be placed to make the distances really equal. Of course, in the actual placing of the coins the false estimation will come out in the fact that the distances in question will not be made equal.

Further interesting studies can be made by

changing the figure about in a variety of ways. Suppose we come back to a figure of the same type as those in Fig. 3. Let us take a line and put at one extremity an arrow-head turning inward, and at the other extremity an arrow-head turning outward, as in Fig. 5. In this figure there is added below, a plain horizontal line equal in length to the upper horizontal line which has the arrow-heads. Comparison between the two horizontal lines shows that the upper figure is ap-

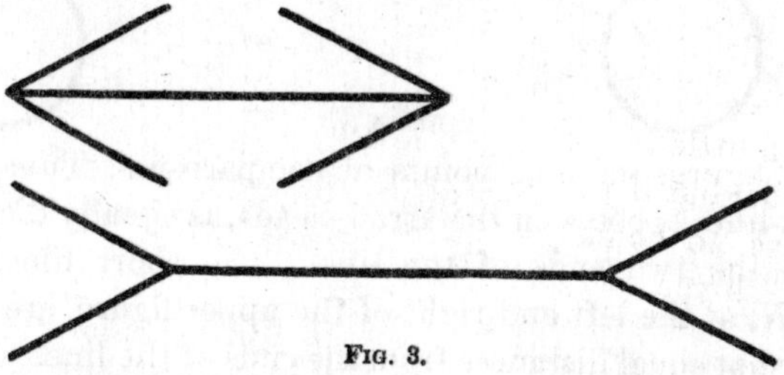

FIG. 3.

parently neither overestimated nor underestimated. I want to secure your special attention to this figure, for it is one of the best possible examples of what seems to be a simple visual process, and it can be shown to be in reality a most complex figure. As it stands in Fig. 5, it seems to be free from all illusion. But this is due to the fact that there is no adequate means in Fig. 5 of judging it. One would say, in similar manner, of one of the figures in Fig. 3, if he saw it standing alone, that there was nothing unusual about it. In Fig. 3 we become conscious of the illusion through a comparison of two different figures which are in reality equal. To become conscious of the illusion in Fig. 5 we must place about it and within it some points of reference which will break it up into equal parts and furnish us with the means of seeing the illusion. This is done in Fig. 6. The short cross-lines, while they add nothing to the

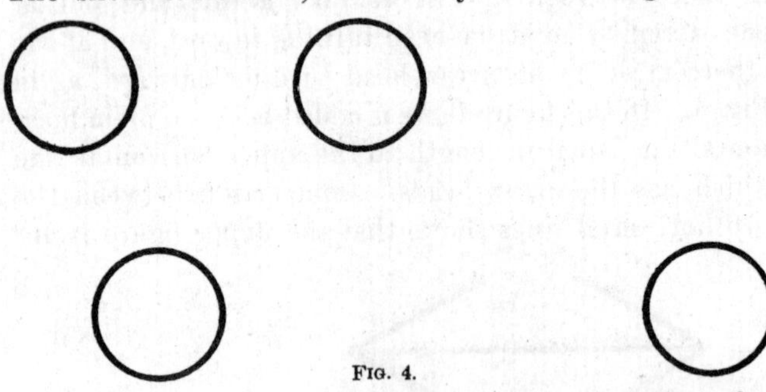

FIG. 4.

main figure, serve as points of comparison. Thus the cross-line *A*, between the arrow-heads, is equally distant from the two ends of the line. The short lines, *M* and *N*, at the left and right of the upper figure, are also placed at equal distances from the ends of the line. The same relative points are indicated lower down in the case of the plain line in the figure. Now we see that the arrow-heads have, after all, had a very marked influence on our visual process. The right side of the upper line, even though we did not know it in Fig. 5, was stretched out in our recognition of it, and the left side was correspondingly shortened. The space outside of the line was infringed upon on the right side, and the end of the line was drawn back out of the empty space on the left. In short, the presence of those arrow-heads changed the whole internal and external character of the line. This is just as true, let me repeat, in Fig. 5 as in Fig. 6. The difference is that in Fig. 6 we have provided the means of bringing it into consciousness, while in Fig. 5 no such means were present. Thus we see that we can not trust our ordinary observation to

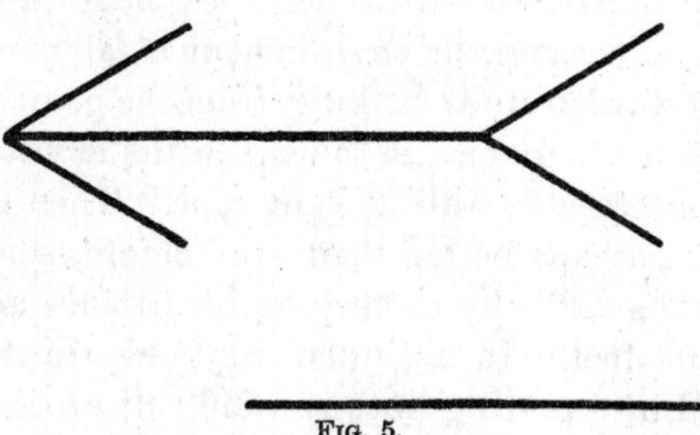

FIG. 5.

discover all the facts in regard to our processes of recognition. Suppose, for example, that we had stopped in our study with Fig. 5. We should have thought of the whole process as very simple, whereas, as a matter of fact, it is, as shown by Fig. 6, very complex.

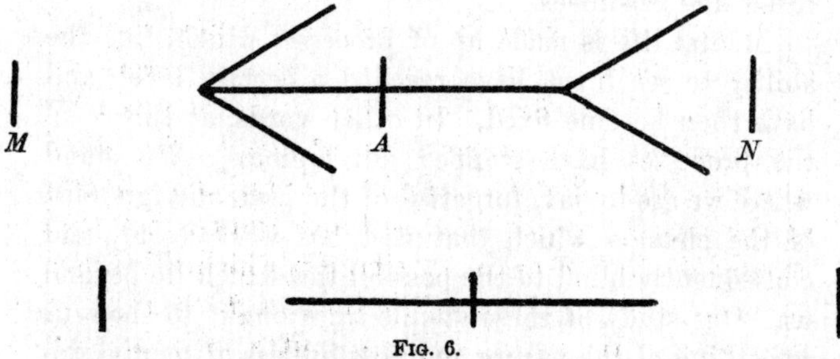

FIG. 6.

Do not try to resist this conclusion to which we have been coming, by an appeal to ordinary experience. Do not say that seeing straight lines seems like a very simple and easy process. This seeming ease, and accuracy of visual perception, is like the seeming ease of walking.

Walking is, however, as we all know, a complex product of development, apparently easy and complete so far as immediate individual experience goes, because of long practise, and because the environment is familiar. One of the best ways to study walking, from the point of view of one's own experience, is to change the environment, as when one tries to walk a tight rope. Then one understands, perhaps better than ever before, something of the child's difficulty in keeping his balance and controlling his feet. In a similar way one realizes that seeing and interpreting lines is a difficult process when he tries to interpret lines in a new environment. Or an adult may realize something of the child's condition when this same adult puts himself under the directions of a drawing teacher, and finds by comparison of his own ability with that of his teacher that the ordinary person is only partially trained in the recognition of forms and distances.

Mental life is made up of processes which, like the ability to see lines, have reached a certain level, and have then become fixed. In other words, at this level the processes have stopped developing. We stand where we are to-day, forgetful of the past, and ignorant of the changes which that past has worked out, and consequently blind to the possibilities which lie beyond us. Our study of these simple lines ought to show us something of the nature and possibilities of mental development. The teacher who gets stranded at one stage of development and knows no past or future, is not fit for his profession, for he can not realize what the child has to pass through, and he has no outlook for his own improvement.

The great lessons that come to us as students of even such minor forms of mental development, are tolerance and sympathy for those below us and ambitions for better thing in our own lives. If even a few teachers would take these lessons in regard to space perception to heart and put themselves through a course of training in drawing, and give us accounts of their experiences, we should have a very valuable chapter added to our teacher-study.

Such a study of our mental development would need to supplement itself with some carefully kept records, for there is nothing so easy as to forget what one did and thought at an earlier stage of development. Have you ever worked at a problem slowly and laboriously until the solution was reached, and then wondered how in the world you could have failed to recognize what is now so clear? The earlier stage of development in which the problem was not solved, is soon forgotten when you take that forward step which brings you to the solution. It is this forgetfulness of where one started which makes it so hard to show the right degree of sympathy for those who do not comprehend at their lower level of mental development what one has learned to see so clearly at a higher level. So I say it would be well for us each to go through some series of mental developments and leave behind him some carefully preserved records. This has been done in one case of space perception with sufficient completeness to furnish us an interesting and helpful example.

The facts I am about to describe now will also illustrate to you what the psychologists call an experiment. We all of us know what an experiment in physics is, or an experiment in chemistry, but it sounds a little odd at first to speak of experimenting with one's mental processes. And yet there is a good deal of psychological experimenting which is going on these days, and we are learning more about mental life than we ever knew before, because of the large possibilities of gaining new information which are afforded by these experiments. Our next description will, therefore, have a double significance. It will be a description of a psychological experiment on the development of perception of length, and as such it will give you some insight into the character of the experimental process and into the method of taking records, and it will also throw light on our problem—the nature of our visual perception of form.

Two figures like those with which we became acquainted in Fig. 3, with the arrow-heads turning outward and inward, were drawn on cards in such a way that by slipping an easily adjustable card backward and forward over a fixed card, one of the figures could be lengthened or shortened to suit the wishes of the person on whom the experiment was tried. Fig. 7 will make the arrangement intelligible. On the fixed card, *A*, was drawn a long line with a single arrow-head turning outward. Over this long line was placed the adjustable card, *B*, on which was drawn the short figure with the arrow-heads turned inward. The cards were then placed one on the other, as indicated in the lowest diagram in Fig. 7. At *A* and *B* we had the two figures, and by moving the card *B* backward and forward, the lines could be made to seem equal. The person trying the experiment, or the subject as we call him, adjusted *A* by moving *B*, until the two figures seemed equal. His only task was to make the lines seem equal, not to make them really equal. When this had been done we had,

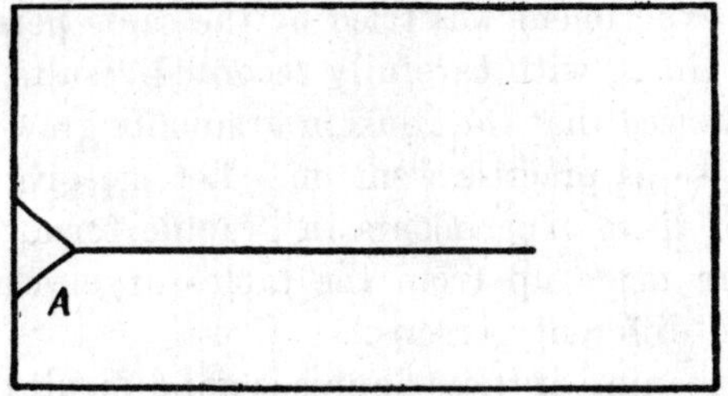

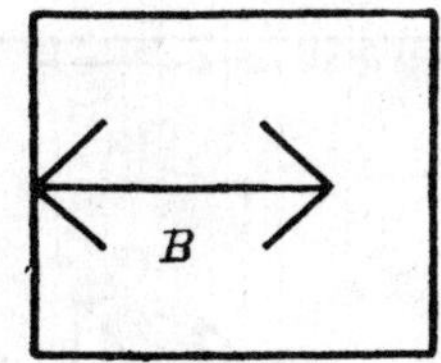

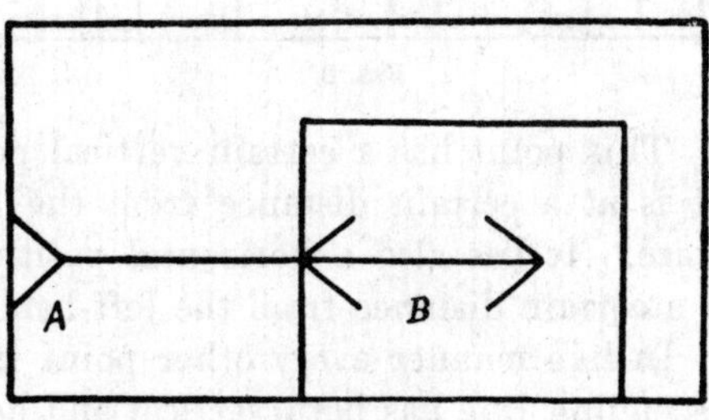

FIG. 7.

in the difference between the lines *A* and *B*, a measure of the illusion; for the greater the illusion, the greater was the difference between the length of the lines.

This experiment was tried by the same person hundreds of times, with carefully recorded results, and the results showed that the illusion gradually grew less and less intense as practise went on. Let me give you the results of these experiments in graphic form. Figs. 8 and 9 are made up from the tables of measurements from two different persons.

The meaning of these figures is not difficult to understand, if one remembers that any point in space has both horizontal and vertical position. Take, for example, the point at which the irregular ascending line in Fig.

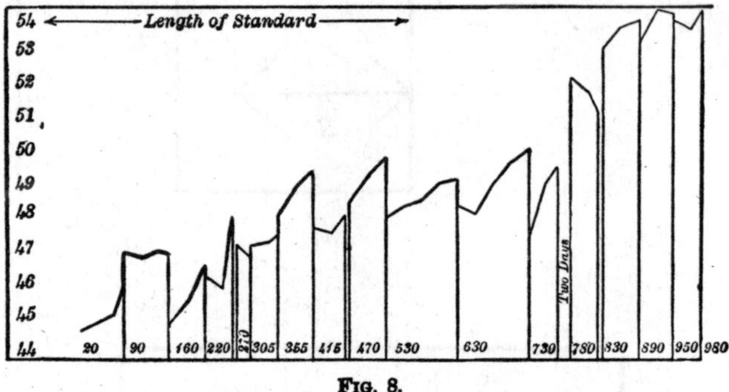

FIG. 8.

8 begins. This point has a certain vertical position—that is, it is at a certain distance from the base-line of the figure. It has also a horizontal position—that is, it is at a certain distance from the left-hand bounding line. In like manner every other point in the irregular ascending line has both vertical and horizontal

position. Now, in such figures as 8 and 9 we use these vertical and horizontal distances to express two different kinds of facts. First, if we want to show the amount of the illusion, we place a point at a certain distance above the base-line. In this way distance from the base-line in Figs. 8 and 9 comes to mean degree of illusion. Along the left-hand edge of the figure you will find certain numerals which make this matter of quantity still more definite. Thus, in Fig. 8, 44 at the very base-line means that the length of the line *A* (Fig. 7) in the first experiments was 44 millimeters. The numerals 45 to 54 then indicate various lengths through which the line *A* (Fig.

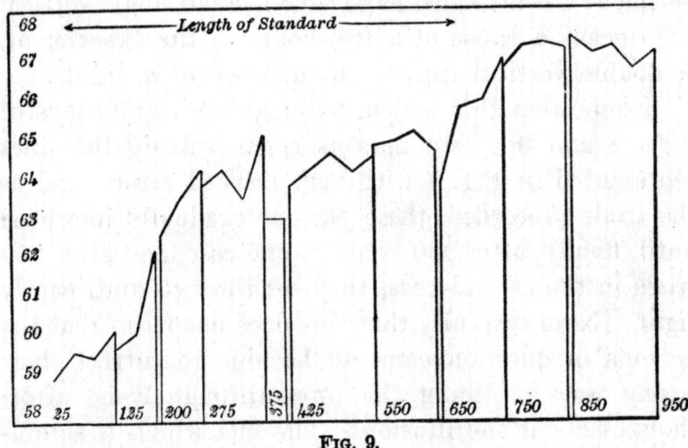

FIG. 9.

7) passed until finally it came very nearly to the length 54, which is the length of the standard line *B* (Fig. 7). If, now, one takes any point in the regular ascending line of the figure, and refers to this series of numerals at the left, he can see how long the line *A* (Fig. 7) was at that stage of the experiment.

At the same time any given point in the ascending line has horizontal position. This horizontal position is used to express the number of experiments that have been tried, and the numbers at the bottom of the figure indicate how many experiments are represented by each point. Thus the line begins in Fig. 8 at 20 and ends at 980. This means that 980 experiments were tried in all. The fact that we progress by twenties is accounted for by the fact that in most cases in this experiment twenty measurements were averaged before being entered in the table. The various vertical lines that interrupt the ascending line tell you how the experiment was arranged as to time. Each single vertical line means a pause of a few hours in the experiment. A double vertical line means a pause of a night.

I hope that this will make clear the significance of Figs. 8 and 9. Two persons began setting the lines represented in Fig. 7 with very marked errors, and as the trials proceeded, these persons gradually improved until, finally, after 980 trials in one case, and after 950 trials in the second case, they set the two lines nearly right. Note carefully that this does not mean that the persons in question came to be able to correct their wrong way of seeing the lines through some afterthought about the illusion. The fact which is significant in this experiment is that, after a good deal of setting of these lines, one gets such complete control of the arrow-heads at their extremities that he sees the lines as they should be. He undergoes the same kind of change in the way of looking at these lines as that which all of us have undergone in our way of looking at big sleeves. The interpretation has changed. Mental life has developed in a small way, and the arrow-heads which were before confusing additions to the horizontal lines, have now been mastered. The arrow-heads are accordingly no longer sources of an illusion; they are regularly interpreted factors.

I wish every teacher could be induced to try this or some similar experiment, so that he or she might learn in his or her own experience what changes in mental life a little training can bring about. The meaning of the statement that children see things in a way that is different from ours would become a living fact, rather than a bare statement. This experiment shows in the brief space of a few days what in ordinary life, where no attention is given to this illusion, would never take place at all. It is therefore an interesting case of development beyond ordinary experience. Furthermore, the fact that a record was kept makes it possible for us to give a very exact account of the way in which the development took place.

Something of the same kind can be seen when one goes back, after a long absence, to the home of his childhood, and notes the smallness of the house and yard and the small elevation of the neighboring hills and the nearness of the next house. To one's childish mind distances were much vaster than they are now in adult life. One has undergone in all these years a slow transformation in his mode of seeing things. The whole interpretation of objects is on a different scale. This is clearly a case of mental development, though it is development in a relatively simple function, the function of seeing sizes: Remember that if such a simple mode of interpretation is capable of such marked transformations through accumulation of experience, then the more complex modes of interpretation must be capable of much greater development through similar processes of experience.

Let us come back, after this description of actual observations and records of the transformations which can be produced through practise, to a more complete illustration of the fact with which we began—the fact that there are a great many illusions into which our undeveloped adult consciousness falls. If you draw two lines of equal length and then break up one of the two with a series of short cross-lines, as in Fig. 10, the two lines will no longer look equal, but the interrupted line will seem longer. The same principle holds for squares which have been broken up by cross-lines, as shown in Fig. 11. This whole group of illusions is described by the general name, illusions of filled space. The name means, of

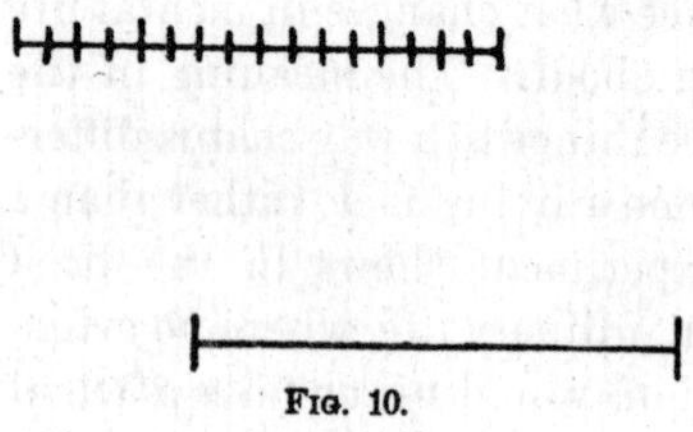

FIG. 10.

FIG. 11.

course, not that one line or one square is absolutely empty space and the other filled, but that in one case the filling is of such a special, noticeable character that it is, as compared with the other, uniform line, or square, much more filled. The illusion is easy to understand. There is more to pay attention to in the filled figure. This moreness we easily turn into moreness of length, while as a matter of fact it is merely moreness of filling. Again it is interpretation that is accountable for the illusion.

An interesting fact in this connection is that with large objects our interpretation is governed by other motives. In the case of an empty room, for example, the barren lack of furnishings calls our attention to the size, and the empty room looks unusually large, not small like the empty square. Or again, when the stripes which in our figure of the square make the figure look wide, are transferred to a garment, the effect is to carry vision up and down the lines and to call special attention to the length instead of to the width, and thus we come to understand the various forms of subtle art by which the rotund matronly figure is elongated to our guileless and undeveloped eyes.

Again we may refer to a group of striking figures in which the false estimation of distances results in a distortion of directions. The earliest figure of this sort to be noted and described was found on a tapestry pattern. It is reproduced in Fig. 12. The long vertical lines are parallel, but they seem to converge and diverge, thus giving the whole figure an irregular character, which destroys entirely the parallel appearance. The explanation of this figure does not seem to be simple. The short cross-lines are evidently the factors which complicate interpretation; but the exact way in which the cross-lines produce their effect is difficult to determine. There is a simpler figure of closely related type to which this complex pattern is generally reduced for purposes

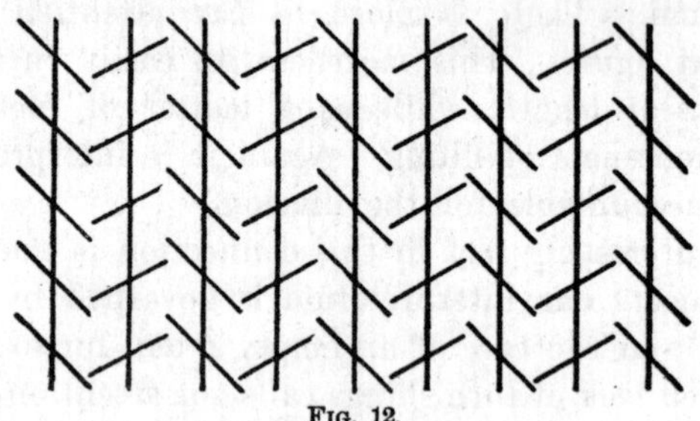

Fig. 12.

of explanation. The simpler figure is presented in Fig. 13. Here the long oblique line is the center of interest. It is interrupted by the space between the two verticals. The result is that one can not see the oblique line as a single continuous line. The left-hand part seems somewhat too high, while the right-hand part is too low. If now one thinks of the oblique lines as increased in number, as in Fig. 12, they become the stronger factors, and they succeed in tipping the interrupting lines, and do not themselves suffer deflection as in the simpler figure.

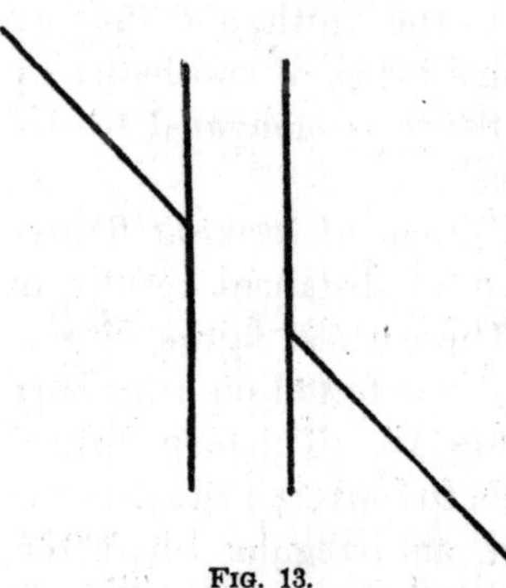

Fig. 13.

Another interesting group of illusions appears in certain architectural forms. A high column, for example, the sides of which ascend in perfectly straight lines, seems to be too slender at its middle point. In other words, such ascending boundaries of a column naturally appear slightly concave at the middle. It has often been noted that the Greek columns were so constructed as to counteract this illusion by having a marked convexity of their ascending lines—that is, the Greek columns were really slightly bulging at the middle, so that they might produce the pleasing impression of straightness rather than concavity.

Enough, however, has been said to make clear the fact which we started out to emphasize in this first discussion. The teacher's own mental life is a world in which marked variations and undeveloped possibilities are always showing themselves, if we will only look for them It is not merely in the more complex processes of reasoning and lofty thought that this holds true. It is true that even in the simplest process of recognition of very commonplace figures, we have much that might be improved by training and development.

It remains, in closing this first discussion, for us to ask, why do we not ordinarily develop further in our recognition of forms. The answer is not far to seek. Ordinarily practical life does not demand it, and we simply live on with half-developed faculties, because these are good enough to meet our immediate needs. We are like men of every age, for in every age there have been intellectual prizes which have awaited the finding; but men have lived on and on, satisfied with good enough, until some vigorous, self-possessed mind has appeared and has boldly sought to improve beyond the immediate practical demands of the lower life. Such a mind always finds effort repaid by further improvement, until finally he comes to live at a new level, with broader outlook in every direction. If we would realize the true meaning of the word education, we must think of it not merely as a word to apply to others; we must think of the possibilities of self-improvement. Teachers often get so absorbed in doling out, over and over again to their children, the same little fund of facts, the same little incentives to new experience, that they come to think of themselves as finished products. The practical lesson of self-knowledge, which will grow clearer to you from any intelligent study of your own faculties, is that you can sympathetically help others to grow only while you are growing yourself.

If you have observed all there is to be seen in a plant or animal, I mean if you think you have observed all there is, then throw it away, it is useless for a lesson in nature-study. The true view, the view you must get if you would be a helpful teacher, is that you have still before you large unexhausted possibilities. You may be a little in advance of the children, indeed you ought to be; but if you are so far in advance of them that you have no bonds of sympathy in undeveloped faculties which you recognize, then you can not understand them and they will not understand you.

And now to make these general statements more specific, and to give the illustrations of spacial form which we have been studying in our recent discussions some direct practical bearing, let it be noted that our recognitions of form and size are in general very much in need of special training.

The subject of form-study, which is gradually coming to have a recognized place in our elementary schools, is one of the most timely additions to our course of study. The reason that the value of form-study is not more fully realized by teachers is that teachers are very generally without knowledge of how exceedingly defective is their own mastery of form. We look at all sorts of objects in adult life in the most superficial way. We have literally cultivated the habit of neglecting form by our failure to develop this phase of our mental lives. The result is obvious in a thousand ways. We miss not only the esthetical pleasures that we might gain, but we miss also the great funds of information which might be had from the mere looking at objects, if we would only look with the mind's eye and not with a vacant and uninterested gaze. I should say to teachers, learn to look at everything that presents itself, and note its form and size and position. If the object has no other value, there is at least value in the training of one of your faculties. Furthermore, such careful observation may bring out values which you know not of. The basis of higher mental life must be laid before that higher life is possible. The trouble with most of us is that we try to carry on the training of our faculties from the wrong end. We get books on art and architecture, instead of going out and getting our eyes open to the facts that would put content into our reading. Let us change all this. We are beginning to do it for the children in the schools, in that we are beginning to train them in the rudiments of seeing. This reform in the schools would stride forward with great rapidity if we could only realize our own needs as teachers. Let us begin this training of ourselves.

One of the best ways that I know of to train oneself in observing, is to begin drawing. Draw some one thing every day. It need not take very much time. Go home and draw something to-day. Do it in the privacy of your own room if you are ashamed of the results. Do not tear it up when it is done, but go out after you have drawn and look at the object again. You will look with keener interest and insight and you will do better next time. Do not do this for the sake of trying to become an artist, and do not drop your practise after the third or fourth day. Remember this is a normal school in which the teacher is pupil as well as faculty. You will be repaid in time more than you imagine. You will not need to worry about examinations in your normal school; you will not need to be afraid of changes in the course of study. And I venture the prophecy that you will not be exhausted by this work. It is not the kind of work that teachers who are overworked, as they call it, complain about. They complain about work that does not contribute to their mental growth and is not done in pursuit of this kind of self-improvement.

But I will not exhaust your patience with exhortation. If the moral of our introductory discussion is not clear now, it never will be. Let us review briefly as we close. Teacher-study will help us to understand ourselves and will indirectly help us to understand the children. If we take some of the simplest acts of seeing lines and figures, we shall find that we have yet large possibilities of development, and we shall find that development means a change of a very fundamental type in our modes of mental recognition. These possibilities of development, as well as the figures by which the possibilities were revealed, all go to show that recognition of size is a fact of interpretation, not a mere fact of impression. And finally, the practical pedagogical lesson is that interpretation of size and form may, and should be more highly cultivated by all of us.

CHAPTER II

HOW EXPERIENCES ARE CONSOLIDATED INTO INTERPRETATIONS OF MEANING

DID you ever ask yourself why it is that we have two eyes and two ears? We all recognize the fact that we need two legs in order to make walking possible; that we frequently need two hands—one to hold the object on which we are working, and the other to do the manipulating. But I venture to say that most people are not aware that seeing is never perfect unless both eyes are cooperating, and that hearing is never complete unless both ears are in use. The truth is that natural and complete visual and auditory experiences are just as much dependent on our two organs of sight and hearing as natural walking is dependent on the combined action of two legs. And the unfortunate individual who is deprived of one eye or one ear, has to make use of unusual and clumsy means of sight and hearing, just as the man deprived of one of his legs has to make use of clumsy devices for walking.

Let us demonstrate this in a simple experiment with hearing. The experiment is one which can be performed very easily by any one. Ask the person on whom the experiment is tried, or the observer as we may call him, to close his eyes, and then let the experimenter make some sort of a snapping sound (snapping the fingers or snapping with a card will produce suitable sounds) just in front of the middle of the observer's face or just behind the middle of the back of his head. You will find that the observer will make the greatest mistakes in trying to tell where the sound came from. Sometimes when it is in front of him he will tell you it is behind, and *vice versa.* In other words, for sounds which are thus half-way between the two ears, there is no means of distinguishing easily the difference between what is in front and what behind. Now let the experimenter move his hand in making the snapping sound slightly to the right or left of the middle line, and it will be found that the observer can give much more accurate localizations—that is, the moment the sound is stronger in one ear than it is in the other, the observer has a complex experience which makes it possible for him to make a comparison and to understand his impressions. The two ears cooperate in these latter cases, in that one reports the sound with a greater intensity than does the other, and by this means the observer recognizes that the sound is on the side of the greater intensity.

We make use of the same principle in ordinary life. When one wishes to locate a sound, he moves his head around in this direction and in that until finally he gets a different impression in the two ears, and then he can locate the source of the sound on the side of the stronger impression. It is probably true that the difference in the way in which the sound gets into the two ears is also of importance, but our discussion need not go into further detail. You see that, after all, there is some necessity in ordinary hearing for the use of both ears, at least, if we are to know accurately where the source of the sound is located.

Similar facts can be demonstrated for the eyes. Most of us believe that the world looks the same when viewed with one eye closed as it does when viewed with both eyes open. A simple experiment will convince you that one-eyed vision is less complete than two-eyed vision. Close one eye. Hold up some small object directly in front of the open eye—a pencil or one of your fingers will do; or it will be better yet if you will let some one else hold something in front of you. Now raise your right hand above your head so that it is out of the range of vision, and rapidly bring it straight down, trying to place the end of your index-finger on the end of the object. After you have brought the finger down and failed to touch the object, open the closed eye and see how clearly the mistaken positions of finger and object are seen with two eyes. One who has tried this experiment a number of times will never be in any doubt as to the fundamental value of two eyes. With two eyes we see the position of objects in depth clearly and vividly; with one eye a great part of this recognition of depth is lost. If you once get into the habit of observing this difference, you can notice it in a great variety of cases. Close one eye and look at a distant group of trees, at a house, or at some object in the room, as a chair, and notice how flat they all look. The best instant at which to notice this flatness is just at the moment when you open the closed eye and see the object fairly leap into depth.

This difference between one-eyed vision and two-eyed vision is due to the fact that the two eyes get different views of any object at which they look. With the right eye you see a little farther around the right side of the object, and with the left eye you see farther around the left side of the object. The result is that the image in one eye is different from the image in the other eye. Our idea of depth depends on this difference. This is very neatly illustrated in the common instrument with which you are doubtless acquainted, namely, the stereoscope. You will recall that there are always two pictures to look at. These two pictures are mounted in such a way that one is seen with the right eye, the other with the left. You may not have noticed it, but the two pictures, the one on the right and the one on the left, are different. They were made in cameras that have two separate openings corresponding to the two eyes. One picture shows a little more of the left side of objects, while the other shows a little more of the right side. If it were not for this difference and for the fact that this difference is now preserved for your vision, in that you look at the two pictures through the stereoscope so as to introduce one picture into one eye, and the other picture into the other eye—I say if it were not for this difference in the two photographs, you could not see the solidity which is the charm of stereoscopic pictures.

The question which arises at once after one has been shown by these experiments the importance of two-eyed vision is, Why is it, that when we close one eye, things are not ordinarily recognized as unusually flat? The answer to this question is to be found in the statement that in ordinary one-eyed vision which is not subjected to close examination, we get the meaning of what we see by the aid of past experience. We do not see things flattened out as they really are presented to the single eye, but we see beyond the flatness and understand what the objects would be if we saw them with both eyes. In other words, we have become so accustomed to our full two-eyed form of interpretation, that, even though only half the usual amount of visual experience is present, we turn it into the usual mold of complete interpretation. In doing this we are aided by the familiarity of the objects and by our knowledge of their surroundings. If we prepare groups of relatively strange objects in a wholly unknown order, as we can easily do by passing threads backward and forward at different levels in a box, then one-eyed recognition of depth becomes almost or quite impossible.

"But," some one will probably ask, "how is it that we never recognize in ordinary life what impressions are coming in at the one eye or the other, and at the one ear or the other? If it is true that the two organs of sense in each case are of such importance, why do we need to make this careful study to find it out?" If you will get the true answer to these questions, you will have one of the important facts in regard to your own mental lives. The fact is that we do not pay attention to sense impressions for the sake of getting the impressions themselves; we pay attention to sense impressions for the sake of understanding their meanings. Now, the differences in auditory intensity which come to us through the two ears, are of no interest as mere facts of intensity, but they are rich with meaning; and that meaning is what we have learned to recognize. Intensities mean, in such cases, position in space. In the same way the different views of objects which we get in the two eyes, are of no interest as different views, but they are of great interest in their meaning, for the meaning of these differences is solidity and depth. The solidity and depth is what we see, for at our advanced stage of mental development we attend to the meaning only, and neglect entirely the simple fact of sensory differences from which we derive the meaning.

Mental life is made up in very large measure of these processes of getting behind experiences and grasping meanings. Take, for example, our recognition of a word. A word taken as a mere sound is a very meager experience. Take such a sound as "cold." Pay attention to it as a sound. It is hard and guttural. There is nothing attractive about it; taken all in all, as a mere sound, it promises little for any one's thinking. Imagine yourself a foreigner, unacquainted with all the fulness of meaning that we put into the world because we understand it, and you will recognize what we are trying to emphasize when we say that our mental states are not bound down to present impressions, but are constantly reaching out, and are attaching to the impressions a rich fund of interpretation.

Or take another illustration. What is a coin to the intelligent adult? Is it a bit of metal with certain decorations? As a matter of ordinary experience, you know how little attention we usually pay to the decorations. It is a commonplace form of amusement to try to see how little most people know about what is on coins. Greenbacks are overlooked in the matter of appearance, even more than coins. Our memory of the size of a common greenback is very defective. But when it comes to meaning, we all have a clear realization of the meaning of currency. We know that there is a certain additional fact behind the mere appearance of the coin or the greenback, which additional fact we call value. Value is the power to bring us desirable things through exchange. This understanding of value is not present in the child's mind, for the child has had no experience on which to base recognition of meanings. He is engrossed in the bright hard metal. Not so with us. We receive the impression, to be sure, but we do not linger even for a moment on the impression. Our attention is upon the remoter significance. Just as we see solidity in ordinary one-eyed vision, which is in reality flat and meager in content, so here in the bit of silver, we realize the possibilities of new experiences not revealed at the moment.

Mental life is full of illustrations of this type. Indeed, so constantly do we attend to meanings instead of to the real mental states that it is for the most part impossible for us to separate the two. When we look away across the landscape, for example, and see the distant green fields, we are having an experience in which the present impression and its meaning are very closely woven together. As a matter of immediate vision, the color which the eye receives from those distant so-called green fields, is a very dark bluish green—indeed, in some cases it may even be distinctly blue; but we do not ordinarily notice that. We have come, through past experience, to know that colors grow darker and milder in tone, as their sources are more and more removed from us, and so we think of the distant blue-green, not as it looks, but as it means. There where the grass is growing it is bright green, and the patch of color in our landscape, which is not bright green, means that grass, and we understand it. We see in our mind's eye the meaning, rather than the present shade of the color. One can convince himself that he has gone far beyond present experience in such a case by pulling up a handful of grass and holding it in the line of vision, and thus helping himself by contrasting the two experiences of color to discover what is the real color of the remote field. Or by an examination of some landscape painting, you may convince yourself that the artists have known this fact about colors for a long time. If they wish to bring up in your mind a distant object of any kind, they tone down its colors and darken the shade, and you see it, not as mere color, but as alive with meaning.

Perhaps some of the best illustrations with which to make clear this fact that we fill out all our lives with meanings, are the illustrations in which we find men attaching the wrong meaning to experiences. One walks out on a dark night and sees the fleeting, shifting darks and shades. What infinite possibility of ghostly interpretation if one is only disposed to read meanings into what he sees! Indeed, I think much of the mystery which men have been wont to read into their environments may well be dwelt upon as showing how much of harm as well as of good may be accomplished by this habit of ours of looking for the meanings beyond our impressions.

The ancient priests knew well how to furnish to the minds of the ignorant people the impressions out of which they could develop the weirdest meanings.

Suppose you did not know anything about the modern stereopticon, with its projection of pictures and scenes in more than life size. Suppose that on some night, or in the shrouding darkness of a temple, you should be confronted with the outlines of a face projected by such a stereopticon. What would you see? You would see with your eye nothing but a flat image. But your active mind would not stop there. You would enlarge upon that image in the only terms that could possibly suggest themselves to your mind, ignorant as we have assumed it to be of the projecting stereopticon. You would literally see a real thing. If you will follow out that line of reasoning, you can understand much of the deception practised by the ancient priests. They knew how to project images, not as we do with the stereopticon through a glass lens, but by means of metallic mirrors, especially by means of concave mirrors, which are fair substitutes for the lenses which we use. For a screen, these priests used the smoke rising from sacrifices, or they used the temple walls. These served very well in place of our sheets of canvas. The people, ignorant of all the machinery back of the image, saw the projections as visiting deities, and the trick is explained.

It is interesting to read some of the accounts. Thus, in the following we can fairly see the priests getting their image into focus before the gaping multitude. It is an account given by Damascius. He writes: "In a manifestation that ought not to be revealed, there appeared on the wall of a temple a mass of light, which at first seemed remote; it transformed itself in coming nearer into a face, evidently divine, of a severe aspect, but mixed with gentleness and extremely beautiful."

An account by the Italian, Cellini, of one of his experiences is amusing in its transparent simplicity. Cellini relates that he became acquainted with a Sicilian priest, skilled in necromancy, and asked the priest to impart some of his knowledge. The priest said that the man must be of a resolute and steady temper who enters upon the study of the black arts. Cellini goes on to say: "I replied that I had fortitude and resolution enough if I could but find an opportunity. The priest answered, 'If you think you have the heart to venture, I will give you all the satisfaction you can desire.' Thus we agreed. The priest, one evening, prepared to satisfy me, and desired me to look out for two companions. Having secured two of my intimate acquaintances, we resorted at night to the Colosseum, and there the priest began to draw circles on the ground with the most impressive ceremonies imaginable. He brought with him several precious perfumes and fire, with some compositions also which diffused noisome odors. As soon as he was in readiness, he made an opening in one of the circles, and, taking us by the hand, led us in, at the same time ordering his partner to throw perfumes into the fire. The ceremonies lasted about an hour and a half. There appeared several legions of devils, insomuch that the amphitheater was quite filled with them. The priest requested me to stand resolutely by him, because the legions were now about a thousand more in number than he had designed, and besides were most dangerous. My companions were in a terrible fright, and even the priest trembled with fear, endeavoring by mild and gentle methods to dismiss the spirits in the best way he could. The priest entreated us to have good heart and take care to burn the proper perfumes. Though I was as much terrified as any of them, I did my utmost to conceal the terror I felt." Does it need any comment to make it clear that the smoking incense was necessary to serve as a screen for the dancing spirits, that the circles on the ground were necessary to keep the visitors in proper range, and that the attending terror of the whole occasion augmented powerfully the natural tendency to see a real being in each shadowy phantom?

Do not fail to keep in mind the general fact which all of these examples are intended to illustrate. The general fact is that the character of any mental process depends, not merely upon the immediately present factors, but also, and very largely, upon what one sees beyond the given factors as the remoter meaning. This fact that we add meaning to all of our experiences is one of special importance to our teacher-study. It is very easy to overlook it from the point of view of ordinary experience. The common man wishes to gain complete knowledge of any object. This he desires without particular reference to the question of what is presented and what is seen as meaning. Now and then, in certain exceptional cases, even the ordinary man becomes interested in the difference between presented fact and interpretation. This is the case when he has to sit on a jury and compare the testimony of two or more witnesses for the purpose of discovering exactly what it was that presented itself to the eyes of each observer, and what each added in the way of perfectly honest private interpretation of meaning. In such a case the ordinary man is, like ourselves, interested in the question of meaning *versus* impression.

The teacher's interest is not quite the same as that of the juror, but is very closely related to it. The teacher wants to know what parts of a given experience which he and the child are having at a given stage in any study, are really common to both. If he could sharply distinguish in his own experience that which is added meaning from that which is immediately presented impression, he would be better able to understand that he and the child may be looking at the same object, and yet be having vastly different experiences.

The illustration that comes first to mind is, of course, the illustration of the new word. I remember the first time I heard the words *Ornithorhynchus paradoxus*. They were spoken by a teacher who knew what they meant, and his whole thought was doubtless off in Australia, where there is an interesting animal bearing that name. What was my state of mind? The name had a sort of impressive sound for me, which I dare say my teacher was not noticing at all. I thought that name over as a kind of mouth-filling combination of rather melodious noises and nothing more. My teacher and I were in the presence of the same experience, so far as the immediately given factors were concerned, but he had the meaning, and I had only the sound.

It is not merely words, however, as common as they are in our school life, which illustrate the absence of meaning on the one side and its presence on the other. Did you ever go with some intelligent teacher of anatomy to examine his museum? Did you ever notice how every ugly bone and jar grows eloquent with interest when he begins to let you into the secrets of what he sees in those specimens? And did you ever note by contrast how barren and commonplace a museum is when you are left to wander about by yourself, with your ideas tied down to the little that can be seen in the merely present fact?

The ability to add meanings to impressions is always a mark of extended experience. The teacher differs from the pupil in the larger degree of ability to see meaning in the objects about him. The expert has a greater range of interpretation than has the novice. Everywhere, richer meanings grow up with fuller experiences. One may almost define what we have been calling the meaning of impressions by saying that these meanings are past experiences brought over into the present. Thus, when one sees a dark blue on the distant horizon and knows that it means a green field, this recognition of meaning is due to the fact that on some previous occasion a dark color has grown brighter and lighter as one has walked toward it. In other words, the present impression has meaning because in some past time we discovered the meaning of a similar impression. The richness of present interpretations will, accordingly, depend on the degree in which one has profited by past experiences, and there is a very large justification for the statement that education consists in the process of adding meanings to given impressions.

Such a definition of education as that which has been offered, requires some further explanation before it can be accepted as entirely safe. Not all meanings are desirable additions to present impressions. Thus, when the savage learns that an eclipse means the wrath of some avenging diety, he has doubtless, in one sense of the word, had an enlargement of experience, but he has hardly been improved, or even educated, in the best sense of the word. What he needs for his education is not merely the addition of meaning to his impression, but the addition of a correct and productive meaning. And just here is the indefinitely large problem: What meanings are correct and productive as additions to given impressions? Here is the serious side of the teacher's task. Be sure, as you face your pupils with a new impression, that they will soon attach some meaning to it. Your problem is to find out what the impression is, and what is the appropriate meaning. Your next problem is to discover what conditions are most favorable to the establishment of proper meanings, instead of false meanings, in the minds of these pupils. And, finally, your constant task must be to discover what meanings are growing fixed in your pupils' thoughts, and to guard most jealously these growing processes, and by constant supervision to see to it that only productive meanings grow undisturbed.

Since this matter of the meanings which are attached to impressions is of such importance for our scientific study of the teacher and the teacher's work, it is worth while for us to dwell upon the nature of these added meanings at some length. And the lesson which one must learn at the very outset of this study and must keep in mind all along, is the lesson which has already been taught by our examples, but can never be too fully emphasized, namely, the lesson that it is one of the most difficult tasks in the world to know in any given case what is meaning and what is impression.

There are certain cases in which impression and added factors are sufficiently separate so that any one can easily discern both of them. Thus, we have all had the experience of meeting some person whom we have met once or twice before and whom we have nearly forgotten. We have to search in the remote corners of our minds for some stray fact which will guide us in what to say and how to treat the person. Perhaps the earlier experience was agreeable, and with a faint recollection of that in mind, we try now to renew the pleasant relations. We are all the time very conscious of the fact that past experiences are being revived to aid us in understanding and dealing with the present. In other words, we are conscious of the fact that the interpreting meanings which should come out of the past and illuminate the present, are separate from the immediate impression. We recognize in our effort to remember, that the process of finding some of the remoter meanings of the face and voice are different from the immediate impressions.

Turn from this stranger to your familiar friend. To be sure, the present impression is again nothing but a face and a voice; but these are now no meaningless visual and auditory impressions. The face and the voice are full of rich significance. You know just how to act, and you have that comfortable feeling of familiarity that comes from a clear and full knowledge of the meaning of your impression. The meaning comes so easily in this case that we do not think of it as separate from the impression. We do not say that we remember our intimate friends—we say that we recognize them, thereby indicating that in this case meaning and impressions arise together. To be sure, the meaning never could have appeared if it had not grown up in past experience, but at this stage of development it is not referred back to the past at all. It is not a memory, it is a present fact. Let us call it a present meaning, in order to distinguish it from something remembered and dragged into the present out of the past. Present meaning and memory are, then, two different forms in which experience gets itself added to present impressions. Memory is the more obvious case of enlarging upon our impressions; present meaning is the more common and the more important case.

Let me impress upon you the difference between present meaning and memory by means of an illustration which was furnished to me by a friend. He feels a very strong dislike for horses. He can not bear to come near a horse's head. This is, as you readily see, a way of looking at the horse which differs radically from the way in which most of us look at that animal. My friend's interpretation is that the animal is harmful, to be avoided, and thoroughly disagreeable. For a long time he said this peculiar personal attribute toward horses remained a mystery to him. No memory served to show him how he had acquired this sort of a present meaning. He knew he differed from most people whom he saw liking and admiring horses, but that was not enough to dissuade him from his view; for him horses were and are thoroughly distasteful factors of experience. He confided his feelings to an uncle one day, and received from the uncle the information which cleared up the whole matter. When he was a boy he had been bitten by a horse. That experience had left its mark on his future interpretations of horse nature, not in the form of memory, for the incident was entirely forgotten, but in the form of a thoroughly established meaning. To-day he looks at horses as that experience led him to know horses; but all he has carried away for his mental life is the meaning of the event, not the actual memory image.

Each of us has had similar experiences, though perhaps less clearly defined. Have you never taken a strong dislike to some one you have just met? Have you not read into his face or manner all sorts of disagreeable traits? And then have you not suddenly realized, as an explanation of the whole interpretation in which you have been indulging, that this man looks like some one you knew in the past? In other words, you have been disliking him because your experience has been such that these special features which he exhibits, mean something unpleasant to you. Notice that in such a case your recognition of present meaning could not depend on memory, for the memory came after the interpretation. The meaning is explained by your recalling after a time some special face in your past experience which has helped to establish the meaning, but the interpretation was something different from the explanation afforded by memory. The interpretation is immediate and definite; memory follows in such a case far behind. If there are cases in which tardy memory arrives to explain our sudden interpretations, how many cases are there, do you suppose, in which the interpretation goes forward in the same way but is not explained at all? I think a careful analysis of experience would go to show that our lives are made up of interpretations that are so settled and fixed that the memory factors which would explain them are long since dispensed with.

Indeed, there are some cases in which memory can not be invoked at all in the explanation of our present meanings, and yet these meanings are the results of past experience. Take the illustrations with which we opened this discussion, the illustrations of ordinary hearing and seeing, and the demonstration of the utility of two ears and two eyes. When one hears a sound in the two ears and receives in so doing, impressions of such a character that the sensation on one side is stronger than the sensation on the other side, he interprets the location of the source of the sound on the basis of the difference in intensity of the sensations in the two ears. This may be stated in other words as an interpretation of the meaning of the experiences brought to him by the two ears. If you will watch an infant you will see that the infant does not interpret the meanings of sounds in any such successful fashion. Indeed, one need not go as far back as infancy. An experimenter [1] has recently demonstrated that adults may, through experience, improve very noticeably in their ability to locate sounds. This shows that adults may become more expert in the interpretation of the meanings of their impressions. What is this process of growing expert in interpretation? Certainly it is not cultivating memory. We do not say to ourselves, this sound in the right ear means the same kind of sounding body as that which we experienced yesterday. Indeed, as we have already pointed out, we do

[1] Professor Pierce, in Studies in Space Perception, p. 98 *et seq.*

not even distinguish the two sounds in the two ears as separate. Experience has grown up in these cases by a kind of blind process of trial. The infant or the developing adult does not so much think about meanings, as he tries to fit himself in a practical way to the impressions. Sometimes he fails to fit himself to the impression, and suffers the consequences; sometimes he succeeds, and enjoys the advantages. Thus he accumulates certain habits of turning in the right direction, not because he knows why, but because his best and most satisfactory experiences are those which resulted in movement in a certain direction in response to a certain combination of impressions. It is this method of blind accumulation of habits of interpretation which gives us, for example, the present meaning of water when we are swimming, or of a turn in the path when we are riding a bicycle. No memory is needed, for the meaning in this case is recognized as a demand for a form of immediate activity and has grown up by personal effort.

Or take again the illustration of seeing with two eyes. When we see a little more of the right side of an object with the right eye, and a little more of the left side of an object with the left eye, we are not surprised. We do not have to refer back to past experience for some explanation. We have had such experiences thousands and thousands of times every day, and the result is we have a ready-made form of interpretation. We know what that means. It means a solid object. So fixed is this mode of interpretation, that if we persuade ourselves to look into a stereoscope, we must interpret those pictures in terms similar to our ordinary experience. We see in the stereoscope a single solid image, not what is really there, namely, two flat pictures.

Our minds are thus constantly seeing in present impressions their meanings. These meanings are the results of past experiences, but they do not depend in any great number of cases on any clearly recognized reference to remembered experiences. You look into a mirror, for example, and you are performing an act of double interpretation. In the first place, you see the object straight ahead of you, back of the mirror. This experience is due to a fixed mode of interpreting experiences which if formulated would lead to a statement of the general principle: light has traveled in straight lines in a sufficiently large number of past experiences so that one is safe in interpreting present cases in the belief that it is always true that light travels in this way. It is hardly necessary to point out that no one ever does, in ordinary life, formulate such a principle as the basis of locating objects in mirrors. Indeed, no one ever thinks about his past experiences in any explicit way. Past experiences have been boiled down into a very safe and practical habit of interpretation. We see objects straight ahead. But now notice the interesting fact that our interpretation of objects seen in mirrors goes further than this. We have, as I said a moment ago, a double interpretation. If we see the frame of the mirror, or if we recognize the presence of the mirror in any way, we know enough about mirrors to interpret our mirror object as a reflection, not a real object. We interpret the light as coming from straight ahead, but we interpret it as coming from what we know through experience to be an image rather than a thing. A savage does not have this added experience which enables us to interpret our experiences in mirrors as images. He takes the image for a real object. We do the same when we fail to notice the mirror. In both these latter cases the interpretation is not double; it is simple, and based on the more common fact that in all our past experience light comes in straight lines and from real objects.

I hope these illustrations have made it clear to you that present meanings are not identical with memories. Our way of looking at things is indeed the product of past experiences, but past experiences are not reproduced in full in the vast majority of our interpretations. Past experiences are worked over, epitomized, condensed, or whatever you please to call it, if you will only recognize that our modes of getting at present meanings are wonderfully economical means of guiding us. They bring all the past into our present lives, sifted and arranged for immediate use.

Indeed, if you will consider carefully you will see that such condensation is just as important a condition for progress as is retention. Suppose every time we were confronted with an impression, we had to go through a long process of passing in review in memory all the related facts out of our past. We should never progress. It is because we do not have to carry the useless parts of this past into the future, because we have the power of selecting and appropriating what we need, that we can profit by past experiences without being burdened with the experiences in full.

If we may borrow an illustration from the life of a nation, we may say that history is the nation's memory of itself. History aims to bring up the past as fully and accurately as possible. It will expend its highest energy in the effort to reach completeness and fidelity. If you would learn, on the other hand, what are the experiences from which the nation has profited, what are the lessons it has carried over into a condensed and immediately useful form, then you must study the present institutions and the life of its people. Our thought, for example, of what an executive head of a nation should be, is expressed in our President. Our President is, to be sure, at the same time an expression of what our fathers, trained under kings of Europe, thought an executive should and should not be; but the chief office of our nation is not an historical record, it is a present institution, an embodied result of condensed experience. It is understood and appreciated in our national life to-day, not because of its reference backward, but because of its present value and utility.

In an analogous way our understanding of a familiar word, such as the word danger, for example, is not due to memory of what that word has been known to mean in the past. When one hears the word danger shouted behind him, he begins to get out of the way. The word with its meaning is a living, present factor in his life, with present meaning and rich content. Experience has entered into the word, of course. You might shout "Danger!" behind an infant indefinitely and the chances are you would get a smile as return for your precautions. But though the meaning of the word danger has been learned through experience, one's present knowledge of that meaning is not to be described as memory; it is much more direct, and therefore much more useful; it is what we have called present meaning.

When we compare memory and present meaning, we find that present meaning is usually the result of more extended development than is found in cases of memory. Thus in the illustration which we used some time ago, of the mental processes which arise in the cases of meeting a comparatively new acquaintance and of meeting a familiar friend, memory is evidently drawn upon in the case of the new acquaintance, because sufficient experience for direct interpretation is not yet acquired. So also in learning new words. One has to go through the memory period in order to reach the interpretation period. This is especially obvious when one tries to learn a foreign language. One finds it necessary to stop and think of meanings, to recall slowly and laboriously what he has learned. In later, fuller acquaintance with words, one will become freer and freer from the necessity of remembering. Spencer has stated this fact in regard to memory and interpretation very clearly in his Principles of Psychology,[1] where he writes: "Memory, then, pertains to that class of psychical states which are in process of being organized. It continues so long as the organization of them continues, and disappears when the organization of them is complete."

One might spend a long time dwelling upon the importance of this statement of Spencer for educational practise. If it be true that memory is a stage of incomplete mental development, that there is a higher and

[1] Vol. i, p. 452.

more perfect form of organization beyond memory, then the fact must be recognized as important for school work. Certain it is that school work has no right to stop when it has trained memory. It must go on to the higher stage, which we have called recognition of present meanings.

There is, however, a much more significant question about the relation between memory and interpretation than this which we have answered by saying with Spencer, that memory, when it is present, is an incomplete phase of development. The question which our present-day education is most eagerly asking is this, How far is there any real need of memory in giving present meanings? May we not pass to present meanings, it is asked, with much greater directness? Some of us are not asking this question in words, perhaps, but we are asking it in a practical way when we try to reduce to a minimum the memory work in our daily teaching of the children. Can we get along with less memory, asks one teacher, when he does not spend much, or even any, time in repeating the multiplication table. Can we get along without the greater part of memory drill, asks another teacher, when he says he would rather develop power in his pupils to deal with experiences as they rise, than cultivate memory of any number of facts which can not be put into immediate use. And so on through the whole list of modern educational reforms, we find this question of memory *versus* direct interpretation, one of the most vital questions in all our thinking and teaching.

It is a question which certainly deserves discussion from the point of view of the teacher's own mental life as well as from the point of view of the teacher's work. How much of our training in methods of teaching, for example, do we owe to memory, and how much do we owe to what we like to call tact or spontaneous power of dealing with situations when they arise? I hardly need to remind you that the common answer to this question in regard to the training of teachers is, like the common answer to the question in regard to the training of children, much in favor of direct ability to interpret and control rather than in favor of memory. So from all points we come to the question, How can direct interpretation be gained with the least possible delay, with the least lingering at the lower level of memory?

There need be no hesitation in giving the answer to this question. The amount of memory drill necessary in order to secure immediate interpretation is reduced just in the ratio in which practical and immediate contact with impressions is increased. Direct handling is the great means of training by which we can obviate the necessity of memory work. The method of learning what things are by using them, is so distinctly the modern method of learning that we all understand its cardinal virtues. Some of the games which we learn almost entirely by practise, and hardly at all by precept, are perhaps the best illustrations of the avoidance of memory work in adult education. If one wants to learn tennis, for example, he commonly goes out and tries to hit the ball. When he succeeds, it is due to the fact that he has tried a variety of ways of reaching the ball and has finally found the right response to his present impression. Success is in a measure the result of past failures, and certainly each success will lead to a higher level of proficiency in the future. But one does not remember in any great degree these various experiences which perfect his ability as a tennis player. He just keeps on trying, each time coming a little nearer to what he regards as a satisfactory degree of proficiency. Again, consider the experience of learning to ride a bicycle, which is much like that of playing tennis. Other examples are, learning to swim, learning some trick of manual dexterity, such as tying a complex knot. In all these cases one learns by trying. Each experience is incorporated at once into present meaning, the useless parts of the experience being dropped on the spot, and only that which is thoroughly assimilated being carried away. That is, if the trial is not successful it is rejected, and just in so far as it is successful it is retained as a present mode of acting in a given situation. The last and most successful movement is recorded in such cases, not in memory images, but in the form of an acquired habit.

Memory is not needed in the cases we have been discussing, because memory would carry forward too much. If memory shows itself at all in such cases, it is usually in the very undesirable form of a haunting recollection of some disastrous failure, which contributed to education only in the most remote and negative way. That the final successful movements are not retained in memory, you can make yourself realize by trying to tell somebody else how you performed the successful move. For example, try to explain how you tie a knot, and see how little is retained in memory. On the other hand, the habit never fails, in spite of your inability to recall how you acted the last time and the time before. In the presence of proper conditions of string and free ends you feel that "warmth and familiarity" of experience which marks it in your mind as an experience which you can easily and directly interpret and manage.

One can avoid memory work through training in the use of things. This is the observation which experience forces upon us at all points, and this is the principle that our modern education is so eagerly taking up in all departments—in the kindergarten, in the constructive work of the elementary schools, in manual training, and in the laboratory work of our high schools and colleges. Learn by use, learn by doing, and you shall have followed the shortest route to recognition of present, practical meanings.

And now I believe that we have said what there is to be said in favor of making present meanings the goal of mental development. We have, up to this point, shown our willingness to join the ranks of those who are striving to improve modern education by making it less a matter of mere recollection of earlier experiences. It is time, after all this emphasis of immediate training in present meanings, to point out some of the limitations of this sort of training, and to say something in favor of a rational form of memory work; for while we should be ready to correct the abuse of memory work in the schools, we should never be so far absorbed in this campaign against memory work as to try to put entirely out of the schools all forms of memory training. Memory work rightly planned and carried out certainly has a place in our school life, and there is danger in our modern pedagogy that we shall be too radical, and shall lose some of the great advantages that come from the cultivation of indirect, memory interpretation.

The great limitation set upon the value of training that includes no memory is that it is inflexible. Immediate interpretation without memory is the mechanical side of thought. It proceeds on its way without variations. Let me illustrate this by referring again to such forms of interpretation as one has when he looks into a mirror. In past experiences the light has so regularly traveled in straight lines that we have a fixed mode of interpretation. This mode of interpreting light, either never had an immature memory stage, or else it very soon passed beyond memory. It is as immediate and complete as any form of recognition of meaning possibly could be. Notice that it does not admit of change even when we know, as in the case of a mirror, that the conditions are changed. We avoid inconvenience in dealing with mirrors by superimposing upon the original fixed mode of interpretation a secondary, or added clause of interpretation, adapted to mirrors as special factors of experience. In other words, we do not attempt to change the first mode of interpretation at all. We let it stand as fixed and safe for most purposes, and simply say to ourselves that it is, after all, not true that the object is back there as we see it in the mirror, that as a matter of fact the object in this case is around an angle.

The fixity of our interpretation of the direction in which light travels would also get us into trouble if we had to deal very frequently with objects under water; for, as you know, a ray of light is bent in passing from water into air. But here, too, it is easier for us to think our way through such unusual cases than to modify our general mode of interpretation. We see objects which are partly under water and partly above the water as if they were bent, but we do not disturb ourselves on this account; we have learned to hold in memory the correction that objects are not bent as they seem to be. We thus make our interpretation by addition, not by any modification of the fixed form of ordinary perception.

Relatively fixed modes of interpretation which have passed more or less completely beyond the memory stage—that is, beyond the possibility of modification—are more common than most of us realize. Such relatively fixed modes of interpretation are not always as unchangeable as is our mode of interpreting the direction from which light comes into the eye. They are sometimes capable of change under very strong provocation, but the provocation must be indeed great. Thus, most of the people we deal with are fixed, so far as our estimate of them is concerned. It would take a great deal to induce us to think well of some people or ill of others. Even if a man whom we do not like does a good thing, we refuse to see it as good. Our mode of interpretation is too fixed. Political faith is proverbially fixed. If one is a stanch partizan he will see things in a way appropriate to his partizan interests, and arguments avail little to change him. In matters of social practise, in matters of taste, and even in matters of religion, we find ourselves fixed and immovable, and our grounds for being fixed passed so long ago out of memory that we can not give an account of the origin of the mode of looking at things which we now adopt.

If you will study the way in which one of these fixed habits of interpretation begins to break up when the sufficient provocation arises, you will see the value of memory. Some fact presents itself which refuses to be interpreted in the old way. If in such a case one can by recollection call up the grounds of the fixed mode of interpretation, he may place the new fact alongside of the older considerations and may formulate a new and broader mode of interpretation. Have you not heard some wise political orator saying to a stubborn audience of opponents: "Let us consider why you belong to your party. Do you not remember how your father was a member of that party, and how it did thus and so in the good old days? Ask yourselves whether it is doing the same to-day." What is our political orator doing? He is putting us back at the beginnings of this political faith of ours. He knows very well how difficult it is to readjust the fixed habit of mature interpretation, even when readjustment is needed, and he knows also how much easier change will be if he can bring us back to the beginnings of this mode of thought. In short, he is playing upon the *variable* element of our mental natures, and that variable element is memory as opposed to fixed interpretation. Memory is characteristic, as Spencer put it, of those psychical processes which are in the stage of formation. If you can get at the memory stage of interpretation you can change it.

I suppose you are already asking yourselves the question to which our discussion has now brought us: Is it advisable in the course of education to keep any of the modes of interpretation open to the possibility of easy revision? The answer to that question can hardly be anything but an emphatic Yes. There are a very large number of interpretations which need constant revisions. Thus, every time a pupil passes from an elementary stage of a science to an advanced stage, there must be a readjustment of ideas. For example, in passing from the arithmetical to the algebraic methods of dealing with the number idea, a very great enlargement of the number idea must take place. The transition from physics to its applications in mechanical engineering, is another illustration of a more practical type. Our social ideas very often need readjusting. Take, for example, all our habits of thought about our fellow men. Take our political interpretations. I remember an old fellow in the country where a part of my boyhood was spent who had voted the ticket of one party all his life. On one occasion a friend of his in the opposing party was nominated for some petty local office. The old hardshell worked faithfully for his friend until election day, and then the habit of thought and action of a lifetime was too much for him, and he went to the polls and voted against his friend, whom he recognized as after all out of the true fold. Such an example as that illustrates, more eloquently than could any argument, the necessity of keeping one's modes of thought ready for revision. If you want to avoid becoming a fossil in any line, keep the reasons for your habits of thought sufficiently fresh in memory to make it possible to reconsider them from time to time.

Take the questions of how teachers shall arrange their work for the class room, and what their methods of instruction shall be. Have you not seen teachers who have thought in certain ruts with such regularity every time a certain subject was presented, that they have become petrified? Given a boy of twelve, a problem in percentage and a blackboard, and such a teacher can not see or expect more than one result, and that result must come in a perfectly fixed, definite way. If some one comes from some other school and says that this method is not right, what can our teacher with the fixed mode of thought do? Nothing. He does not remember now why he adopted the method. It is fixed, that is all there is of it; new methods are not wanted.

Mark you, I do not say that every time some one comes to you with a new method you should adopt it. What I do say is, that if you want to keep yourself from getting into bad ruts, you must be intelligent about what you do and about what you think; and the way to be intelligent is to be able to remember why you do, and think, as you do. Pedagogy is little if anything more than a means of waking a teacher up to the importance of understanding his or her own modes of thought and action. Why does a child mean this or that to you? What are your reasons for your attitude toward your pupils? Why do you think geography is an important subject? Why do you use the inductive method? Why are you prejudiced against manual training? These are questions which, if you can not answer, you are a slave to blind attitudes of mind. You may even be a fair teacher and not depend on anything but these blind and thoroughly established modes of thought, but the chances are against you. You should give your habits of thought, as I said a moment ago, a periodic looking over, and, if necessary, a periodic revision.

And what is true of teachers and other grown-ups is true of children. They can learn to be in a sense expert by the mere methods of trial and retrial, by the methods of practical manipulation. They can be *intelligently* expert, however, only when they add to their ability to do things, some knowledge of how things are done and why they are done. In the good old days, boys were sent out as apprentices, and they learned by trial. To-day we give our boys a thorough course, in which, if we are wise, we mix with trial some memory work. I think that the day is not distant when we shall recognize in all departments of our teaching that memory work has its large and proper place along with the more direct forms of learning. And for ourselves, I think we can find, if we study the matter closely, as we shall try to do in the next chapter, that many of the great difficulties that beset teaching are due to the fact that teachers do not try in a practical way to be something more than routine teachers; they do not try to keep alive their memories and to understand the reasons for their present modes of looking at their experiences.

CHAPTER III

THE ORIGIN OF SOME OF OUR EDUCATIONAL IDEALS

In one of his letters, Stevenson sums up the discouraging side of educational efforts by saying that one must keep chopping and chopping and never have the satisfaction of seeing the chips fly. What teacher has not realized keenly at times this feeling of vagueness and uncertainty as to the effect of class-room and school work? We seek to render this uncertainty somewhat less trying by holding now and then what we call tests. We are ready to admit that these periodic tests do not give us an entirely satisfactory indication of what has been accomplished, but we want to see some of the chips flying, and so we get what meager satisfaction we can out of examinations.

How different it is in other callings! The carpenter looks over his work as it progresses day by day; the merchant takes his inventory and account of stock at least once every twelve months; the lawyer knows when the verdict comes what has been the effect of his plea; the doctor finds his patient better or worse; and so on through the whole list of professions and occupations. The results are obvious, and they come soon enough to serve as guides for new efforts. If this or that method of treating a disease does not produce the desired result, the doctor soon knows it and changes; if this or that method of advertising is successful, the merchant soon finds it out and develops it more fully. With teaching it is different. We think we have a new and most successful method of teaching, and we use it with unrestrained enthusiasm, only to find that the children on whom the method has been tried are being hindered in their general mental development by their special devotion to this one subject. One can not cast up accounts in matters of education until that far-off period when the boys and girls shall show themselves well or illy equipped for life outside of the schools. And even then, who shall separate the results of school training from the results that grow out of the influence of home and social life? Surely the teacher's task is one in which it is not easy to weigh and measure methods and results.

Did you ever consider the effects of this remoteness of results on the teacher's conduct and mode of thought? Of course we all realize that just because we are not brought to a practical test day by day, we are, more than most people, open to the temptation of shirking. But I do not intend to dwell on that phase of the discussion. I wish rather to assume that a teacher has unlimited devotion and untiring zeal, and to point out that even under these conditions, the remoteness of the end of education has its marked effect on thought and conduct. The best way, perhaps, to describe this effect is to say that, deprived of the obvious guides which the carpenter, or merchant, or members of other professions have, we as teachers are dependent on the ideas which we hold as to our aims and purposes. In other words, we set up as substitutes for unseen and remote ends, a variety of theoretical ends. We do something to-day and to-morrow, not because we expect to find our efforts ripening into immediate fruition, but because our thoughts as to what we should accomplish lead us to take this step and the next. I think such a line of consideration as this serves to explain and justify very fully the large amount of discussion which educational questions are everywhere receiving. Certainly there is no profession more in need of good ideals and strong ideals than is that to which we belong.

So necessary, indeed, are ideals to guide the work of the teacher, that history is full of illustrations of the fact that where no carefully thought-out educational ideals have been at hand, the necessary ideals have been seized up from this or the other outside source and have been made to stand as guides for pedagogical endeavor.

Let us consider in detail one of the best historical illustrations of such borrowing of ideals. Just at the beginning of the eighteenth century there grew up in the little German city of Halle an educational movement which was destined to have a far-reaching influence on the development of Germany's school systems, and indirectly on the development of our own school ideals. An enthusiastic professor in the University of Halle saw what seemed to him to be the possibility of developing a new and more practical form of school work. He organized a school for waifs, and attached to this general school, a training-school for teachers. The results of this movement are still alive in a vigorous normal institution bearing the name of the founder of the earlier school, the name of Franke. Franke's school made some innovations in the subjects chosen for instruction and in the way of teaching these subjects, but in these innovations we shall not interest ourselves now. The fact of chief interest to us here is the thoroughgoing application of a certain narrow religious ideal which Franke worked out in the organization and discipline of his pupils. "Play," said Franke, "must be forbidden in any and all of its forms. The children shall be instructed in this matter in such a way as to show them, through the presentation of religious principles, the wastefulness and folly of all play. They shall be led to see that play will distract their hearts and minds from God, the eternal Good, and will work nothing but harm to their spiritual lives. Their true joy and hearty devotion should be given to their blessed and holy Saviour and not to earthly things, for the reward of those who seek earthly things is tears and sorrow."

There is something strangely narrow in that ideal which Franke set up for the discipline of his pupils. We shall miss the significance of Franke's work, however, if we fail to recognize that this was with him a true and clear ideal. It did not arise from any careful study of children; it did not arise from any broad historical study of what education had been; it sprang rather from a deep religious conviction. It was an ideal which the teacher relied upon to guide him in the task of preparing his pupils for life here and hereafter. It was an ideal which I dare say Franke himself would have admitted was beyond the possibility of any immediate test. Indeed, it was enthusiastically adopted by him just because no test was undertaken of the value or limitations of play. It was a borrowed educational ideal.

And now that you have seen the narrowness of Franke's educational ideal, borrowed from his religious beliefs, let me ask you where our own ideals of play came from? Or, to relieve the discussion of direct personal applications, take the schoolmaster of a generation ago; what did he think of play? I remember some of my own experiences which lead me to believe that if some of my teachers were not inspired by profound religious zeal, at least they were inspired from some other source, perhaps opposite to that of Franke's inspiration, by prejudice against play equal to that of Franke, if not exceeding it. The changes which our own ideals of play are undergoing at this very time serve to call our attention as teachers most emphatically to the prejudice against play so prevalent in the schools of yesterday, and give us at the same time good ground for the question, Whence came these earlier educational ideals, and whence are coming the newer ideals? In short, we have here a phase of the large question of the teacher's professional ideals. Whence do they arise, and what are they?

Professional ideals are to be distinguished from ideals in general. There are some teachers who have a kind of schoolroom manner and mode of thought, different from the manner and mode of thought which they carry into every-day life; these teachers illustrate the strength of special ideals adapted only to the professional life of the teacher, and unfortunately they illustrate too often the peculiar and narrow character of these special ideals. Professional ideals are not, however, always bad. The term "professional" refers to all these special ideals about the aims of education which we as teachers take up from this source or that, and use to guide our steps along the by no means obvious path of educational work. Very frequently we do not realize whence these ideals came, or how appropriate or inappropriate they are as guides. They are like the modes of present interpretation of which we spoke in our last chapter, always present in developed mental life, but frequently so far beyond the memory stage that their sources are forgotten and the possibility of changing them is very limited.

Many of our professional ideals are borrowed from tradition; such ideals have, in a double sense, passed the stage of memory. In the first place, those who transmitted the ideals to us have commonly lost sight of their first sources; and in the second place, we have forgotten in turn whence we drew the tradition. We teach, in short, as we were taught, and we do this because it is easier to take up with ready-made ideals than it is to make new ideals for ourselves. When some educational thinker steps out with a new ideal for the school, we all stand back and refuse to have anything to do with the new ideal. If we recognize his proposition as a call to defend our old views, we find out very soon that the justifications for these older views are long lost in misty antiquity. The curious fact is, that even if we do become convinced of all this, we do not, or can not, muster energy enough to reopen the whole question and revise our ideals in the light of the new facts. Or, at least, to put the case somewhat more mildly, the process of revising our ideals is exceedingly slow, and requires a generation or two before new traditions can grow up. Would that we might have a body of teachers so well informed as to the traditions of their profession, and so constantly in touch with the helpful new considerations, that revisions of educational ideals would not be so difficult and tedious! And this is, in other words, nothing but a plea for more study by teachers of their own ideals and of the grounds of these ideals.

By way of illustration, let us push that question of discipline in the school a little further than we did in our discussion of Franke's methods with his children. What is your ideal of good order? Where did it come from? I venture to say that we all of us have a notion that we are not responsible for the imposition practised on children in the schools. This idea, to which we cling more or less tenaciously, of making children sit in one place for long periods of time, is gradually being given up, it is such an ignoble failure. But how many generations of children have suffered in the years past because of this notion of order, a notion which any intelligent mother could have told teachers was, to say the least, defective!

By way of contrasting other ideals of order with our own, it is interesting to know that in the schools of Hindustan and of many other Oriental countries, the boys are allowed to sway backward and forward and to read aloud from their books as they study, each in his place. The way in which the teacher picks out the good boy there is to select the one who is wiggling most energetically and talking to himself the loudest. They have a form of order which agrees with our view that doing is essential to the learning process, very much better than does our own form of order.

Even in the old Roman school, from which our schools borrowed much, the boys had far greater freedom than in the later medieval schools which followed the Roman schools. As Laurie puts it in his history: "The pupils seem to have spoken out loud when learning, and the masters outshouted them." Our ideal of order evidently did not come from this old Roman school.

Furthermore, the changes we are now making show that our older ideal did not come from a careful study of children and their needs.

We sometimes try to justify the ideals of rigid order by saying that quiet is necessary to concentration of attention, and bodily repose is necessary to mental activity. But all this is shallow fiction. Bodily activity is always present in connection with vigorous mental activity, as we shall see more in detail in our later discussions. Indeed, in children this bodily activity is of a very pronounced type. We are coming, as every student of present-day education recognizes, to see more clearly the necessity and value of proper movement as an aid rather than a hindrance to education. And as to the necessity of quiet for mental concentration, do you think your boys and girls will get quiet when they go into the activities of real life? And if not, do you think we are preparing them best for life in our quiet schoolrooms?

No; if we are to understand the present organization of our schools, we must go back through the centuries, stopping for a moment to see how the stern Puritans of New England enforced the law that all things pertaining to this life are trivial and fit only to be eradicated by the schoolmaster. We must pay our respects again to Franke and his school; we must go back of the Reformation, with its schools for the people conducted on the same plan as the earlier church schools. Here in the church schools we have the beginnings of our modern ideals in more than one particular, but in no particular more clearly than in the matter of discipline. The medieval schools conducted in connection with the cloisters were organized on the same stern principles as the whole life of those institutions. The silent monks, given over to meditation, withdrawing from the frivolous and untutored world without, these were the only schoolmasters of that day. They marched to and from the service with bowed head and lips moving only in silent prayer or devout hymn. They learned the words given them by the authority that presided over them. They suffered in confinement and with cruel tortures for the slightest infraction of the laws under which they lived. All this they thought to be necessary in order that they might free their spirits from degrading association with the unspiritual body. And when they took boys into their cloisters to prepare them for intellectual and spiritual life, these zealous monks naturally followed in great detail the lines of discipline through which they themselves had come to their high estate. What did these sequestered monks, cut off from all the real life even of their own times, know about the child's nature? To them the child was nothing but a soul to be saved at any cost of self-sacrifice and mortification of the body. To them anything which looked like play was a reminder of the vulgar, wicked world outside the cloister walls. To them sternness and severe discipline were the only means of salvation. And since their day, teachers have gone on accepting this false notion of play and school discipline. Now and then there have appeared extremists like Franke, or like the teachers in the Port Royal schools in France, or like the Puritans in our own New England—all of whom have tried to be more consistent than most of us. These extremists said that if our school discipline is right it should be extended so as to cover all the hours of the day; no half-hearted compromise like ours of half a day of play and half a day of severity would do for those eager souls. And then, on the other hand, there have been men like Robert Ascham, who have pleaded for humanity and mildness. There have been men like Rousseau and Froebel, and a host of others, who have said to us in no uncertain terms: Give up the harsh and artificial rigor of the school. Bring back this institution to real living and natural enjoyment, and let us recognize the children's rights of body and nervous organization as well as of what we call soul.

The trouble with us as teachers has been in the past that we have never waked up to the fact that our ideal of order is a mechanical, traditional idea. I am not going to say that the new ideal on which we are working in our American schools will not contain something of the spirit of the old sad-eyed monk's view of life. There is some truth to my thinking in that medieval idea, carried in those olden days to an extreme and accepted blindly by generations since. But that truth must be mixed with other truths. The other truths are rushing in upon us in these days. They come from child-study, from our study of biology and sociology. We are learning the lesson that an act does not need to be disagreeable to be virtuous, that pleasure is compatible with highest effort. And it is possible that we are being a little carried away by these discoveries. If the old monk was a hard master, some of our modern schoolmasters have adopted what Professor James has so aptly called a "soft pedagogy." This violent swing from one extreme to the other is due to the fact that in neither case is the idea an intelligent one. It is adopted blindly from tradition, or it is seized up from modern science. Teachers need to become more intelligent as to the grounds of their practises.

If we turn from school discipline to the matter of instruction, we come upon a group of traditions that it is almost impossible to bring teachers to realize are mechanical and often dead. A subject of study gets itself petrified very rapidly. One generation learns it in school in a certain way, and when that generation has grown old enough to be in charge of the work of teaching, it is almost impossible to introduce a new element or phase of instruction. If you ask why we teach thus and so, you will be confronted with a whole series of artificial excuses; the real reason is that we, as the older generation, are so fixed in our modes of thought about the subject in question that we can not realize that there is any rational ground for change.

Take such a question as that of the desirability of changing the character of geography in the schools.

I have seen whole bodies of teachers protesting against commercial geography. They have tried to brand commercial geography as mercenary and materialistic. They have tried to point out that there is less exactness and less discipline in such study than in the minute scrutiny of the map which used to be demanded. Such teachers would rather locate the most northerly town in the State of Maine, than know the way in which cotton is gathered and packed for market. They would rather mark a pupil down for forgetting that one corner of the State of Pennsylvania touches Lake Erie, than teach a class how coal is blasted and carried out of the mines, or how iron is turned into steel. It is not true that these facts of industrial life are unworthy of careful study in the schools. It is true that the average teacher will not arouse himself to revise his notions of geography. I venture the remark again, that our teachers are not so much intelligently opposed to the new demands made upon them by the new curriculum as they are blindly worried on imaginary grounds. A new geography is demanded of them. The traditions of a lifetime rise up in rebellion against this innovation. Nine times out of ten the teacher begins by feeling imposed upon, and ends by rebelliously thumbing over the new requirements, and goes away worrying because the new requirements and the old ideals do not agree.

Which is right, the old ideal of what geography is and ought to be, or the new requirement? Again I shall venture to formulate the results of observation in the statement that probably neither the new requirement nor the old ideal is entirely right. They both need careful examination and criticism. They need intelligent study on the part of class-room teachers. The trouble in our school systems is that there is not enough of this constant comparison in an enlightened way, of new demands and old ideals.

If in a large mercantile house the methods get ever so little behind the times, the results show themselves in a falling off of profits, and there is a constant spur to keep one's eyes open in the observation and study of methods. But in the teaching profession there is no such constant spur. One may fall years behind and not realize it. One may be so blind as to be quite unwilling to see even when the new subjects and methods are brought to his door. Or one may, if he will, be progressive, and realizing the character of his own profession be his own spur.

I have used the illustration of geography first, because that composite science is so clearly one of the storm-centers in our present-day discussions of education. Physical geography on the one side, commercial geography on the other; nature-study in all its manifold departments; political history and social science as studies of the human institutions of which geography used to give us a glimpse—all these new subjects are calling for recognition in a larger measure. These are the subjects under which teachers are chafing. What shall we do with them? I think there is only one answer that can be given to this question with any hope of bringing about a satisfactory solution. The individual teacher must examine for himself the new claims. He must bring out his old geographical ideals and prepare to understand them. Above all things he must not put himself blindly on the defensive. Never hold to an educational ideal as if it were infallible. Remember that it too has real grounds on which to rest, and the value of the ideal will depend on the validity of these grounds. Prepare to know the grounds, that is the rational line of defense. Do not turn this task over to the superintendent, especially if you have the mental reservation that, whatever he concludes, you will hold to your old ideals.

The conflicts between reform and pedantry which we have seen so often in our schools, are due to the fact that one or both parties to the controversy are unable to see back of their particular ideals to the underlying justification.

One could pause and draw from history illustration after illustration of how bitter conflicts have been waged in breaking up petrified ideals not only in education, but in other realms of thought as well. We have a kind of admiration for the men who laid down their lives for the ideals represented in the crusades, when the nations of Europe determined to repossess the Holy Sepulcher. And yet, after all, the greatest good accomplished by the crusades was not the protection of the medieval religious ideal, but the renovation of this ideal. The verdict of history is clear. The crusades were blind struggles for an imagined and unsubstantial good. In that struggle the medieval man learned the difference between the good to which he had falsely held and the real good. One can not read that lesson of history aright without applying it to his own life. We fight blindly for educational ideals, only to find in the course of the struggle that we were perhaps partly right, but seldom wholly so. Let us take the lesson as a warning against that kind of defense of our educational ideals. Let us do the intelligent thing, the rational thing, and before we become militant and rush to arms, let us use our minds, which we as teachers hold to be the safest guides in life.

It is hardly in place in a general discussion of the teacher's attitude toward the subjects in the curriculum to devote much time to the detailed discussion of the separate subjects themselves, and I shall recognize that limitation of our present opportunity. I shall not enter into any defense of nature-study and commercial geography, except to repeat an incident which seems to me to be full of the kind of meaning which my whole argument has tried to convey to you. I once had the opportunity of speaking to the teachers of a small Ohio city in defense of certain changes which had recently been introduced by a new superintendent into their course of study. The argument ran something like our present argument. The accepted studies of our curriculum have not always been the accepted studies. Arithmetic was once recognized as valuable for school discipline only in so far as it was needed to make possible computation of the church calendar. Geography of the sailor type is a comparatively recent subject. The earlier forms of geography used to be more like our present astronomy. And so on, I was trying to show how the school course is a gradual growth, and was drawing the conclusion that what has grown up to its present stage of development must be expected to grow further. After that teachers' meeting was over an old gentleman came up and said to me, "Young man, you might have made your statements a little stronger if you had had the experience of one as old as I am. I can remember when a young New England girl who had come to teach in the school which I was attending, introduced a new subject into the course of study of that school, and that new subject was geography. There was a good deal of excitement about it in the community and much skepticism on the part of the sages as to the propriety of the innovation. Especially the teacher in the next district was disturbed that the good old traditions of the schools thereabouts were thus ruthlessly set aside by that young New England girl." I asked the old gentleman what the outcome was, and he laughed and said for his answer that his daughter was now teaching nature-study in the school.

Of course geographical ideas are not the only ones that are getting a renovating these days. We do not have to go far into any of the lines of instruction to find changes. I shall content myself, however, with reference to one of the more general of the proposed changes in the course of study. Why is there such opposition to the new ideals that are being offered to us in the so-called constructive work, or manual-training courses in the schools?

The common attitude toward constructive work can be discussed from several points of view. In the first place, we may undertake a description of what the attitude really is in the mind of the average teacher. And here I think we may safely say that most of us think of constructive work as a sort of secondary mode of training, closely related to pure physical training or even to recreation. We seldom find a teacher who would be willing to defend the position that constructive work is coordinate in importance with reading or arithmetic. We usually think of constructive work as less intellectual than the other subjects mentioned. We think of it as less ennobling, as less characteristically human, as less highly developed. Consequently, we feel at liberty to neglect constructive work more than the other subjects. We do not feel that it is anything of a stigma upon ourselves when we admit freely that we are not able to conduct constructive work successfully. If too much of this kind of work is demanded of us, we chafe under the requirement and wish for a special teacher to relieve us of the work.

Another point of view from which we might discuss constructive work is that of the teacher's equipment. Most teachers are not prepared to take up such work. They possess no manual dexterity, no knowledge of tools and materials, no imagination with which to plan such exercises, and worst of all no desire to correct any of these limitations.

Again think of the relation of constructive work to our present school organization and equipment. Our desks are not adapted to such work. The arrangement of our desks in the rooms is not suited to it. The supplies ordinarily furnished by boards of education do not include the necessary tools or raw materials for constructive work.

Finally, from the point of view of the parents of the children, constructive work is not what is expected of the schools. I once heard an irate parent sum the matter up by saying that his children did not go to school to cut and fold papers or whittle wood—they could do that at home without the help of a teacher.

Certainly such considerations as these which we have been briefly summarizing, show beyond the possibility of doubt that constructive work is not a fully accepted or willingly accepted innovation in our school work. Men may argue as they will at teachers' meetings and in the educational journals about the advantages which arise from the introduction of constructive work into the school. The simple fact is that most of us listen to these arguments in the proverbial fashion, with both ears, one ear serving, however, as an exit for what comes in at the other.

Why is it that an average teacher is so prejudiced from the outset against constructive work? I find it very much more difficult to give a definite answer to this question than it was to give an answer to the question of the source of our ideals of school discipline. The difficulty of accounting for our prejudice against constructive work in the schools lies in the fact that this is not a prejudice peculiar to teachers. It is so wide-spread, I was about to say so universal, and so old, that it is impossible to get at the special period when it came into the school or even had its origin. The fact is that men of all classes have long drawn a sharp contrast between bodily activity and mental activity. The Hindu devotee who sits in one position year after year busy with high and holy thought, the Greek laughing at the philosopher so lost in meditation that he clumsily falls into the well in his path, the religious ascetic of the medieval world who sat and gazed for hours and even days into blank space—all these are witnesses to the antiquity of the contrast between bodily dexterity and mental activity.

Taking up the matter from the point of view of the science of psychology, especially from the point of view of the psychology which has been written by the so-called English school, mental life has been treated for the most part as if it were made up of impressions and of ideas resulting from these impressions. Until very recently no one thought it necessary to say very much about expression, or the active side of knowledge. If expression was mentioned at all in the earlier psychologies, it was treated as a kind of unessential after-effect. Thus we have all of us come to think of action as something which one may or may not enter upon after he has had a thought. We consider the thought as a kind of taking-in process, and as a kind of turning over in the mind of what is thus taken in, but we have not been in the habit of expecting action unless the thought is supplemented by a process quite apart from the thought and additional to it. We all of us tend even now to believe that one may think intently and be perfectly inactive so far as his expressive muscles are concerned. In short, the tradition of our psychology, both scientific and popular, has been that bodily dexterity and mental life are distinct and separate.

I suppose that it will require a generation or two of teachers to root up these ideals and to clear the way for a new and better ideal in the art of teaching. I suppose that the strongest evidence will have very little force in assaulting this stronghold of tradition, and so I shall feel quite satisfied with the results of my efforts during the remainder of this chapter if I can only set you inquiring into the validity of your idea as to the relation of mental life and movement.

In order that there may be no ambiguity as to my position in the matter I will say to you frankly at the outset that I believe we have been all wrong in this matter. I believe we have enough facts now to make it perfectly clear that bodily movement is present in a very pronounced form whenever there is mental activity, and I believe it can be shown that the training of this bodily movement is an essential part of the general training of the individual. If these beliefs are justified by the facts, then the conclusions will not be very difficult to draw, our educational ideals are sadly in need of revision, and the sooner we can effect this revision the sooner we shall undo the harm that has been done by accepting a false ideal.

Let us turn now to a consideration of some of the facts which support the statements just made to you. There is a very simple experiment which any one can easily try. Take two bottles of different sizes, cover them so that one can not see what is in them, and then put shot into the smaller one until it is exactly equal in weight to the larger, empty bottle. Then take up the bottles in your hands and you will find that, in spite of your knowledge that the two weights are the same, the small bottle will seem very much heavier. That is, you are subject to what we have already learned in another connection to call an illusion. It requires no great degree of insight to see in a general way what is the cause of the illusion. There are plenty of other illusions of the same type. You take up a small bottle of mercury and it will seem very heavy, much heavier than you expected from looking at the bottle. The sudden difference between what you expected and what you really get in the way of a sensation, increases very much the effect of the weight. We say that the apparent weight has been increased by contrast. Now, in our experiment of the two bottles of the same weight but of different sizes, there is such a contrast. Bottles of different sizes are commonly different in weight. But if the expected difference in weight does not really appear when we pick up the bottles, then we are led through contrast to perceive just the opposite of what we expected.

There is a not uncommon trick which is of the same type as this illusion of the bottles. Five or six of us stand around some person who lies on two chairs and at a given signal we each lift with one or two fingers of each hand, and the person seems to be very light. We do not pay attention to the fact that the weight is distributed so as to be very little for each of the lifting fingers. We expect to lift 150 pounds, we actually lift about 15 pounds or less with each finger, and the result is we do not notice the 15 pounds as being at all heavy. The contrast between 150 and 15 is great enough to account for the whole illusion. The holding of one's breath and the other mummeries that are generally added to the experiment, help to distract one still more from the 15 pounds that have to be lifted and so aid the illusion even further.

Up to this time we have spoken of these illusions in the usual terms of impression and mental contrast, and I venture the guess that most of you have thought of mental contrast in this connection as a sort of conflict in the mind between what is expected and what really came in. That is, you have been satisfied to think of the whole matter as a mere comparison of impressions. But there is a great deal of bodily activity involved in this illusion of which the explanation by mere impression does not take account. When you looked at the two bottles, or when you prepared to lift the person lying on the chair, the sight impressions that came in at your eyes were not the only facts which we need to consider. Your consciousness went beyond the impressions and interpreted them. The interpretation involved as its most important factor in this case, a recognition of what you could do with the objects at which you were looking. What you could do was added to the incoming sight impressions and your real idea of the objects before you was not merely "that thing," but it was rather "that thing which can be lifted with more or less effort." Even before you did any actual lifting your impression was joined to the possibilities of expression. In some other cases, the expression factor is more elaborate. For example, if one of the bottles is full of medicine and you look at it, you see not merely "that light-colored bottle which can be lifted," but you see "that light-colored bottle which is to be turned up and a part of its contents swallowed." In other words, there is no idea which is made up entirely of mere impression; there is always a factor of expression. This factor of expression is so closely related to one's personal use of the object that we may say that the personal phase of all knowledge is the expressive phase. It is because there is something that I can do with objects that these objects are of interest to me. Anything which I never can use, is of little importance to me, and I am sure to overlook it. What I can use, I look at sharply. I recognize, accordingly, when I look at such an object not merely its color or its form, but also its value to me. I add meaning to the impression in the manner described in our last chapter. *And this fact of value or meaning is paralleled on the bodily side by an actual preparatory contraction of my muscles.* If, as in the case of the bottles in our experiment, the object is small, the contraction of the muscles will be very slight, but it can nevertheless be demonstrated as present by means of appropriate recording apparatus. And what is of greatest importance to us here is that the intensity of muscular preparation for lifting agrees with our interpretation of the object as heavier or lighter. That is, in the case of the two bottles of different sizes and like weight, our muscular preparation is controlled by the different sizes, and we get ready in the case of the larger object to lift a heavier object. When now, we do the lifting, the larger object seems light because our actual muscular preparation was too great and the object was therefore very easily raised. The contrast, you see, is not a mere matter of comparing impressions in the mind, it is a question of the kind of interpretation which was added to the impression, and the interpretation in this case, as in every case, involves certain factors of bodily action. Bodily action is present before the lifting really begins, and before we recognize that we are in action through any impressions of actual movement. Bodily action is the expressive side of the experience. We see accordingly that an incoming impression and the expressive interpretation, are mutually interdependent; that they supplement each other; and that together they constitute the total unitary experience.

The reason why we do not recognize in ordinary life the constant relation of bodily activities to impressions, is that we have a wrong notion of what goes to make up bodily activity. Most of us think of bodily activity as consisting in a movement of some of the external parts, such as the arm or face. We forget that there are certain inner movements which are always changing with every incoming impression. Take, for example, the action of the heart. We all know that in extreme cases of strong or sudden impression, the heart beats violently, or seems suddenly to stop. We see the face grow red or white when the appropriate impression is received, even when there are no signs of external movement. What we see in extreme cases as noticeable changes in the action of the circulatory system, gives us a clue to the general fact which scientific investigation has fully established. This general fact is that every impression, be it ever so weak and insignificant, affects in its measure the distribution of the blood in the body. Put in other words, this means that one of the forms of bodily activity which regularly accompanies impressions is the internal change in the way in which the heart and the blood-vessels do their work. And this is a very large expressive factor; it is an important form of activity, even if it does not involve external muscles of the hand and face.

One of the simplest ways of demonstrating the constancy and delicacy of these inner activities is that devised by Mosso, an Italian scientist. He balanced a man so carefully on a balance-board that the slightest increase in the amount of blood in the head would be indicated by a tipping of the board downward at the head end. Then he found that even if he let the man go to sleep, and thus made him less susceptible to impression than usual, the slightest noise would have as its immediate consequence an increase of the amount of blood in the head. Just as hard study or excitement results in a rush of large quantities of blood to the head, so a slight impression produces in its degree a slight increase in the amount of blood. The carefully constructed balance-board showed what the coarser observation of ordinary life shows only in extreme cases.

What is true of the activities of blood circulation is true also of activities of breathing and of digestion. One has felt himself stop breathing when listening intently to some piece of music or to some patriotic orator. One has seen a whole company draw a long breath of relief after an exciting scene on the stage. The holding of the breath and the long after-breath show how very strongly our activity of breathing is affected by the impressions that come in at ears and eyes.

As for digestion, we all know that excitement is very far from conducive to the enjoyment of healthy life; and recent researches carried out with the aid of the Röntgen rays on the movements of the stomach of a cat during digestion showed that these movements stopped with surprising promptness and invariability whenever the animal was disturbed by any external impression.

All of these facts serve to call attention to activities

accompanying impressions, and they ought to enlarge our common view of what activity means. When one sits still and listens, he may be very active in some one of these internal systems, even though he presents to himself and to the world at large a placid and unruffled exterior.

It remains to mention another group of activities which are not internal, but commonly escape attention because they are so constant. Did you ever stop to consider that each one of us is constantly active so long as he sits up and holds up his head? One has only to watch a nodding, drowsy man to realize how much muscular energy is involved in our ordinary sitting up. The muscles of the neck are always in a state of tension during waking hours, and their activity must not be omitted when we are making up a list of our ordinary bodily responses to impressions. For is not hanging the head a proverbial expression for shame? Do we not recognize the man of buoyant spirit by the proud carriage and the head thrown back? Do we not notice the straighter walk of the soldier when the thrilling martial music is ringing in his ears? Indeed, one can notice on every hand the close relation between the way one carries himself and the way one looks at the world about him and sees in its impressions hope and promise or envy and enmity. One's bodily activity can not be described without full recognition of these forms of muscular activity which appear in our attitudes. They are not forms of rapid movement, and that is why they do not impress us very strikingly. They show all the better the fundamental distinction between the activity and what we ordinarily mean when we use the term movement. The body is always active, internally and externally, whether its parts are noticeably moving or not.

This distinction between activity and movement is significant for the teacher. Do you think that the boy who sits still in his seat at school is not active just because he is not moving? Watch him a little more closely and you will see that the true description of what he is doing involves a good deal of attention to forms of activity that are no less real because they are not forms of external movement. That boy would, if he did the natural thing, get up out of his seat and come up to you, as, indeed, he often starts to do when he forgets. He would naturally start and go to his neighbor who has something interesting under his desk, if it were not for the law of the school. He would jump up and look out of the window at the slightest provocation. The reason why he does not do this is that a kindly Providence has furnished him with two sets of muscles, one which would fain do the forbidden thing, and the other set to hold back these unruly members. And when the boy wants to look out of the window, but seeing the threatening look of the teacher, holds himself in the seat, he sits still by sheer force of muscular activity. His warring activities are not as obvious to the eye as they would be if he started up and then sat down again in a hurry, but he is in reality getting up and sitting down at the same instant, so that what may look to the superficial observer like sitting still is in reality doing much hard work.

You have felt like sneezing or coughing, have you not, when you were obliged to go through the excruciating experience of keeping still? You have had a tickling sensation on the end of your nose at a time when you did not dare, out of respect to your social environment, move your hand up to that irritating organ? How did you manage in these cases to sit still? Was it not through an effort, and was that effort any the less real because it did not involve actual movement? Such an experience ought to help you to understand why it is that a boy has such difficulty in keeping still; for the sights and sounds out of doors which stir our torpid grown-up blood all too little, are to him the most attractive objects in the universe, and the thought of running about the room is as irresistible to him as is the most inviting allurement to our adult ambitions.

But we must draw this discussion to a close without entering into any of the applications of this principle that mental activity is always paralleled by bodily activity. It is to be hoped, however, that the impression begins to grow in your minds that we are very active beings, and that our usual prejudice against activity in the school is not altogether justified. The activities which we are exhibiting in larger measure than we usually realize, are of great importance to the teacher in his study of himself and in his study of his pupil. The traditional notion that the school is a place in which impressions are merely to be poured into the mind has had its day. We are beginning to enter upon a new era with new educational ideals, and it will be well for us to get out our old ideals about the nature of mental life and give them a thorough renovating. The fact is that most of our notions about bodily activity are due to the fact that we have overlooked the inner activities, and that we have overlooked those constant external activities which do not result in actual and obvious movements. But these large groups of unnoticed activities are very closely related to our impressions. A given impression results in its own appropriate activity, and that activity is just as much a part of the bodily condition of the experience and of its interpretation as is the process in the eye or ear which we call a sensory excitation.

We shall take up next some discussion of the general principles upon which we are reconstructing our educational ideals. The work of this chapter has been largely negative. We have attempted to call attention to the fact that the teacher's professional ideals frequently rise and get themselves established on wholly inadequate grounds. The teacher then forgets where the ideal really came from, and holds to the unjustified ideal with all the greater tenacity because its grounds are lost from view. What we need in our study as teachers, is to become conscious of our ideals, to think of their grounds, and to recast many a false belief in view of fuller and better knowledge.

CHAPTER IV

THE NEW IDEALS OF DEVELOPMENT

The last chapter closed rather abruptly with a negative conclusion. In that discussion we were showing how unfounded is our ordinary notion that mental life can be understood without attention to accompanying bodily activities. There was a very large positive principle involved in that conclusion, the principle that every mental state has its parallel bodily expression, but we did not there attempt to work out that positive principle with all its pedagogical corollaries.

The negative conclusions of our earlier discussions were, however, merely preparatory to the positive, constructive treatment of educational ideals. Certainly there could be no justification for mere negations in a series of discussions of this sort. Indeed, there is no justification for mere negation in the thought of any teacher. We should never stop working on our ideals until we have something positive. See to it that you never cultivate that chronic state of doubt which makes it impossible for you to believe in the validity of any ideal. You will never have peace of mind in your teaching, you will never overcome the fretful wear and tear of seeking after petty devices, until you have found out some broad positive principles which can be relied upon to guide your work.

Fortunately there are many positive ideals and positive principles with which to replace old and worn-out prejudices. These newer ideals are being offered to the teachers on many sides. Sometimes the new principle is only half formulated. Sometimes the enthusiastic advocate is disposed to overemphasize the value of this or that new educational doctrine. Indeed, there is much sinning by way of omission and commission; but through all the error and the misguided enthusiasm, one can see the outlines of a few of the great fundamental principles which promise to furnish our educational practise with a firmer and broader basis than has ever been known before.

One of these general principles is the principle of expression, with the negative side of which we closed our last chapter. No one has given this principle a clearer statement than has Professor James in that admirable book of his, Talks to Teachers. He defines education[1] as "The organization of acquired habits of conduct and tendencies to behavior." Such a definition throws the whole weight of attention in teaching, not on the impression which is given to the child, but on the expression which is to result from the impression. In the chapter following the one from which we just quoted, Professor James confirms the position taken in his definition of education with these strong words:[2] "An impression which simply flows in at the pupil's eyes or ears, and in no way modifies his active life, is an

[1] Page 29. [2] Pages 33, 34

impression gone to waste . . . . It leaves no fruits behind it in the way of capacity acquired. . . . Its *motor consequences* are what clinch it. Some effect due to it in the way of an activity must return to the mind in the form of the *sensation of having acted,* and connect itself with the impression. The most durable impressions are those on account of which we speak or act, or else are inwardly convulsed." Such an ideal as this which Professor James gives us is certainly full of positive suggestions for the class-room teacher.

One might seek out other examples of strong positive contributions to educational thought, but we shall not content ourselves with a mere review of these principles as they are given to us by our leading thinkers. We are fortunate in being able to seek the same source of inspiration which these great leaders have sought, for the whole thought of our times, not only in education, but in every sphere of natural science and sociology and psychology, is dominated and controlled by the one great principle, the principle of development.

Within the last half century we have seen this idea of development rise and spread over every domain of human thought. The geologist seeks to know the development of our planet. The astronomer inquires boldly into the secrets of the great cosmic development that brought forth our sun and our sister worlds. On the other hand, delving down into the infinitely small, the biologist seeks to know the development of the minutest living cell. Even the student of human life in any and all of its phases, has adopted the same point of view, and whether he be historian, or economist, or psychologist, his chief problem is to trace the course of human development.

I need not tell you that in the educational world this same idea of development is everywhere being recognized. The development of the child, the development of our school organization, the development of the curriculum—all these are common subjects of investigation. Has not our own subject up to this time been the subject of the development of the teacher's ideals? And so we are introducing no strange question when we ask what is this general idea of development. What is its value to the teacher, and how can we get some help from it in our school work? If it is true that Professor James in his Talks to Teachers is only working out this idea; if it is true that Professor Dewey is seeking to realize the same ideal in his experiments; if it is true that President Hall has to thank his grasp of the same idea for what of value there is in his writings—if all these men come back to the one broad idea of development as their starting-point, then, certainly, it is time that the individual teacher should turn with all despatch to a study of this fundamental idea.

True, this is no easy task which I have proposed to you, for all the recent writings in the sciences and in education have been trying to work out the details of this idea. The story is told of Huxley, the English scientist, that on one occasion a narrow-minded opponent wrote, demanding that Huxley send him a brief summary of all the arguments for evolution, in order that this same opponent might refute them. Huxley replied, advising his correspondent to take a complete course in the science of comparative anatomy, in which science Huxley assured him he would find many of the reasons in favor of evolution. And, perhaps, some captious critic will be disposed to set aside our suggestion that the individual teacher acquaint himself or herself with the meaning of this fundamental idea of development on the ground that such an acquaintance would involve a study of all recent science. But I think we can meet our critic by admitting frankly the truth which there is in his remark. Certainly the individual teacher can not read all the modern literature on development. On the other hand, no teacher should fail to read some of this literature, enough at least to grasp the meaning of the idea. If each teacher will get the broad outlines of the idea, he or she may leave it to the specialists to work out the details in this direction and in that, devoting himself or herself to the narrow and yet thoroughly productive task of working out the details of the idea in the class-room.

The educational world has need of a vast army of investigators to settle some of the unsettled questions about mental development. The various forms of development of the mind in the course of its learning to read, or write, or count, are phases of development with which no one is fully acquainted. These are phases of development that no one has any better opportunity to investigate than the individual teacher. Let us not give up this task because we can not solve it before we begin our work. Let us, rather, boldly enter into the investigation, first getting something of the inspiration and guidance that is to be derived from a survey of the general principle of development as it has been formulated by the leaders in science up to this time.

The idea of development was first worked out in the science of biology. The other sciences, such as sociology and psychology, have borrowed a great deal from the earlier studies of biology. Perhaps we shall do well to go back to the biological formulation of the principle of development as the basis for our present discussion.

The biological notion of development may be defined by the use of three phrases. The first of these is the phrase, individual variation, the second is selection, and the third is hereditary transmission. The best way in which to get at the meaning of these three phrases will be to take a concrete illustration.

There is a little mouse-like animal which lives in our fields and burrows under the sod for earthworms. It is called a ground mole, and has broad shovel-shaped forefeet by means of which it does its digging. This same little animal has very small, weak eyes. Indeed, at times the eyes are not only much reduced in size, but are covered with a layer of skin so that they are useless for vision. The mole spends most of its time underground, and digs out intricate passages for itself in its search for food.

We know something of the history of the mole species through our study of embryology, for the embryo repeats in a large measure the typical stages of the development of the species. Our knowledge of the history of the mole species teaches us that generations and generations ago, the ancestors of the present moles were of a different type. They were small, mouse-like creatures which devoured insects and worms, but lived above the ground and had strong eyes and no broad digging forefeet. In other words, the first moles were not like the present moles either in habits or in structure.

Let us carry ourselves back in imagination to the early moles that lived above ground and had strong eyes and slender toes. We know what happened with a good deal of detail, for the biologist has seen similar facts over and over again in our modern world. There was a day on which some mole in foraging for food got hold of an earthworm. It turned out to be good food, and the fortunate mole began to look for more. Finally, it found that it could get earthworms best by doing a little digging. A good many animals have learned to dig to some extent; think of the fowls. But this digging meant a great change in the mole. It began to be interested in a wholly new kind of life. The earthworms had never been the prey of animals of this kind before, and they were very plenty. The whole mole family began to dig for worms.

By and by there was born in the family a little mole which had broader forefeet than moles had been used to having. Whether this was due to the fact that the parents of Broadfoot had been getting stronger and broader feet by digging, or whether it was a mere accident, is hard to decide. The fact is that the little mole arrived with a broader foot. This *individual variation,* as the biologists call it, this deviation from the usual structure of the family, gave Broadfoot a great advantage. He could dig faster and could get more worms with his improved shovel than could any of his family. He even grew bold and went clear under the ground, and in that way he escaped the enemies he would have met above ground, and had an easier time under ground where there was less competition. The experiment which nature had tried of giving one little mole broad feet was a great success. The advantages which Broadfoot enjoyed made him live longer, and he had a larger family and supported them better, so that ultimately broad feet came to be the most common form among moles, and the moles with slender feet had a harder and harder time, and ultimately died out. This preservation of the stronger type and decline of the weaker type is what the biologist calls natural *selection.* Natural selection is no premeditated choice on any one's part; it is, to use another current phrase, merely the survival of the fittest. And the fittest who survive, transmit their strong characteristics to their young through *hereditary transmission.* Some of the young in any family get more and some get less of the desirable characteristics. Thus, we have a new series of individual variations and a new series of selections of the fittest, and a new series of transmissions.

The broad feet of the mole have thus, through long generations, been gradually improved until they have reached their present form. In the meantime let us not forget to include the eyes in our study of development. The first moles probably had a good deal of inconvenience under the ground with sand which kept getting into their eyes. By variation the eyes of some moles turned out to be very small and weak—all the better for the underground burrowing. In fact this seeming weakness was a positive advantage. What a fortunate mole among moles must have been the one born with a layer of skin completely covering the eyes!

Development is thus a progressive fitting of a species more and more fully to its environment. Whatever is desirable in the structure of any member of the species is fostered and improved. Whatever is undesirable is cut off. But desirable and undesirable in this case are relative terms. Desirable means helpful in the given environment. Thus we should speak of characteristics as being, not absolutely good or absolutely bad, but as suited or unsuited to the environment.

The principle of adaptation was forcefully stated by Professor Minot in his address as president of the American Association for the Advancement of Science. His statement was as follows: "Vital functions have a purpose. The purpose is always the maintenance of the individual or of the race in its environment. The entire evolution of plants and animals is essentially the evolution of the means of adjustment of the organism to external conditions." And after making this general statement, Professor Minot applies the principle to human progress, so that there may be no doubt as to the man's share in this progressive adaptation to environment. He says: "In practical life it is convenient to distinguish the works of nature from the works of man, the 'natural' from the 'artificial.' The biologist, on the contrary, must never allow himself to forget that man is a part of nature, and that all his works are natural works. This is especially important for the present discussion, for otherwise we are likely to forget also that man is as completely subject to the necessity of adjustment to external reality as any other organism. From the biological standpoint all the work of agriculture, of manufactures, of commerce and of government is a part of the work of consciousness to secure the needed adjustments." [1]

It should be noticed in this connection that development for adaptation may reach a stage of relative completion. That is, progress in adaptation may go so far that an animal is sufficiently well adapted to the particular environment in which he lives, and then change either stops entirely or goes forward only very slowly. Thus, the forefeet of the ground mole represent what is, in all probabilities a completed adaptation. If the forefeet should by variation appear in any given mole wider than the average, this would be no advantage, for an increase above the average width of the digging foot would require an increase in muscular strength in order to manipulate the wider foot. And this increase in strength would require in turn a larger body, and a larger body would mean that the mole would have to make a larger passage through the ground. These larger passages would require more digging than the smaller mole has to do with the average forefoot, and this requirement of more digging would neutralize the advantage of the broader forefoot. There is thus a certain equilibrium where the animal is better off than it would be through further increase in the size of its organs. Many animals which have been long in a given environment have reached such a state of relatively complete adaptation.

We turn now from the kind of development which we have been discussing, the structural development, as we may call it, to consider another phase of develop-

[1] Science, July 4, 1902, pp. 9, 10.

ment. There is a social development as well as a structural development. Every species of animals develops certain common habits of life, and these are transmitted to the young of the species through the example set by the older members. The social tradition is very strong in certain species. Think, for example, of a little ant or a little bee coming into their respective communities. The military order and division of labor in an ant-hill or in a bee-hive, are matters that could not be transmitted to the young of the species in the form of bodily structures, but they are a part of the lesson of living which the species has learned in its long struggle for existence. The young addition to the community must learn to fit into the cooperative life of the community. This process of learning what are the rules of community life, will be a great benefit to the individual, and he will gain from it lessons which he never could have worked out for himself if he had not seen the whole community in action. The individual, therefore, gets, through imitation, a kind of social inheritance which is different from the structural inheritance with which we are well acquainted. Imitation has accordingly been called the means of *social heredity*.

Social heredity is one of the most important phases of human development. To be sure, we are in very large measure what we are as individuals because of a long process of structural development in our race. Think of our hands and feet, for example, as illustrations of structural adaptation. In the other higher animals the fore extremities and hind extremities are much alike, but with us the legs are long, strong, supporting organs, ending in feet which are very advantageously supplied with broad flat walking surfaces and with short and little developed digits. The arms are light and muscular, with free joints, and they carry hands which have long flexible digits adapted to the most delicate kinds of manipulation. Surely this differentiation in the structure of our hands and feet shows a very high degree of adaptation of the purely physical or structural type. But think of the immensely higher form of development which comes in the life of every one through social heredity. Think, for example, of the student of art, supplied with hands through physical development, but learning the use of those hands only through the careful training of some master. This master's training is a part of the student's social inheritance. Or think of the athlete supplied with legs and feet through structural inheritance, but learning the use of these organs under the social stimulus of competitive races. Our social training is, after all, our highest inheritance.

Before we turn to the direct application of all these general terms which we have been defining, to our own special problem of school training, it will be well for us to recognize the fact that variation, and selection, and adaptation have a narrower meaning and may be applied to strictly individual life. Not only does the individual as a member of a species profit by advantageous variations, but the individual develops in the course of his own life through a similar series of discoveries of new adjustments. Thus, take the case of a man who has always done some act in a given way, until suddenly he finds by a chance variation or by a carefully premeditated variation in his mode of action, that some other way is better. This is a personal variation. The savage who first discovered that arrows would fly straighter if feathers were added to the bare shaft, contributed an important fact to general knowledge through individual variation.

The period in life when variations are the predominating facts is the period of childhood. Did you ever notice that children learn to ride a bicycle sooner than old people, and are very much freer in their actions after they have learned? Their greater facility in learning is due to the fact that they begin to learn at a period when all their movements are much more variable than they will be in later life. Consequently, children discover the right movement to make in balancing themselves on a bicycle sooner than adults, because they naturally make more different kinds of movements. They have, to use the technical terms, a greater series of variations in action from which the best and most adaptive movement may be selected.

After this general discussion of the nature of development, let us turn to a consideration of some of the modifications which the acceptance of this general idea has wrought in our pedagogical ideals. Take first of all the question which Franke discussed so seriously, the question of whether the child is by nature good or bad. You remember Franke's answer. He said the child is low and earthy in his nature. His play is an exhibition of the evil in him, and so on through the whole list of childish characteristics. This view was perhaps more than usually emphasized by Franke and his followers, but it represents fairly well the generally accepted notion about the child even less than two centuries ago. Rigor and constant suppression of the childish nature were the accepted practises of the school, so long as this view prevailed.

Suddenly, in the midst of all this rigor of practise and strenuousness of ideal, there came the teacher of a new educational gospel. That new gospel was given to the world by Rousseau in his book on the education of Émile. If Franke and others had thought the child's nature evil, hear the opening sentence of Rousseau's book: "Everything is good as it comes from the hands of the Author of Nature, but everything degenerates in the hands of man." [1] And then if you will follow the later argument of the book, you will find Rousseau carrying out the idea that the child is good and needs only to be allowed to grow up in a perfectly natural way. We are warned against the harmful influences of social life, against the artificial practises of the schools. Back to nature! Back to the primitive forms of life! These were the doctrines of Rousseau and his school.

With this fundamental disagreement between those who believe the child to be good, and those who believe the child to be bad by nature, what is the individual teacher to accept as the true ideal? I confess I do not wonder that teachers feel confused. Take, for example, the modern form of this same dispute about the goodness or badness of the child's nature. It centers around that word of which we hear so much from the Herbartians, the word interest. There are those who tell us that the child's native interests are the safest guides to lead us in the tasks of selecting and arranging educa-

[1] Payne's translation, p. 1.

tional materials. We have heard educational writers and speakers enforce this argument in favor of natural tastes and interests by such statements as this: "Physicians are coming to agree that in cases of convalescence from disease, when there are no known rules to guide the patient's diet, it is safe and expedient to follow the patient's own wishes." "Hence," runs the argument, "when we do not know what is the best course to pursue in directing the development of the child, it is safe to follow the child's own interests."

Opposed to all this unqualified acceptance of the child's interests, as guides of our educational practise, stands our knowledge that children's interests are very transient and often very trivial. Some would say that it is obviously best at times to make the children do the hard and uninteresting things. I am not sure that the highest wisdom does not favor that strenuous form of training which one of our Chicago educators is said to have adopted. He is so opposed to the doctrine of natural interests that he gives his children each day, at a certain hour by the clock, a short course in bodily chastisement as a supposedly helpful, though probably uninteresting, preparation for the hard, uncompromising duties of life.

So the dispute goes on, and there seems to be little light on the difficult question of whether the child is good or bad. As for most of us, we work out a sort of average between the two extreme views. We applaud the eulogizing of the child nature in public, and we reserve the right to think a great deal in private about the child's innate wickedness. We urge leniency on our fellow teachers in view of our confidence that the child is by nature tending toward better things; and yet for ourselves we sometimes mourn that the day of the rod as the symbol of pedagogical authority is rapidly passing. In short, we have most of us patched up a compromise between Franke and Rousseau, and believe in both. The child is bad, yes, that is too true! The child is good by nature, yes, that is the saving clause in our creed!

The gratifying fact about the doctrine of development is that it makes it possible to continue in our average belief that the child is neither wholly good nor wholly bad, and at the same time it places this average belief of ours on a firm rational foundation and explains it and illuminates it in the most complete fashion.

The doctrine of development says of the child, here is an immature being. He is not adapted to the environment in which he has to live. He does all sorts of things that would injure him, and fails to do a great many things that are quite essential to a happy and successful life in this environment. In short, considered with reference to the immediate present, this child is about as poorly adapted to life as any one easily could be. But, continues the doctrine of development, this is, after all, not so bad as it might be, for the child has certain redeeming characteristics. He has the possibilities of variations and adjustments in a much higher degree than we older people have. Where we fail to fit our environments, we are generally so fixed in our habits that we can not easily change. If we are unadapted now, we continue unadapted to the end. The child, on the other hand, has the largest possibilities of fitting himself to his environment. In this he is much better off than any mature person in the world. If the child's lack of adaptation is a bad characteristic, then certainly this adaptability is one of his most hopeful characteristics, and quite compensates for his lack of present adaptation.

Do you not see where the fault has been in earlier discussions of this subject? Teachers have applied adult standards to the child's life. According to adult standards, lack of adaptation is an evil. We must come to recognize the fact that in judging the child's nature no such standard will apply.

See how this new view of the child as a developing individual is modifying our notion of punishment. We do not punish a child now because we wish to meet out to him vengeance for his infraction of law. We punish a child these days only when we deem pain helpful to him as an aid toward his more complete adaptation. The law of the school has a deeper meaning to us. It is a rule which if obeyed will help the child to pass from an unadapted state to one of adaptation. If the rule is not strong enough to lead the child pleasantly and without compulsion in the right direction, stronger measures must be adopted. Teachers of to-day who understand the real meaning of punishment do not get angry at children. I think the greatest advance in school discipline that we have to record in recent generations is the advance which has been made in the teacher's attitude toward the child. To-day we look upon the child's mistakes and failures as phases of the process of development. We correct these shortcomings as a part of our general duty of supervising development.

While we are on this subject of punishment as one phase of the process of education, it is interesting to note that we who teach in the schools are not the only ones who have come to take a broader view of the meaning of the terms good and bad, because of this increased insight into the nature of human development. Go to any one of the well-conducted penitentiaries of the land and you will see that there too, men are treated, not as if confinement were society's revenge, but as if confinement were society's means of education. There are a great many men to-day who are studying the criminal, and they are very generally of the opinion that the typical criminal is a man whose development has been arrested in some way or other. Give this undeveloped man an opportunity to get some further training and see if we can not in that way adapt him to life in the community. That is the way in which those who study the criminal are arguing, and their principle is exactly the same, if you will only recognize it, as that which we are adopting under very much happier conditions in our schools.

You can see, I think, that the far-sighted application of this principle of punishment as a means to education does not forbid the use of pain. We are not to make the developing process at all stages one of easy concession to individual preferences. The fact is that every now and then the individual needs a sharp turn in development. Even nature, to which appeal is so often made by those who would have the child's life one unbroken day of sunshine—even nature uses pain as a means of development. The unpleasant consequences from any form of overindulgence are nature's punishments. They are not nature's revenges, but rather her lessons to guide us in the future.

Another change in our educational views which has resulted from our new insight into the nature of development is that we do not regard the child's early unsuccessful efforts in any line of thought or action as culpable mistakes. When our fathers and mothers went to school, the teacher used to blame the boys and girls for not being able to write well or pronounce well, or for not being able to do this or the other thing correctly. The teacher merely heard lessons; sat as a sort of judge of the perfection of the child's adaptation, and measured out reward or punishment according as the child was successful or unsuccessful. To-day we think of the child's errors, not as culpable offenses, but as indications of a need of fuller development. We do not demand of the immature child that he shall fulfil the same requirements as those which we impose on adults. In short, we consider perfection to be a relative term, to be applied with a clear recognition of the stage of individual development.

The adoption of different standards of judgment for different levels of development is a phase of our application of the new ideals of development to which we have already made frequent references in earlier chapters. We pointed out, you will recall, in our first discussion of visual perception, that the same image falling on two different eyes will be differently interpreted. These different interpretations, even when they are what we call illusions, are not to be classified as right and wrong, but rather as more or less fully developed. And so through our whole discussion of the teacher's life, we have been seeing again and again the same general principle illustrated, the principle that different stages of mental life are different in character and require different standards of judgment.

This difference between different levels of development is sometimes overlooked because we see the same person passing through the different stages of progress. We see the same boy, for example, taking work in arithmetic and then in algebra, and we somehow think of the boy as just getting more and more mathematics. In other words, we overlook the fact that the general word mathematics covers a number of different modes of thought, and that the word boy covers a great many different levels of development. Sometimes we have a striking illustration which calls our attention emphatically to the fact that the boy studying arithmetic is quite a different grade of boy from the same boy when he has, later in life, grasped the mode of thought appropriate to algebra.

Let me give you an illustration which brings out the difference between the arithmetical stage of development and the algebraical stage. Some years ago some students of education and of mental life discovered in a country district in Indiana one of those interesting characters known as a mathematical prodigy. This boy could add great columns of figures with astounding rapidity. He had a multiplication table that ran up to 150. He knew all the short methods of calculation given in the books on rapid methods, and he had invented other rapid methods unknown to the makers of books. In short, he had more arithmetic in his head and at his ready disposal than any of the skilful mathematicians in the land. They took this boy from his home to the State University and tried to train him so that he might find a higher use for his mathematical bent. But just at this point they discovered the fact in which we are now interested. They found that this boy had so much arithmetic that he could not, or would not, learn any algebra. In other words, he had developed all of his powers in one way, and that, too, at a relatively low level, and now the next step upward was impossible to him. Algebra was not according to his mode of thought.

Nothing could show more clearly than this example of the arithmetical prodigy the fact that modes of thought at one level of development are not the same as modes of thought at higher levels. The most obvious warning which comes from the case cited in our illustration is the warning not to let children stay too long at one level of development. But deeper than this warning, the student can see in the example a most admirable illustration of the broad principle that different stages of mental development are essentially different, and require different standards of judgment.

What is perhaps the clearest recognition of this principle, appears in the recent scientific studies of the mental lives of animals. Animals have often been credited with marvelous mental powers. Who has not heard that crows and cats can count? Who does not wonder at the geometrical knowledge of the bee which builds its cell in the perfect hexagonal form, and so on through the whole list of animal achievements? And now we are coming to recognize more and more clearly that in none of these performances of the animals is there any justification for assuming the existence of marvelous mental powers.

The crow sees five men go into a hut and four come out, and he does not allow himself to fall into the trap and come into dangerous proximity to the one remaining man. But that does not show that the crow counted the men who went in and the men who came out. It might show ability to count if mental life were all at one level, and that the level of mature counting consciousness at which we live. But even you and I have methods of dealing with number relations without resorting to our usual method, which is the highly developed method of counting. Did you never go to the store and make a number of purchases and then start home with a haunting feeling that you have left something unpurchased? You did not count, that is obvious, for if you had, you would have been sure whether you had left something undone or not. Can you explain that feeling? Certainly the feeling is not the result of counting.

Or take an illustration from some of the experiments which the psychologists try in their laboratories. Sit down at your table and with a pencil make a series of taps. Do not count, but just make a short series of about eight to twelve taps. Now pause for a moment, and make another series of exactly the same length. You can do it with a certainty which will surprise you if you have never tried it before, and all this without counting.

The fact is, we have in mature mental life a good many different ways of dealing with number relations —some higher and some lower. The highest way of dealing with these relations is that of counting; one of the lower ways is that which we have just described of grouping objects without counting. The crow probably does not count, he recognizes groups.

Or take other relations than the number relation. Take some of the animal instincts that make animals appear to have such great foresight. Take the persistent and highly commendable devotion of the setting hen to her eggs. We shall be deceived if we attribute all this to any clear-headed maternal foresight or prophetic imagination. Her action is rather, as Professor James says, to be attributed merely to a blind feeling uppermost in her consciousness that those eggs are the never-too-much-to-be-sat-upon things.

Or another illustration given us by the naturalist Wallace, may be used to illustrate how animals come to deal easily with distances and with falling bodies. Their knowledge of these subjects is not of the high type of the scientist who lays his yard-stick upon the distances and times the falling body with his delicate chronometer. When you hear this illustration repeated you should think of that blind form of feeling for distance which the ball-player has when he pitches a curved ball or bats at one. You should think of the way in which a billiard-player knows his angles of rebound without the higher abstract forms of measurement. The illustration, which I wish to borrow from Wallace, is a description of the skill in flight exhibited by certain sea-gulls in the Southern seas. Far from land, and quite unable to light in order to devour the fish which are their prey, these gulls develop the ability to feed in mid-air. After catching a fish, one of these birds soars far above the surface of the water and there it cuts the body of its prey in two with its sharp beak, and lets one part fall while it swallows the other part. Then, with incredible rapidity, the bird swoops downward, overtaking the falling part before it reaches the water, and, recapturing it, rises again and repeats the process until finally it has devoured all of the fish. Such activities as these are more accurately adjusted to the relations of space and gravity than any of which the child or even the most highly trained adult is capable. And yet we do not think of the bird as higher in its intelligence than man. The fact is, we recognize the general principle that the level of mental development attained by the bird, and hence its whole mode of mental action, is different from that exhibited in the highest processes of adult life.

This principle of mental development is coming to be very fully accepted among scientific students of animal life. It is also coming to be recognized more and more by teachers as they study the levels of mental development at which they find children. Children, too, have a certain recognition of number. Is it the same as adult recognition of number? Evidently it is not, for we find children quite unable to manage some of the relations with which we deal easily. But is this the only difference between children and ourselves, that we can manipulate more relations than the children can? Is the difference merely one of the number of processes with which we are familiar? Do children and adults think in the same way about even those relations with which they both deal? The answer to this question we are coming to understand in the light of our principle of development. Even when dealing with the same relation, children's modes of thought are not like ours. They are at a different level of development, and that different level of development means a different mode of thought.

Thus, when the child first learns addition, the process does not have the same meaning for him as it does for the adult who knows the relation of addition to the higher process of multiplication. And when the child learns multiplication, the process does not have the same significance for him as it does for one who understands the use of logarithms. With each step in advance one sees richer and richer meanings in the processes which he half grasped in childhood. The man reads Robinson Crusoe or Gulliver's Travels and sees, not only the story which interested the boy, but he sees the literary art and the deeper satire on social life. His view is, as we say, broader and fuller. This is what we expect of a developing individual. We apply different standards of judgment to different stages of mental life, and it is well that we should. The duty of the teacher is to recognize this as a sound principle of educational practise.

The general principle of differences in mental processes at different stages of development, opens up a whole series of questions for the teacher to investigate. How does the child deal with number relations, how does he read and write? The details of mental development call for investigation, for we understand as yet very little of the different stages through which children pass. Even memory of our experiences, as we have already pointed out, helps us but little in understanding the details of development, for our own earlier experiences did not consist in attention to the processes of development.

This leads us to a consideration of the fact that the child, though he is all the time developing, is wholly without knowledge of his own process of development. Take, for example, the child at play. We are coming to recognize the great importance of play for individual development. The child has weak muscles and organs of sense which have never had their full range of experience. Nature does not send such an untrained child into the serious struggle of real life, but lets him spend a few years in a sort of sham struggle. This sham struggle the child takes in all seriousness, and enters into it with all enthusiasm—for him it is real life, though we call it his play. The child sees only the things with which he plays. He does not look beyond the play and see the development for the future which he is getting. He just romps, and has a good time. There is nothing premeditated or reasoned out in his conduct. He is developing in what may be called the natural or wholly non-rational way.

In calling the child's development non-rational we must make sure that the word non-rational is not misunderstood. Non-rational does not mean irrational or contrary to reason. The child may grow into an adult, and, looking back on his development, he will see how the struggles through which he has passed all contributed to his better adaptation. He will then recognize the reason for this or that impulse implanted in him by nature. He will see, for example, why nature gives to every child a play impulse. He will also come to understand why it was advantageous that this or that variation which he exhibited as a child should be checked before it became a burdensome habit. In other words, he will see as an adult, beyond the immediate facts which engaged his attention as a child. He will see beyond mere play, and discover that play is in reality a process of development; beyond the painful experience he will later recognize nature's helpful lesson. In short, he will see how fully in accord with the principles of his reason it has all been. His development will thus appear as rational, though he did not know it before, and though he did not plan it—though it was wholly non-rational when it was actually taking place.

Again, when we say that the child's development is unpremeditated and non-rational we conceive ourselves as standing in the child's position. From the teacher's point of view the child's development should not be non-rational. The teacher should know why play is good for the child. The teacher should always be considering the process of development rather than the immediate facts of the child's experience. The teacher's place in the development of the child might be defined by saying that the teacher is a rationalizing factor—a kind of higher intelligence furnished the child to aid him in passing through the dangerous non-rational period of childhood. As the child takes step after step thoughtlessly and unknowingly, it is the duty of the teacher to stand by him and to prepare the way for each of these steps of development, so that nature may be supplemented in bringing the child safely and well to maturity.

Do we as teachers succeed in this rationalizing of the

child's development? Let us ask this question specifically, with reference to one of the subjects that we shall take up later. Do we as teachers know how to develop the writing habit in children any more rationally than they themselves? Is not the writing lesson too often a blind struggle in which teacher and pupil unite in a sort of try, try again form of procedure, which never realizes whither it is leading? Is it rational to leave our children to work out their own educational salvations with a mere engraved copy to guide them? The copy merely shows them the end to be attained. Between their undeveloped efforts and that goal lie leagues after leagues of development. How shall they best find their way along that weary road? Who among us is ready to answer clearly? Who among us knows the steps by which fingers and arm and hand grow more and more responsive to the demands of brain and eye? Who among us is prepared to do his full duty until all these stages of development have become parts of his rationalized knowledge?

Such questions as these are questions that every teacher should face. They are the questions which arise the moment one realizes that the teacher stands by the child to rationalize the child's non-rational development.

Another line of thought, which we may take up briefly, enforces very greatly the principle that the child's development is non-rational. It is the line of thought which grows out of a consideration of the facts of imitation. Modern science has given a good deal of attention to imitation. It is one of the means of transmitting habits from the older generation to the younger. It is a channel of what we called a little while ago social inheritance. The infant sees its mother smile, and there spreads over the infant's face a reflected smile. Do you suppose that the infant realizes that this is one of the means by which his development in the social habits of expression is being accomplished? Of course not. The infant just imitates in a wholly unthinking, non-rational way, and the development goes on as nature has prescribed.

We can understand this sort of unthinking imitation when we catch ourselves imitating a yawn that we saw a moment ago. Or let some member of our social circle set some fashion, either of conduct or of dress, how meekly we all follow! Fashion is the blindest, most non-rational thing in the world, and it owes its power to the trait of human nature which we are discussing, namely, the tendency to imitate.

The teacher does not need to be told that children are great imitators. For weeks after a Buffalo Bill show has been in town the boys will be lassoing posts, and small domestic animals, if not, indeed, passers-by. Let a company of soldiers pass through a city, and the boys will do nothing but think of military affairs during the next month. The girls, too, have their milder imitations, as one can see when some little six-year-old daintily prevents her perfectly safe skirts from getting into the dust of the crossing, by holding them as her seniors do theirs. And the teacher who recognizes this tendency toward imitation in children, recognizes also that it is wholly non-rational. The child does not sit in judgment on the habits of his elders. He simply follows blindly whatever they do. Education would be very far advanced if it did nothing but select and set before the children good examples for imitation. The teacher certainly can not afford to overlook the fact that blind non-rational imitation on the part of the child, places on the teacher a very heavy burden of responsibility for the setting of clear-sighted, rational examples to be imitated.

There is a final lesson which must be added to this discussion of the non-rational character of the child's development. The child should not always remain non-rational in regard to his own development. He should gradually be brought to the stage where he can become his own rational guide, his own teacher. The educator who does not see to it that children are made independent of him, has not done his whole duty. And this process of rendering the child independent and rational is not a task to be undertaken suddenly at the end of school life. We used to think of graduation day as the commencement of independent self-guided conduct. We are coming more and more to see that all along the course of the school life the lessons of development may be learned in two ways. First, nonrationally. That is nature's first method. And then as soon as some experience has been gained by nature's first method, this experience should be turned to account in the development of a higher stage of mental life, and at that higher stage it will be possible to advance not merely non-rationally, not merely by blind struggling, but also by self-conscious struggling, which is self-directed, rational conduct.

There are other lessons that come to the teacher from the study of the principles of development. Some of these are of such importance that we shall be justified in taking up another chapter in considering them. Then we shall pass on to some detail studies of how children develop in the lines which we try to cultivate in the schools.

The main underlying thought which we have been working out in these first four chapters, should be clearly before you now. All mental life is of interest to us because it develops. The subtle changes in the processes of thought and perception which go to make up individual development, will escape us if we do not make them subjects of careful study. Even our own modes of thought are but half understood until we begin to look into their sources. If we will but have the courage to undertake this study of ourselves and of the ideals of our times, we shall see that just now we are taking up a large idea which is destined to modify our educational thought and methods more than they have ever before been modified in a single period of the world's history. This new idea, with all its derived principles, is the one which we are discussing—the idea of development. Get at this idea from many sides. Study your own development. Study the development of your pupils. Study the stages and ends of development. Recognize education as one phase of the broad process of development.

CHAPTER V

INDIVIDUALITY, ADAPTATION, AND EXPRESSION

In the last chapter we introduced the discussion of the general principle of development, beginning with an illustration from biology, which served as the basis for the explanation of the terms variation, selection, transmission, and adaptation. We then pointed out how the doctrine of development disposed of the old dispute as to the goodness or badness of the child's nature. We called attention to the growing recognition in science and in practical education of the characteristic differences between different stages of mental development; and, finally, we concluded by pointing out the relation of the teacher, as a rationalizing factor, to the child's development, which, in its first stages, is wholly non-rational.

The first new application of the general idea of development to which we now turn, grows out of a recognition of the significance of the term variation. We have already seen that variation is the necessary first step in both individual and racial progress. And it is obvious also that the advantages or disadvantages of variation are most keenly felt by the individual, for where the variations are advantageous the individual is selected and becomes an important factor in turning development in the direction of his own superior characteristics, and, conversely, where variations are disadvantageous the individual suffers, and is selected for elimination. In the same way where one institutes a new mode of action in his individual life, and thus produces what we have called a variation in individual action, selection retains what is advantageous, and eliminates what is disadvantageous. And this process of selection goes on whether attended with pleasure or with pain.

Judged from a narrow view of individual life, it seems hard at times to see a single human being suffering the consequences of an unfortunate variation. Indeed, we have been passing, as a people, and as a body of teachers, through a period of thought in which we have rebelled against the mere suggestion that an individual could be sacrificed for the larger good of the race. The principle that all men are created equal has seemed to us so eminently desirable an ideal with which to inspire one's efforts in life that we have held to it as one of the dearest dogmas of our democracy. We have held to it in a form in which human experience never justified our stating it. For if there is one thing that appears clearly in all human life, it is that individuals are not born with like tastes or capacities. Men are differentiated through the appearance of inevitable individual variations. Let men be equal before the law all you please. Let them seek on a common footing, even with equal opportunity, if you will, life, liberty and happiness, but their lives will be different, they will make different uses of their liberty, and their happiness will be of the most varying types.

The doctrine of development did not discover this

fact of the existence of variations, it simply pointed out the value of variations for development. We can now recognize in a clearly explained fashion the necessity of individual variations. Variations are the first steps in development, and without them the larger progress of the race and of the individual would be impossible. Our view of life thus expands so as to include not merely the moment when there is pleasure or pain from the selection, but so as to include also the remoter and final advantage from the whole process of consummated development.

Gradually we are coming to accept a higher form of the idea of individuality. We are beginning to grasp the new idea in our school life. A few generations ago when our public schools were first organized, the children began at a certain age in the first grade and went on through the years of school life on the theory that they were always equal. Teachers knew that they were not equal, of course, but the theory was maintained. The theory was maintained sometimes in the expensive way of holding back some bright boy, or else of pushing some stupid boy forward. Teachers had no courage to face parents with the statement that all men are not created equal. So firmly were our schools based upon this principle of equality that to separate a child from his fellows was a most noticeable fact.

How different it is coming to be! The school of to-day is striving for a new ideal of the child's individuality. If a boy has variations that are advantageous to him, we recognize it. Most boys have some advantageous variations, and we see that it is the business of the schools to find these and give them the emphasis they deserve. In short, the school is coming to recognize individuality as a mark of differentiation rather than as the stamp of uniformity. A boy or a girl is seen to have individuality when he or she does things in his or her own way. If that individual way is good we foster it, if it is bad we cut it off and develop a substitute; for our work is to help make permanent the child's advantageous variations, and to eliminate his disadvantageous variations.

I need not dwell upon the changes in school organization which exhibit this change in our attitude on the question of individual character. We are coming to promote children now as individuals, not in droves. We allow boys and girls to follow, before they leave the higher grades of our schools, some of the subjects that shall best develop their natural powers. But more significant than these external changes in organization, are the changes which show themselves in the class room in the individual teacher's ideals. To the old pedagogue every shivering child was but another unit in his school attendance. Each pupil went through the same strenuous ordeal in the same way. The public school was, as some one so aptly put it, a great machine for polishing pebbles and taking the edges off diamonds. The teacher of to-day is, more and more, grasping the ideal of individuality, and school work is showing the results in a broader, more human relation between the teacher and each individual child.

The broad way in which the ideal of individuality is being taken up is in no way better illustrated than it is in the clearness with which we recognize the harmony between our ideal of individuality and our ideal of education in classes. We never think of putting a boy off by himself with a tutor, as the highest form of instruction. That is a treatment of individuality which seeks to draw the lines of exclusiveness about the boy. Individuality fostered by exclusiveness is not the kind of individuality we want. We want the boy to test the utility of his variations in contact with his fellows. We want him to profit by the advantages of imitation, and in this way to acquire some of the variations in action which originate with the other boys. In short, we know full well how to hold at once the ideal of social development and the ideal of individual development. We have the broader view of individuality, which means contact and relation with the world, not separateness. And so we are glad to put boys and girls into classes. We are sorry sometimes that the classes have to be so large, but better large classes pulsating with individual life than the rarefied atmosphere of the exclusive circle of an individual or two withdrawn from social contact.

Coordinate with the individual, in our discussions of development, stands the environment. No one ever thinks of the process of development without recognizing the fact that the individual variations are selected and preserved or rejected because they either fit or do not fit a certain environment. You recall our earlier illustration of the ground mole with its broad forefeet and weak eyes. These structures are fully developed in the sense that they fit the environment in which the mole lives. Examined by themselves, out of relation to the environment, the eyes of the mole would be judged to be failures, and the feet would probably be considered clumsy. It is only when we recognize the fact that sensitive eyes would be worse than useless in the dark underground channels in which the mole lives, that we comprehend the reason for the line of backward growth of the eyes. But once we comprehend the relation of the mole to his environment, we see the reasons for it all. The failure of the eyes as eyes is entirely explained by the successful adaptation of these eyes to their particular environment.

One way of putting this matter of relation to environment is to point out that true development does not consist in mere refinement of functions for their own sake. Thus, if in contrast with the mole's eye, you examine the eye of the hawk or trout, you will find a very highly refined organ of vision. But you will have no reason for changing your verdict about the mole's eye in the presence of these examples of higher refinement of vision. The mole's eye is adapted to the mole's environment, though it is not as highly refined an organ as is the hawk's eye or the eye of the trout.

Or to transfer the discussion from the mole to human life, we too have certain functions which are very little refined. Among the human senses, for example, smell and taste are notably defective as compared with the smell and taste of many of the animals. We have heard educators of rank assuming that development meant refinement, and deploring this lack of sensory refinement in the human race. Indeed, I know of one family where, through the persistent efforts of the father, the children have been so trained in the detection and discrimination of odors that they can identify their friends in the dark through their keen olfactory sense. These children have a refined sense of smell. If refinement of the senses were the goal of education they would be far nearer that goal than most of us. But I venture to say that even before we have argued the matter out in detail, we shall all feel that human development has not been entirely wrong in its neglect of the senses of taste and smell. The truth is that even before men understood that true development meant adaptation rather than mere refinement, they had the word pedantry with which to characterize those forms of ultra-refinement which extended beyond all practical purposes. As for the deficient faculties which most of us cheerfully acknowledge in many directions—in smell and taste, for example—these are like the mole's eyes, faculties which we do not need in our lives. We should be distracted from the more important concerns of our environment if we were devoted to tastes and odors. We live in a social environment where the sense of hearing gives us more important information than could possibly be obtained through the sense of smell. A refinement of the sense of smell would be wholly useless to our ordinary mode of action and thought, and would be quite out of harmony with even our bodily structure. Did you ever notice that the animals which have the most highly developed sense of smell are so constructed that the organ of that sense is carried close to the ground where alone it can be advantageously used? Think of the dog or of the beasts of prey. And what have we as men to do with that ground environment? An African traveler tells us of a tribe of natives who rely much upon the sense of smell, which they have developed to a very high degree of perfection. But, he adds, they generally go on all fours when they are following a scent.

Mere refinement of functions should never be the end of educational training. This has not always been recognized. There have been periods in the history of education when men devoted themselves so closely to the refinement of their use of classical Latin that they had no energy left for the real facts of their immediate environments. There are teachers to-day who would rather get at some detail of the Revolutionary War than have an intelligent understanding of their duty as citizens in a great peaceful republic. There are pupils who are led to believe that arithmetic consists in those intricate puzzles which get nowhere on this earth, and have no value, unless, indeed, the refinement of arithmetical acumen beyond all degree can be defined as having value.

There are certain difficulties in the application of this doctrine of adaptation, and we shall not overlook them. But before we come to these difficulties in the way of application of the doctrine to school work, let us pause for a moment and consider whether there is not a lesson for us as individuals in this principle of adaptation. How many of us are fully adapted to the environments in which we live? There is the young man or young woman, just out of one of the higher schools of the State, suddenly plunged into a farming community or into a small manufacturing or mining town. What is he or she equipped to do in such a community? Generally the teacher is equipped only to enter into the details of this or that form of thought and study, such as mathematics, or Latin, or literature.

Now, mark you, I have nothing to say against mathematics or Latin, or literature. The more the young teacher has of all these the better. But the trouble lies in the fact that this young teacher too often has no ambitions except to go on and on along these same lines. To use the technical phrase, the teacher is ambitious to refine more and more these particular forms of training. The doctrine of adaptation ought to come to such a young teacher with a new view of his duty to himself. There is nothing so worthy in life as to meet successfully the environment into which one is thrown. Even if you are going to outgrow this environment very soon and go to another, do not deceive yourself into the thought that you do not owe it to yourself to fill this environment with a well-adapted personality. A teacher in a farming community who knows so much mathematics and literature that he can find nothing of interest in the scientific studies of soil and insect life which are engaging the attention of many of our scientists—such a teacher has begun refining functions without laying the broad foundation of adaptation. He will find that he is not a force in the community. He will be regarded as curious and foreign to the life of the people among whom he moves, and it will be his own fault. And when he leaves that community, as he is very likely to, and goes to another, the probability that he will find a purely mathematical or literary environment is so small that it is safe to assume that he will again find himself an outsider. And with each successive move he will find his powers of adaptation growing smaller and smaller.

This fact that we as teachers spend our lives pursuing refinement of functions is what makes people look on our schools as out of date, and it is a realization of the necessity of giving up the ideal of mere refinement for the broader ideal of adaptation, which is fortunately shaking us out of our slumbers and setting us about a complete and thorough revision of our courses of study. Who is not familiar with the demand which is nowadays so frequently made that our school courses shall train boys and girls for life in the working world into which they are soon to pass? And who is not aware of the change in the spirit and content of our education, which is coming as a concession to this demand? We see the increase of practical courses in business methods and in manual training. We see the physical environment of the child presented in courses of nature-study. We see the social environment taken up in elementary civics and history. In short, the movement in all parts of the country and in all grades of schools is in the direction of adaptation of the child to his environment.

Indeed, so overwhelmed are we with the new practical ideal of education that there is some danger of our failing to weigh carefully the true difficulties in the way of its application. Let us stop and ask ourselves what we mean when we speak of the child's environment. Think, for example, of the boy, who, instead of the course in history, is given a course in business arithmetic. What is the interpretation of the principle of adaptation in such a case? The teacher has evidently said to himself, this boy is going into business. He will come into contact every day with business problems. The historical facts, on the other hand, are facts which lie far in the past, and will never enter directly into the boy's life. The conclusion seems to be direct, give the boy business arithmetic, and let history go. Again, here is a boy who will leave school at an early age and take up a trade. That boy does not need very much geography; he would be better off if his hands were trained in the use of tools. Let us give him manual training instead of geography.

One of the clearest indications of our general acceptance of the principle of adaptation is to be found in the fact that we are perfectly familiar in these days with such arguments in favor of business arithmetic and manual training. The argument does not shock us as it would have shocked our fathers. And yet I believe that most of us feel that there is something lacking in an ideal that is so directly and exclusively practical. We feel that the child's environment has been defined in too narrow terms when we see in the environment of the boy going into business merely the humdrum of commercial competitions and successes, or when we see in the environment of the laboring man merely his tools and his trade. One feels like saying, "Yes, let us recognize in our schools all these practical demands, but let us try to see more in the child's possibilities than is included in this narrow definition of environment." We feel, even where we do not see them clearly, some of the difficulties in the way of applying the principle of adaptation to our school work.

Let us face the question that we have raised. What is the true environment of the child? In the first place, we see more clearly to-day than ever before that the child must live a real life in the school and home communities in which he grows up. Do we regard these as his true environment? In some sense, yes. We must treat of this immediate environment in our study of education. There are some teachers who have not yet waked up to this fact that they must pay attention to the life in the school and in the home. They think only of the large world which lies beyond the child's present grasp. They would distinguish between the child's immediate environment as transient and unimportant, and the future environment in which the child is to live, and would consider the latter as the real environment to be recognized in education. For such teachers, education is always an anticipatory adaptation to something yet unseen. On the other hand, there is fortunately an increasing group of educators who regard it as a mistake to think exclusively of the future. They would define the child's environment in such a way as to recognize very much more fully the present. Hear, for example, the words of Rousseau, where he says: [1] "What must we think, then, of that barbarous education which sacrifices the present to an uncertain future, which loads a child with chains of every sort, and begins by making him miserable in order to prepare for him, long in advance, some pretended happiness which it is probable he will never enjoy?" And, later, hear him lay down the positive side of his doctrine: [2] "The first education," he says, "ought to be purely negative. It consists not at all in teaching virtue and truth, but in shielding the heart from vice, and the

[1] Payne's translation of Émile, p. 44.
[2] Ibid., pp. 59, 60.

mind from error. If you could do nothing and allow nothing to be done, if you could bring your pupil sound and robust to the age of twelve years without his being able to distinguish his right hand from his left—from your very first lessons the eyes of his understanding would be open to reason. Without prejudice and without habit, he would have nothing in him which could counteract the effects of your endeavors." Certainly this is an unambiguous plea for the school to think of itself as the child's true environment. To be sure, the present environment in such a school of negative education would not be a school with desks and blackboards. It would be rather a playground with objects of nature about the child.

Conceiving of the child's immediate environment as rich in present experiences, there can be no doubt that our modern education is coming to give more and more attention to present adaptations. We show the children a plant and tell them how to cultivate it and use it. This is adaptation to the natural surroundings of the child, and it breaks in upon the monotony of ever preparing for the future as they used to in the school of yesterday. This is a step toward practical education. We see the schools of to-day taking up studies of domestic occupation, and of healthful recreation. We see the boys and girls trained in play and in physical exercise. To the old-fashioned educator all these activities were too trivial for the school. The natural surroundings of the child were supposed to impress themselves upon the child without any supervision, and the school concerned itself only with the remote future. Certainly we have gained much by these changes.

In our high schools we see the same tendency. The school community organizes itself into athletic associations, literary associations, and even into general governing bodies controlling the whole life of the school. There is in all this a recognition of a real social environment in the school itself, not in some remote social world of the future. This attention to present adaptations is in keeping with the highest and best understanding of development as a process of adaptation to environment, a part at least of that environment being the immediate surroundings.

While we laud these efforts to bring about adaptation to the child's present environment, let us not fail to see that there is danger that in the midst of all this attention to present environment there shall be no adequate recognition of the larger problem which unquestionably lies beyond. For we all of us know that the child must some day live in an environment which is not like his present environment. We know that his present adaptations must be made the stepping-stones to the larger adaptations into which he is to rise. The mistake of the old education was that it neglected the present too much. The danger of our present system is that we shall make no explicit provision for the future. There is such a thing as studying occupations in the home city so long that the boy and girl shall have no adequate notion of the large world beyond. There is danger that plants and animals shall be studied to such an extent as to exclude the boy and girl from a thorough mastery of the elements of some of the less immediately applicable, but no less essential, adaptations of arithmetic and reading. We must not lose sight of the fact that adaptation to any given environment is never of the true type unless it leaves a certain amount of energy and attention free to go still higher and to seek out wider ranges of environment.

The great difference between the lower grades of human and of animal life and the higher grades, is that the lower grades of life are limited in their adaptations to certain narrow environments. All these lower adaptations consist in changes due to direct individual contact with the facts to which one is adapted. Think first of animal adaptations. The ground mole, for example, develops a broad foot for digging. That is a direct adaptation, and it serves only to fasten the animal to his narrow environment. The street gamin becomes adapted in very much the same direct fashion to his environment. But direct adaptation is not the highest form of development. Man's adaptations at the present stage of development consist chiefly in indirect adaptations. Thus, man has developed a variety of indirect devices for digging, and he does not need to develop individual bodily organs such as the mole has. Man may have a variety of methods of meeting the same situation. This makes possible the use of one mode of adaptation, while at the same time it permits the enlarged development of a higher, broader mode, without impairing the first.

This is exactly what we should aim to recognize in our education. Suppose we want to train the boy to meet advantageously his relations to his physical environment. The first and most available method is to bring him into direct contact with the natural objects which are a part of his immediate environment. This is the only way in which the animal or any undeveloped individual comes to know nature. But it is not the only, or even the most comprehensive way that man has, for man has, besides direct contact, a way of gathering into books observations from all over the world, and laying them before the boy. The boy can not go to Greenland or to the equator. If his only method of development were that of direct contact, he could not know nature in these remote regions. There is need, accordingly, of training in the indirect modes of knowledge. We recognize in present-day education that it is a great mistake to take the book method of bringing the boy into contact with nature before we use the direct method, for books are good to enlarge the boy's environment, but they do not constitute his most direct path of approach to immediate environment. Clearly the true method of training the boy is to give him first direct contact with nature and with the social life about him, and then give him the means of enlarging his natural environment by means of books. Do not become so absorbed in either direct environment or in the books that you neglect the other. The neglect of direct environment was the mistake of the bookish education of the past. The neglect of the more general, indirect means of adaptation through books, is one of the menacing dangers of our present devotion to direct adaptation.

It ought to be clear through such discussions as these which we have been following, that man's development, while it has much in common with the lower forms of development, has a range which is immensely broader. The young animal endowed with the structures of his species has only to grow up and come in contact with his social and physical environment, and exert himself in the regular activities of getting food and providing for himself and family, and his work in life is done and his development is complete. Such an animal has a narrow range of environment to which he is adapted, and in which he must live. A man might develop in very much the same way. The savage boy does, indeed, follow the same formula of education. And it looks very much as if the highest ambition of certain educators is to foist upon the human race this same formula of direct adaptation, as the highest definition of education. The truth which these educators have is by no means to be overlooked. It is the great truth that, like the animal, the human being needs much direct adaptation. But there is the larger truth which must also be recognized. Man has multiplied vastly the range of his adaptations by the development of the power of indirect adaptation, and now a single man may come into contact with a vast environment and may fit himself to it. Spencer, at the close of one of his chapters, calls attention to this vast extension of human environment in the following examples:[1] "From early races acquainted only with neighboring localities, up to modern geographers who specify the latitude and longitude of every place on the globe—from the ancient builders and metallurgists, knowing but surface deposits, up to the geologists of our day whose data in some cases enable them to describe the material existing at a depth never yet reached by the miner—from the savage barely

[1] Principles of Psychology, vol. i, p. 318.

able to say in how many days a full moon will return, up to the astronomer who ascertains the period of revolution of a double star—there has been a gradual widening of the surrounding region throughout which the adjustment of inner to outer relations extends."

The broad range of human adaptations, and of the human environment, is a fact which teachers should keep in mind as they try to work out the problem of school training. It is not full human adaptation when a carpenter is adapted merely to his bench and tools. It is not full human adaptation when the young man becomes a cog in the wheel of business and nothing more. Our schools have a higher duty than mere commercial training. They have a larger task than to keep children at the level of the narrow-sighted present. They have it as their best function to prepare for the narrower and also for the broader adaptation. They should show the boy what is about him, and they should also show the boy how to reach what is beyond.

Thus, we see that the acceptance of the principle of adaptation does not in any degree curtail the largest hopes or ambitions for school training. Let us not be narrowed by our new ideal. For while our new ideal is giving us much firmer ground to stand on, while it is clearing up for us the relation of school-life to the present, it is in no way lessening our duty to the future. *Practical education as the basis for liberal education is the true ideal.* Never confound this with the false maxim that practical education is a substitute for liberal education.

We have come back, as you will see, through this discussion of adaptation to environment, to the point at which we began our study of the idea of development. The ideal of adaptation is one which lays greatest stress upon activity, not receptivity. An individual adapted to his environment is not an individual who has passively received something, he is rather an individual who has met his environment in an active way, and has fitted himself to that environment through his own exertions. The whole modern discussion of education is ringing with the word activity. We do not give children their mental development, we help them to get it through their own endeavors. We talk of expression and self-activity as the fundamental necessities for individual development. And we have come to think of both mental and bodily activity as most intimately related in working out the ends of individual development. Some of the facts which go to establish the relation between bodily and mental activities have been reviewed in an earlier chapter. Let us come back to the discussion with more facts to establish this relation and show its significance for development.

Every one recognizes the importance of what we call attention. The children in the school are urged to give attention to this or that. Taken in a broad sense, attention to an object means making it a center of active adaptation. The boy is attending to the ball, which he tries to catch. In terms of his development this means that the boy is concentrating his whole nature for the time being on that ball, and is striving to fit himself and his ball environment to each other. Nothing could show better the completeness of this relation of attention to adaptation than a study of the bodily conditions of attention.

The bodily conditions of attention consist in a series of activities. In the first place, every sense organ fits itself by activity to the object of attention. Both eyes move in their sockets so as to look directly at the object. Within each eye, the fine muscles which control the lens are straining to get the lens in the best possible condition to give a clear, sharply defined image of the object. Even the head may be bent forward so as to bring the eyes nearer the object, and at times we literally get up and move toward the center of attraction. If the object is one that gives forth sounds, there is a similar adjustment of the ear. There is a contraction of the little muscle which stretches the ear-drum so that one has a well-stretched receiving surface, sensitive to the slightest sound. The head is turned so as to bring the ear toward the source of sound, and one investigator reports that he was able to demonstrate even in human beings, movements of the outer ear of the same type as those which we see very clearly in the animal, though these human ear movements were fortunately less intense and much less noticeable.

The senses of taste and smell also have active adjustments. Thus, when we attend to tastes, the salivary glands become very active, and furnish the liquid in which to dissolve any substance coming to the mouth. This is an important active adjustment, for only fluids can affect the organs of taste. Similarly, when we attend to odors we snuff the wind and the nostrils dilate, even though we make little use of this sense. In the case of animals, of course, there are very noticeable movements accompanying the active turning of the senses of taste and smell upon a given object.

The sense of touch is perhaps the most actively adjusted of the senses. We can not attentively see or hear, or otherwise recognize the presence of an object, without making an active effort to grasp it. This active adjustment of touch has been suppressed in part through long periods of social training which forbids our seizing everything which we see, but the movement is there, nevertheless. Attach the hand to any delicate recording apparatus and you will see that it moves in the direction of any object of attention. Some persons have grown very skilful in leading others to the object of their attention by holding their hands. This so-called mind-reading, or better called muscle-reading, is by no means a difficult task. You can usually find in any party of five or six, some one who makes sufficiently intense movements of the hands toward objects of attention to become a suitable subject for even amateur muscle-reading.

A great many experiments have been made to show the presence of involuntary hand movements toward objects of attention. Professor Jastrow has recorded[1] a series of experiments with the planchette, or writing board. A sheet of glass placed on rollers and having a tracer attached, is brought under the hand. The subject without looking at his hand, thinks intently of reading across a page of print, or he recalls a poem, or thinks of a tower, and the hand moves noticeably, following the shifting of the attention.

One of the best practical illustrations of hand movement following attention is to be found in the case of

---

[1] **Fact and Fable in Psychology.**

the learner on a bicycle. Let such a learner try to pass some approaching object which attracts his attention, and the chances are he will run into the very object which he was trying to avoid. The explanation is very simple. He could not help moving toward the object of his attention. The hand movement, which turned out so disastrously on his bicycle, would not have been noticed if he had been walking. But a hand movement when a hand is guiding a bicycle is a much more important matter as the consequences showed.

Attention means, as these facts indicate, the active concentration of the senses on the object attended to. But it means more than this. Have you not felt the mustering of all your vital forces as an essential part of the most intense attention? One holds his breath in order to keep his trunk muscles ready for action. One feels the muscles of legs and arms grow tense. The very beating of the heart stops, ready to begin again at a furious rate as soon as the suspense of waiting attention shall give place to the attention of real action. All this shows how the mental state of attention is a process of active adaptation.

Or turn the matter about and see what are the effects of activity upon the character of ideas. What part of the streets of your native town do you recall most clearly? Not the long, uninteresting stretches where you never stop. It is the corner where you make the turn, it is the house at which you are accustomed to stop, that you think of most clearly. These are the parts of the street which are of practical importance. They are the parts to which your actions are directed, and where action is directed there attention is directed.

Nothing can be clearer than this conclusion that mental activity and bodily activity are both working toward the practical adaptation of the individual to his environment. The chief consideration in our present-day study of mental development is not the impression that goes in at the eyes or ears, but rather the way in which attention is adjusted to these impressions, and the way in which action is directed by attention.

Again turn to that whole group of mental processes known as the emotions. A few years ago two scientists[1] advanced what was at that time a novel and bewildering proposition, namely, the proposition that the emotions are not conditioned merely by impressions, but are conditioned also by the way in which the individual reacts to these impressions. There is much scientific truth, they said, in the old advice to keep up your courage by whistling, for no matter what your surroundings are, if you can act as if you were cheerful, you will find that your emotional state will correspond to your actions rather than to your impressions. This theory of the emotions, now known as the James-Lange theory, has leavened the whole lump of our psychological thought. We no longer think it strange that one should emphasize the active conditions of emotional life, or, indeed, that one should emphasize the active conditions of any phase of mental life. We are quite willing to accept in some form or other the proposition that action is quite as important as impression.

All the careful experimental studies of the emotions

---

[1] **Professor James and a Danish physiologist, Professor C. Lange.**

recently made, go to show that the different types of emotions are directly connected with different forms of action. Let us review one of the typical experiments. Train a blindfolded person to move the arm back and forth through any convenient distance, say, for example, a distance which measured at the fingers amounts to about a foot and a half. One can learn to make this movement with a good deal of uniformity. The movement depends on two groups of muscles: those which carry the arm outward and are called extensor muscles, and those which draw the arm inward and are called flexor muscles. Both extensor and flexor muscles are more or less active during the entire movement, even when not drawing the arm in the direction of their special contraction. Suppose now that some influence should make the extensor muscles at the beginning of the movement tenser than usual, and should leave the flexor muscles unaffected. The result would be that the arm would move in the direction of the tense extensor muscles easily, and in the opposite direction less easily. This is exactly what happens when one is given a pleasurable sensation of any sort. Give a person a sweet taste, for example, and you will find that his outward arm movements are longer than they normally were. These longer outward movements show that the extensor muscles are unusually tense. Conversely, if one gives the subject a bitter taste or a disagreeable sensation of any sort, the flexor muscles will be unusually tense and the outward movements will be curtailed.

Other experiments also confirm the general principle that all pleasurable experiences express themselves in large expansive movements, or in tensions of the muscles favorable to such movements, while unpleasurable experiences express themselves in contracting, withdrawing movements. And even passing from these to other forms of experience, we find everywhere the same characteristic fact, that each emotion has its characteristic motor conditions.

The value of emotional reactions in the development of the individual can not be doubted. Darwin[1] was the first to attempt a detailed explanation of the utility of emotional reactions. Whether we agree with his analysis of the various emotions or not, we have to recognize the fact that he set the pattern for modern explanations of the emotions in that he sought to find their value for development. The great value of many of the human emotional expressions is probably to be found in their utility as means of social communications. But some have other values as we see, for example, in the protective function of the emotional reactions which withdraw the body from disagreeable stimuli. Or again, the reaching out after objects which give pleasure is evidently in keeping with the general fact of development that in the great majority of cases pleasant experiences are favorable to individual life.

These special groups of facts which appear when we study the active conditions of attention and of the emotions, are typical of all phases of development. If one wishes to understand individual development, he must study not merely the impression side of the individual's life, he must study more especially the expression side. Impression is, of course, necessary to develop-

[1] Expression of the Emotions.

ment. Impression is the means by which the environment produces its first effect upon the individual. If an individual were not sensitive to his environment, the later adaptive process would be impossible. But impressions are present in superabundance at all stages of human life. So far as the sense-organs of the boys and girls in our schools are concerned, we have no reason to believe that they do not receive the same number and kind of impressions that our own sense-organs receive. Nature has thus provided that the environment shall produce its first effects, long before the boys and girls can fully make use of these impressions. The raw materials for adaptation, the impressions, are there very early, waiting for the individual gradually to adjust himself to them.

The active adjustments of oneself to impressions is the real adaptive process. All the sensations must be distinguished from each other and the individual must learn how to react to each impression. Certain groups of impressions must be treated in groups, not because they are alike as impressions, but because they are all objects of a single form of reaction. In short, so far as this raw material for development which presents itself in the form of impressions is concerned, it must all be worked over and connected with individual reactions before it can be regarded as really assimilated by the developing individual.

Take the form of training which we call sensory training in the schools. We present certain sense stimuli, such as colors, and sounds, and sensations of touch. Do we do this for the sake of developing the receiving organs? Not if we understand the process aright. The colors that fall on the eyes, the sounds that fall on the ears, are all received, so far as mere reception is concerned, by organs that were given to the individual through the development of the race. The individual life is too short a span in which to modify appreciably the development of eye or ear as sensitive organs. This appears in the fact that certain eyes which are defective in sensitivity, the color-blind eyes as we call them, can not be improved by individual development. Indeed, it often requires two or three generations of fusion with well-developed individuals to correct color-blindness, so thoroughly is the condition of the sensory organ determined before individual development begins. Individual development begins at the point where racial development ends. Our sensory training takes the sensory impressions after they are received, and, first of all, sharply discriminates them, and then organizes them.

Discrimination is not a process of impression. How often one has heard two sounds, for example, two sounds in a foreign language, and has confounded them. When we hear Chinese, for instance, or even French, if we do not understand it, the sounds all seem to run together in a confused mass. The different sounds are there so far as the receiving process is concerned, but we do not discriminate them. Now, instead of merely listening to these sounds, begin to try to reproduce them. That is, change from the attitude of impression to the attitude of expression, and as you try to fit your active life to each of the different impressions, you begin to discriminate and recognize. In other words, you begin to have more than the mere impression, you begin to have *recognized* impressions. This is sensory training. It is not training of the sense-organs, it is training in discrimination and in reaction to sensory impressions.

Nowhere does the relation of mental development to activity appear more clearly than it does in the unities which we build up in experience and call ideas. Every experience of visual or auditory recognition is, on its impression side, a complex. Every object at which we look, makes a series of impressions upon us. But we do not get an idea which is broken up into parts. We see things in the same unitary way as that in which we react to them. The fact that our action and thought are adapted to unitary objects rather than to single attributes of objects, is evidence of a close relation between ideas and actions, not between ideas and impressions. Thus, when we look at a piece of iron, the sensory stimulation received by the eye is not separated in our action or in our thought from the other attributes of the object. The color fuses in our idea with the weight, and the weight fuses with the roughness and coldness, and altogether we act toward the piece of iron as toward a single object, not as toward a group of colors, weights, roughnesses, and temperatures. The action and the idea correspond in that they are both unitary complexes containing in modified form the net results of all the varied sensory antecedents.

Striking parallels can also be found between the more complex unities of consciousness and action. Thus, take the case of the piano-player. At first his activities are a series of single, separate responses to separate notes. But later he strikes a whole chord in a single moment. Or take the singer; one may be able to sing each note of the scale separately and not be able to sing even a simple line of music. What must be learned in these cases? It is the combination of the elementary movements into new wholes, so far as the action is concerned. And when such combinations of activities are once established, we have corresponding complex ideas. The ideas of a musical chord, and of a vocal transition, are to the trained mind, unitary wholes, not mere aggregates of impression elements. And while these wholes contain, in a certain sense, the different sensory elements, they are in a much larger and more important sense, unitary processes with characteristics depending upon the fact that the elements are united into a single idea.

We have, however, dwelt long enough on these illustrations. The general principle to which they all lead is the general principle that development is adaptation, and *adaptation is an active process.* The individual has many functions, but all these functions cooperate in his higher and higher development, and that means that they all cooperate in working out more and more adequate forms of activity.

These, then, are some of the new ideals that are growing up in our education. We shall be blind to our own individual advantage if we do not see that the new spirit which springs from these new modes of thought is worthy of our individual study and acceptance. We shall be equally blind to our own advantage if we do not see that we can not fully grasp the newer spirit without understanding the fundamental ideas which underlie it.

There is a good deal of doubt in the minds of some teachers as to the value of their taking up some of these general lines of consideration. Give us methods and devices, they say. Let the leaders in education, let the superintendents, if you please, work out the larger problems and give us the result. But this is an idle demand. The method may be ever so perfect, the device may be ever so well wrought out, and yet fail unless administered in a right spirit, and the spirit can never be cultivated by mere superficial imitation.

Our educational life is full of dangerous opportunities to cultivate false and superficial ideals. Teachers are, as we have already said, more than most people dependent on their ideals. And especially at this period when the air is full of pedagogical doctrines from the North and from the South, from the East and especially from the West, it behooves each one of us to have a real, genuine ideal to save us from errors.

The history of the past has been a history of vague striving after such safe ideals. Men have borrowed their ideals from the church, from their philosophy, from their neighbors, from their teachers, who in turn borrowed their ideals from earlier teachers. Slowly the struggle has gone on and has brought us to these times. Here again there is large opportunity to borrow if we are so disposed. The traditions of the schools are ever present as fertile suggestions. The suggestions of our neighbors are offered even more freely than in former times. We may borrow; but you know the result of such borrowing. We can not borrow any more as they used to in the good old days, for we are in an age of rapid progress; the next piece of borrowing that we try, may upset our whole system. It is the blind borrowing of ideals that makes the teacher of this generation anxious and worried. It is the Babel of tongues without any single voice of authority, and this is what makes us feel confused. What is to be the relief? Are you going to wait until some one shall come and silence all this wrangling? If so you have a long dreary life ahead of you. There is to be much discussion of educational doctrines from this day on. You can not silence it or suppress it. The thing for you to do is, prepare to meet it. Have some ideal of your own. Get a broad principle, and then enter into the active discussion of details yourselves, and be, each one of you, a factor in the educational thought, not a confused outsider.

This is certainly not too large a demand to make upon our teachers. I do not suggest that you try to write articles for the educational reviews. That seems to be a dangerous sort of dissipation at the present time. I do not even suggest that you write a book. I certainly do not ask you to read all the books. But I do ask that before you let yourself adopt a plan of work in your classes, you consider some of the reasons for your plan. If it is writing that you intend to teach, or reading, or arithmetic, do not simply go ahead without any consideration of what is the value of this study for the boys and girls. Do not enter upon a lesson without thinking over its aims and purposes. You try to make the boys and girls think about what they are going to do before they do it, why should you not think about what you do?

And so I bring this general discussion to a close with

an urgent recommendation to you that each one of you think himself or herself into the modern view of education. There is not one of you who could not, and should not, understand the main outlines of this broad and fruitful idea of development. It is an idea that will illuminate your whole work. It will make it easy for you to understand that children improve slowly. It will give you a new spirit of tolerance of their undeveloped states. It will give you a broader ideal of the purpose of education and its relation to the other phases of the child's life. And above all it will give you a basis on which to build your methods, and it will give you suggestions as to the particular problems which you should take up for further investigation.

CHAPTER VI

THE TEACHER'S WRITING HABIT

In the preceding chapters we treated of some of the general characteristics of our mental lives and of some of the general ideals which influence us in our work as teachers. We turn now for a time to more special topics. How we write, and read, and use numbers, are the topics to which I shall now ask you to direct your attention. These are, in a general way, certainly not new subjects, and I am well aware that you have, before we enter upon the discussion, a good many valuable ideas on how children should learn to write and read and use numbers. But I wish we might set aside for a little time all that we know about how children should do these things and might approach the familiar subjects from a somewhat different point of view—the point of view of our teacher-study. How do you and I actually behave when we write? This is a somewhat different question from the one with which we are more familiar, the question which asks how we shall teach children to write.

Our question is one of self-study. It is not especially a question of self-examination, for I do not wish you to examine your writing with a view to comparing it with some copper-plate model. I wish rather to induce you to stop and think that you, as a trained adult, have the habit which your children are working most earnestly to acquire. You, as a trained adult, can take a pen or a pencil, or a piece of crayon; and you can, rapidly and without apparent effort, express ideas by means of written symbols. What is this habit of which you have such complete control? It certainly is not an abstract or theoretical affair. There is a very great deal of your concrete personality involved in it. Did you ever stop in the midst of all your pedagogical struggles to think that in writing, as in many other respects, you are your own best subject for study? Did you ever think that when you sit down and study this or that so-called system of penmanship, you are studying something very remote and abstract, something that contains very little of the human beings who have to produce such letters and use them in real life? I wish I might draw your attention to the habit of writing as a human performance, to your own habits in writing as profoundly interesting illustrations of what education is aiming at. For, if I mistake not, education aims to cultivate human habits of thought and expression—not forms and symbols. One of the troubles with our teaching of writing has been that we have had our eyes too much on the lifeless, material paper and ink, and not enough on the pulsating human being back of these material things. The habit of writing is not to be found in lines on paper—it is in human beings.

Perhaps it will not be amiss for me, as we enter upon this study of ourselves and of our ability to write, to assure you that this is no subtle scheme by which to induce you to accept some new form of penmanship. I solemnly promise not to turn out to be an advocate of some new series of writing books, or even a representative of one of the publishers now dealing in writing books. If I were to give an opinion growing out of a careful perusal of a good deal of what has been written for teachers on the subject of writing, I should not hesitate to say that the multiplication of new writing books and the multiplication of pamphlets and even volumes in support of these numerous systems of penmanship, must be recognized as very largely accountable for the deflection of the attention of teachers from the really important questions of the nature of writing habits, to the less essential and often wholly unessential characteristics of this or that system of copies. Let us agree, then, that this is not a study of systems of penmanship, but a study of the nature of the writing habit, beginning with a careful examination of developed writing as exhibited in the teacher.

Writing involves as its most obvious factor a complex muscular movement. Our study of developed writing may well begin with this obvious factor. One does not need to know very much about the muscles of the hand and arm to recognize the fact that there are a great many of these muscles involved in writing. Thus, one must carry his hand across the page on which he writes. This movement across the page is performed by the larger muscles of the arm. It is a movement in the shoulder-joint and at the elbow. This movement is very different, in regard to the muscles which it involves, from the finer finger movements which ordinarily make the pen-strokes. I say ordinarily, for there are, of course, certain special modes of writing in which all the movements are arm movements. And even if one insists on talking about these relatively unusual forms of arm-movement writing, the same general proposition is true. The lateral movements across the page are different in character and in the muscles employed from the rotary movements by which the letters are formed.

When one begins to notice this fact, that writing movements are made up of a number of different factors, he begins to notice in the same connection that all the different factors fit each other perfectly. The finer pen-strokes and the movements of the arm across the page do not interfere with each other. The arm muscles do not contract too soon, but wait until the finger-work is done, and then easily and fluently, without our noticing that an entirely new movement is being woven into the total complex of action, the arm muscles carry the hand forward to a new point where new pen-strokes are to be executed.

Or consider the ordinary finger movements by means of which most of us make the pen-strokes. It will be clear to you after a little observation, that the thumb does not perform the same kind of movement as the first finger, and that the middle finger does not perform the same movements as either thumb or first finger. The first finger makes the downward strokes. In these downward strokes the thumb and middle finger simply guide the downward movement and give to it its inward and outward curves. The returning upward strokes of the pen are very largely the work of the thumb. The guiding of the upward movements is the work of the first finger and the middle finger. Put in a general way, one can say that thumb and first finger do most of the active work in the upward and downward pen-strokes, while the guiding of these strokes is the complex result of the cooperation of all three fingers.

The cooperation of the three fingers is, like the larger cooperation of the arm and fingers, so nicely adjusted that we do not notice the complexity of the movement in ordinary experience. We should ordinarily describe the stroke of the pen as a single movement. It is in one sense of the word a single movement, but it is single only in the sense that its factors, which are many, are perfectly fused so that there is no interference or lack of harmony. The various muscles are perfectly timed to each other and perfectly regulated with respect to intensity of action.

All this cooperation of the different muscles must, of course, be due to some controlling system which sends to each muscle at the appropriate moment the proper command to act. The muscles themselves have no power of uniting with each other. They are separate organs. Their cooperation is due to the nervous center with which they are all connected. And so our first consideration of the external muscular movements in writing, leads us to a study of the way in which these movements are controlled and initiated.

Every muscle is supplied with a delicate nerve-fiber. You know enough about nerves and their connections so that we need not go into any extended discussion here of the details of nervous structure. No muscle ever moves except as it is aroused to action by its nerve-fiber; and no nerve-fiber ever arouses a muscle except as it receives its impulse in turn from the brain. When, now, we find a group of muscles acting in perfect harmony, as do the writing muscles, we can explain that harmony by the fact that in the brain there is a group of nerve-cells all connected with each other and so organized that they produce from a single region the combined harmonious action of the different muscles. We speak of this organized group of cells as the center of muscular coordination. And by muscular coordination we mean the fact of cooperation which we described a moment ago.

Developed writing movements depend, then, on the existence of a group of brain-cells which are interconnected and interrelated in a most complex way. The growth of this series of interconnections between the cells was a process that required time and practise. At the beginning of this practise each cell acted in a large measure apart from its fellows, and there was no well-organized cooperation, or muscular coordination as we have learned to call it.

One can get a notion of what the condition of things must have been before the cells became organized, through certain disorganizing experiences which one has in adult life. Suppose you are writing and a sudden peal of thunder sounds in your ears. You know the result. Your pen flies off in some unexpected direction, spoiling the line you were just about to complete. Even a milder noise than thunder will often make one start and spoil a pen-stroke. These failures of the writing muscles to cooperate in the usual fashion when one hears loud, sharp sounds, are explained by the fact that the thunder, or the other loud noise sounding in one's ears, sends into the brain very strong excitations which stir up the whole brain. The excitation is so great that it does not respect the usual channels of well-organized discharge into the muscles. Instead of flowing out as a well-coordinated impulse, this strong stimulation leaps forward on its own arbitrary paths, and those cells which it excites most intensely simply break away from the system to which they belong and act independently of the system, just as in earlier times they acted independently because the system was yet unformed. This independent action of certain nerve-cells breaks up immediately the harmony of the movement. We see the value of the ordinary coordination in contrast with this lack of coordination.

Nothing could be more instructive for the teacher than to study these irregular movements which are made under the influence of some sudden, strong stimulation. You find it impossible to make a regular movement under these conditions. If some one should, at such a time, preach you a long sermon on making the letter correctly, it would not help matters any. The fact is, the wrong movement was due to a lack of ability to make the right movement. The machinery of coordination broke down at that instant and the false movement appeared. Now you know how to sympathize with your pupil whose machinery of movement has a good many weak points. Impulses go astray in your pupil's nervous center because the center is not completely organized. It does no good to preach to him about correct movement—at least, if you preach to him in the spirit of blaming him for the wrong movement at the wrong time. He does not choose the wrong movement. He has before him a problem very difficult for us to understand, namely, the problem of making any movement that shall even approach what you want and what he wants.

There is another kind of experience in adult life which will help us still further in our effort to comprehend what is meant by a coordinated movement. Think of a movement which even in adult life is wholly unorganized. There are muscles in our bodies which are supplied with nerve-fibers but which we have never learned to use. For the sake of understanding the child's feelings about his writing lesson, try sometime to write with your own undeveloped muscles in your feet. This is not an absurd proposition by any means. There are a great many people in this world who, for one reason or another, have learned to use the feet very dexterously, and some have even learned to write with them. Of course the feet are not as well adapted to fine work of this kind as are the hands, but if you will make the trial you will find that your immediate difficulty is not that there is a lack of muscular activity, or even that there is a lack of general adaptation of the organ to this kind of movement. There will be movement enough and to spare, and there will be movement which, if trained, would do the work very well. The first fact which you will discover is that the movements which are present, are not coordinated. They are not under control. A little experience will show you how hopeless it is to try to do anything with these untrained movements except through patient practise. You must have the nervous organization before you can have the coordinated movement. And this is exactly what is true of the muscles of the child's fingers, hand, and arms.

If, now, the general character of the writing movement, as a coordinated movement, made up of many factors, is clear to you through these contrasts, we may turn to the study of some of the characteristic forms of writing movement. It is obvious, of course, to all of us that there are great individual differences in writing movements, and it is also true, as we shall see, that the explanation of these individual differences must be sought in the individual modes of coordinating movements. It is not chiefly, if indeed it is at all, differences in the shape or size of the hand, or differences in the character of the writing materials, which determine these individual differences. The way in which one writes will be determined in a measure by the materials which he uses and by the strength and shape of his muscles. But these are very secondary factors. The chief consideration is the nervous organization which controls the coordination of the muscles. In other words, one's individual writing is the expression of his individual habit of movement. His hand may be large and strong, but if writing is for him a series of fine delicate coordinations, then his writing will not show the size or strength of his hand, but will express rather, by its fine delicate lines, the character of the coordination.

We can see even by superficial examination of a number of adults that their habits of movement are very different. Ask two persons to sit before you and to write a given word over and over again, and watch their hands and arms and compare their modes of movement. You could tell that the products of these movements must be different from the very fact that there are such noticeable differences in the movements. But we shall not be satisfied with this superficial observation of what can be seen directly. Let us resort to a thoroughgoing experimental analysis of a number of individual coordinations.

Such an experimental analysis is not difficult, at least in so far as the grosser coordination between the arm movements and other movements is concerned. One can arrange a tracer in such a way that while one is writing as usual with the fingers, the tracer shall record, not what the fingers do, but only what the hand as a whole does. All that is necessary in order to make such a tracer, is first to find some part of the hand that does not participate in the finger movements. Such a part of the hand is, for example, the hand bone, or so-called metacarpal bone, just back of the little finger. This metacarpal bone moves every time the hand moves, but it has no part in the movements of the thumb and first two fingers. A simple tracer of the sort represented in Fig. 14 is fastened to this bone.

The tracer consists of a spring (*A*) which fits closely on the hand and carries the light rod (*B-B*) which runs forward far enough so that the distance of its end from the wrist and elbow is the same as the distance from the wrist and elbow of the pen held by the thumb and first finger. This equality in length ensures a record of the hand movement which is on the same scale as the writing, and thus comparison is made direct and easy. At the end of this rod is placed a perpendicular glass tube (*C*), and through this falls a closely fitting pencil (*D-D*). The record in any given case is made by writing naturally and allowing this tracer, which is fastened to the hand during the writing, to make a record on the same paper as that which receives the writing. The written letters are the records of finger movements plus all the hand and arm movements, except such hand and arm movements as are made during the intervals between words, when, of course, the writing pen is raised from the paper. The tracer-pencil is kept by its own weight constantly on the paper, and records all that the hand and arm do, but nothing of the pure finger movements. By a comparison of the written letters and the tracer-record we can therefore easily determine what part of the whole work is done by the arm and hand and what part is done by the fingers.

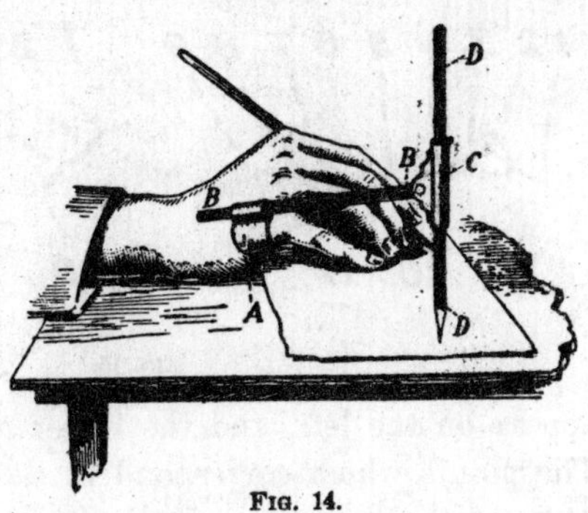

Fig. 14.

A large number of records have been taken by means of such a tracer. Many of them were made by teachers, so that we may use the results directly in our study. Of course your individual record would not be exactly like any one of the records which I have to show. But out of the many records which I have taken, I have selected examples which seem to illustrate the general types of handwriting, and so your general type of writing is doubtless here represented.

The first typical record which we shall take up for detailed study is shown in Fig. 15. The letters written

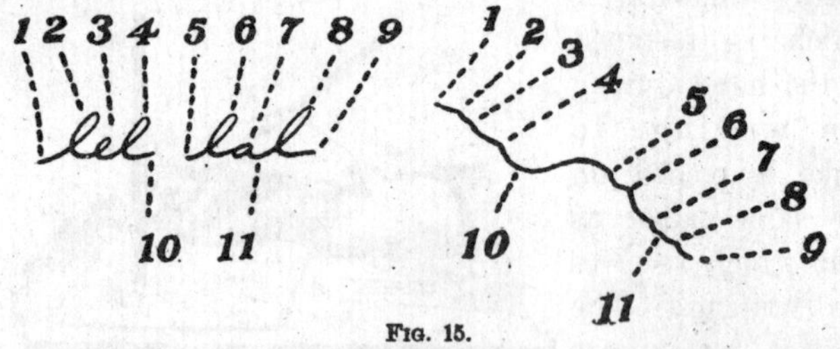

FIG. 15.

appear on the left, and the tracer-record on the right. The points which correspond to each other in the two parts of the figure are similarly numbered. The most obvious fact is that the hand participated only in the forward movements, while the fingers did all of the finer work in forming the letters. Thus, the lines between 1 and 3 in the tracer-record represent the whole movement of the hand during the writing of the letter *l* and the first stroke of the letter *e*. A still more striking illustration of the relation between hand movements and finger movements is found in the case of the letter *a*. From 6 to 8 in the tracer-record, we have the total movement of the hand from the top of *l* to the top of the next succeeding *l*. The movement 6–7 in the tracer-record, represents the part played by the hand in making the downward stroke of the *l* and in carrying the fingers forward to the position from which they did the larger part of the work of forming the *a*. If

6–7 is contrasted with 2–3, which represents a similar movement from the top of an *l* to the top of its next succeeding letter, which was in that case *e*, a very characteristic fact in all hand movements will be observed. It is the fact that in most cases the hand does its part in the formation of a letter before the fingers begin their finer formative work. Coming back now to the *a*, we see that after making the long movement 6–7, the hand participated in the completion of the *a* only to the extent indicated by the line 7–11. The point 11 is somewhat less definite in its location than are the other points, and is consequently indicated below, rather than above the line.

Another important feature of this tracer-record appears in the differences in slope of the three parts 1–10, 10–5, and 5–9. The part 1–10 indicates the movement of the hand during the writing of the first group of letters. Its slope indicates that the hand executed a considerable movement from left to right on its own center in the wrist. During the pause between the writing of the two groups of letters, an entirely different form of movement was executed, as is shown by the new slope in the line 10–5. In the first place, the slope indicates that this movement was made from an entirely different center. It was indeed an arm movement centered at the elbow, instead of at the wrist, as was the movement 1–10. But it also included a wrist movement from right to left, as is indicated by the convex form of the line just before 5. The interval between the groups of letters was, accordingly, employed in executing an arm movement which carried the hand forward, and in executing a backward wrist movement which prepared the hand for the new series of forward movements which we find recorded from 5–9. This new series was made up again of wrist movements from left to right.

Fig. 16, from a different writer, presents a somewhat different type of coordination. Here the hand

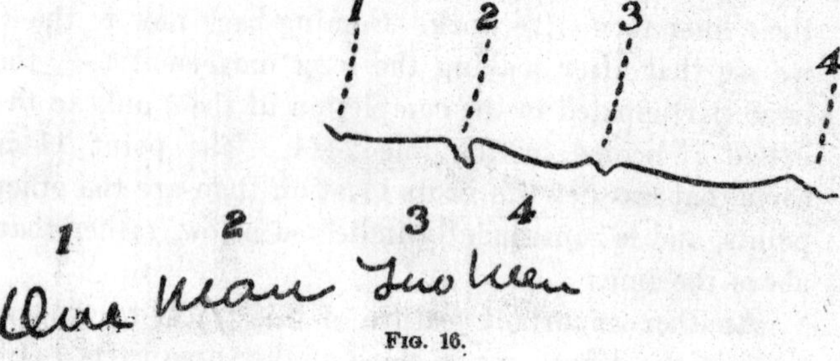

FIG. 16.

movement during the writing of the letter was much less than in the case of the first subject. The arm movements were longer and freer. The hand and fingers were carried forward by the arm during the intervals between words, to positions corresponding to the middle of the word to be written, and then the fingers executed the major part of the writing movement.

This is, because of the limited amount of hand movement, a very excellent illustration of the relation of hand movement to the word. Any group of letters which is written with a single progressive hand movement, as were these groups in the figure, will be seen to have a kind of unity which can not be overlooked. It is not the unity of a single letter, to be sure, but it is a higher form of complex unity. It should be noted also that such hand movement units are not always coextensive with single words. A long, complex word is often broken up into two, or even three, such hand movement units with a regular arm movement between. Sometimes, on the other hand, two short words are united into a single continuous phrase and are written with a single unitary hand movement.

Records essentially identical with the one reproduced in Fig. 16 were secured from a number of persons who wrote " round " letters, and from every case investigated in which the writing was of the type known as vertical. There is, accordingly, ground, as far as these cases are concerned, for the statement that broad, round letters, indicate a preponderance of finger movement.

While the relative importance of the various movements is different in the cases reproduced in Figs. 15 and 16, yet the same general statement which was made in the analysis of Fig. 15 can be repeated for Fig. 16: the function of the hand is to participate only in the forward movements, while the fingers do the work of constructing the letters, and the arm acts chiefly in the intervals between words in such a way as to carry the hand forward. It is only necessary to note that in this second case special emphasis is given to the constructive finger movements which have a relatively larger part to perform than they had in the first case.

A third type of record is reproduced in Fig. 17. This record shows a very pronounced preponderance of arm movements. The movements recorded in 1–6 and 7–11 differ little in slope from the recognized arm record between 6 and 7. The hand reproduces the letters in much more detail than in the other cases, because it is carried along in the process of writing by a general arm movement. To be sure, the finer details of the letters are here, as before, formed by the fingers, but there is more of the general work done by the hand, and arm muscles. The writing here reproduced is obviously bolder and more angular than that in the earlier records. This writing is typical of a whole group of cases

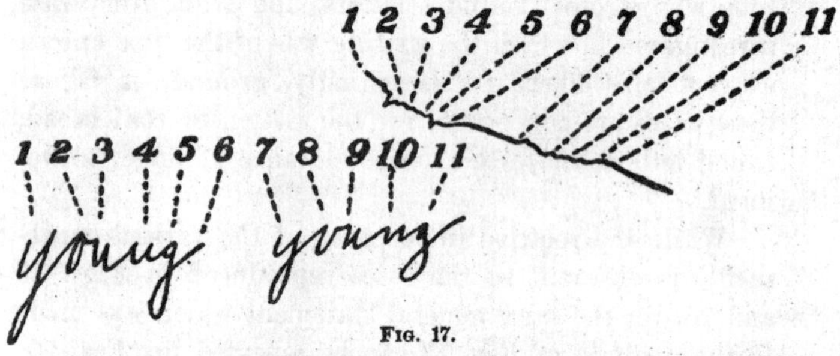

FIG. 17.

in which the movement is coarse and more general, and in which less attention is given by the writer to questions of form.

It remains for us to notice that there are certain forms of writing in which the individual has trained himself to make no use whatever of the fingers. It is not our purpose at this time to deal with such unusual and extreme forms of writing movement. Enough to say that they require long periods of special practise. When the ordinary individual is asked to write without moving the fingers, the records generally make it very clear that some finger movement has crept in, in spite of the effort to exclude it.

The general conclusion from the comparison of a large number of records, of which the three reproduced represent the chief types, may be summed up briefly in the statement: in ordinary writing the fine formative movements are executed by the fingers; the movements which carry the fingers forward are executed by the hand or arm; and the pauses between groups of letters are utilized for longer forward arm movements which bring the hand back into an easy working position.

The different types of coordination are well illustrated in these three records. Let me repeat the statement that each individual has his own peculiar combination of arm and hand and finger movements so that while these three records represent types, they do not by any means represent all possible forms of coordination. The forms of coordination are as numerous and as various as are the individuals who write.

Let us carry the experiment further so as to see what are some of the influences which effect even a well-established habit of movement. A subject was required to make a record of a series of free upward and

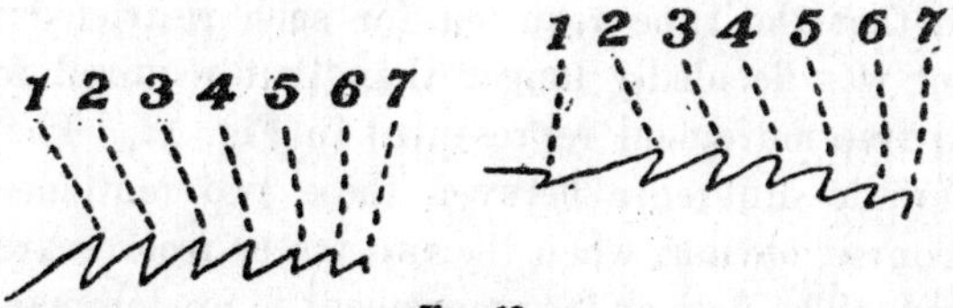

1 2 3 4 5 6 7   1 2 3 4 5 6 7

Fig. 18.

downward movements such as those represented on the left of Fig. 18. In this first experiment no restrictions whatever were placed upon the subject; he was allowed to make each line in the freest possible manner. The corresponding tracer-record is given on the right of the same figure. The presence of some finger movements appears in the fact that there is a lack of sharply defined angles in the tracer-record. The tracer-record shows, however, by its general form and slope, that it is due very largely to free arm movements which carried the whole hand over the same path as that traversed by the writing pen.

The lines which the subject had prepared in this first free drawing were then set for imitation, and in order that the imitation might be exact, the extremities of each of the upward and downward movements were indicated before the movement began by means of dots. A typical result of such restricted movement is presented in Fig. 19. It should be noted

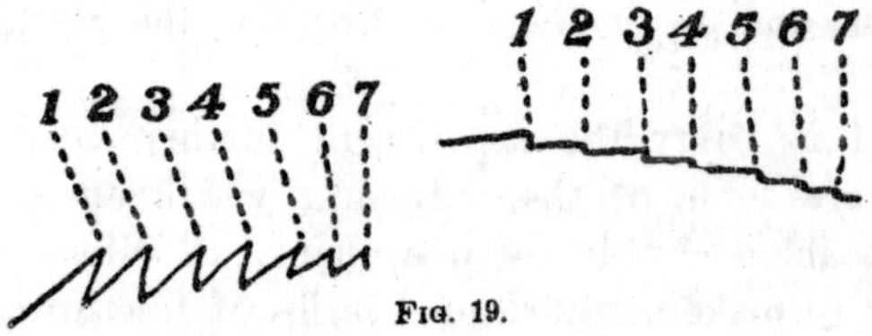

1 2 3 4 5 6 7

1 2 3 4 5 6 7

Fig. 19.

also that the time required for such restricted movement was decidedly longer than that required for the first free movement represented in Fig. 18. The characteristic difference between these two movements is, of course, obvious when the two tracer-records are compared. The first or free movement is predominantly an arm movement, the second contains a very much larger element of finger movement, especially in the downward strokes. The subject finds that in order to meet the points prescribed, it is necessary to make a finer, more accurate adjustment than was necessary in the first drawing.

A fact which appears very clearly in Fig. 18 may also be made a subject of special comment. The movement is not the same in character at the outset as it is later in the course of the drawing. This same fact appears in almost every record of writing. The hand is evidently not in position at first, but requires a few strokes to adjust itself. Sometimes the necessary adjustment is brought about by a greater emphasis on finger movement, sometimes by a more pronounced hand movement.

Another group of results is as follows: Any change in the conditions under which the subject writes will modify the character of coordination. A change from a hard pencil to a soft pencil, or a change from a vertical position of the paper to an oblique position, will be sufficient to produce noticeable variations in the character of the muscular coordination, even when the product of the movement—that is, the written letters—conform very closely to the same type.

There is one movement which enters into the total complex of writing movements which requires special attention. It is not recorded by our tracer and consequently must be studied by itself. It is a movement which the physiologists describe by the name pronation. It consists in rotating the hand, so that it tends to lie flat on its palm. This rotary movement is possible, as you know, because the lower arm is supplied with two bones—the ulna and radius—which fasten at the wrist in such a way that they can turn the hand so that the palm lies either upward or down-

13

ward. When the palm is downward, or prone, the position is due to the movement which we mentioned, the movement of pronation. Most adults make a slight movement of pronation in the course of writing a line across the page. The motive and effect of this movement can be easily understood. Let us first note that the position of the hand and fingers at the beginning of the line of writing is such that the movement of the first finger (which, as we have seen, is the most important movement in directing the pen in its downward strokes) will give the letters a certain slope with reference to the edges of the paper. This first slope may be to the right, or it may be vertical, or it may be to the left; but in any case it is the result of a pen movement which depends for its direction upon the total position of the hand, arm, and fingers, with respect to the edges

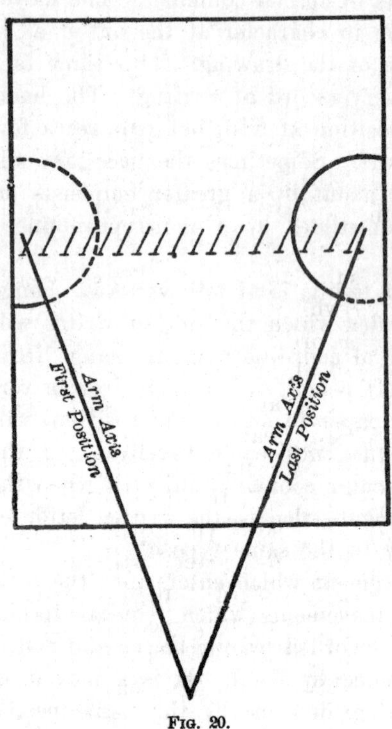

FIG. 20.

of the paper. As the hand moves across the paper during the writing of the line, it is obvious that the position of the arm and hand with respect to the paper must undergo a change by virtue of the movement of the arm about its center in the elbow. To make this statement definite we may study the angles with the aid of Fig. 20, and we shall find that the angles formed by the axis of the arm and the left edge of the paper are, at the beginning of the line, acute below the point of intersection and obtuse above; while the angles formed by the axis of the arm and the edge of the paper, at the end of the line of writing, either are, or tend to be, just the reverse. If as sometimes happens the center of arm movement—that is, the elbow—is itself moved forward during the writing of the line, the above statement in regard to angles holds with this change: each period between movements of the elbow is to be treated as if it were a separate line.

The gradual modification in the position of the arm axis with reference to the edge of the paper, which takes place during the writing of a line, requires some definite form of compensating movement, if the slope of the letters is to be kept uniform with reference to the edges of the paper.

It should be noted at this point that a compensating movement of less degree is required to counteract the changes in the direction of the axis of the hand which are due to the wrist movements that take place as we have seen in writing a word (see Fig. 15, p. 172). This lesser corrective movement is of the same type as the greater movement which is the main subject of discussion; it therefore needs no special discussion. Another preliminary remark is that if one examines many specimens of handwriting, he will see that only partial corrections of the slope of finger movements have usually been effected by ordinary writers. The slopes of letters at the end of a line, and the slopes of letters at the end of a word, are commonly greater than the slopes at the beginning. This failure to correct the slope, gives to the line and to the word, the somewhat irregular appearance usually noticeable in ordinary writing.

Coming back to our main discussion, we may say that, so far as any correction in slope is effected, this correction results from a movement of pronation which tends to throw the upper end of the pen toward the writer and thus to give the pen a movement more nearly parallel to its first movements at the beginning of the line. This movement of pronation is one which most adults have, but have in only partially developed degree. It is a kind of added refinement which gives uniformity to the slope without interfering with the continuous arm movement across the page. If the movement of pronation is present only in small degree, another way of securing uniformity of slope is to keep moving the elbow forward every time the slope of the letters begins to grow noticeably different. This repeated change of position of the elbows is, however, neither easy nor conducive to fluency of writing.

The corrective movement of pronation which we have been discussing, is required no matter what the slope of the letters. It is not a factor which will help to settle any of the disputed questions in regard to the slope of writing, it is rather a factor of movement necessary to secure uniformity, whatever the slope. It is one of the nicest refinements of the whole complex coordination, and when fully developed it can be observed as a regular and very gradual adjustment as the hand travels across the page.

This movement of pronation furnishes a favorable subject for investigation, just because of its incomplete development in most adults. A group of ten teachers was once induced by the present writer to give some attention to the regularity of the slope of their letters. The members of this group were asked to pay attention as closely as possible to the conscious processes which accompanied their efforts to improve, and they were also asked to make daily records of their observations and to note whether or not they really improved in the regularity of slope during the period of practise. These ten teachers were all trained in careful observation and could consequently be depended upon to take up the practise with intelligent interest. On the other hand, they had no special preparation for the particular form of practise which was prescribed. No one directed their attention during the first period of the experiment to the movement of pronation, and they were asked to put themselves as far as possible in the normal attitude of one who is trying as earnestly as possible to improve his writing, rather than in the studied attitude of one who is investigating the problem merely as an outsider.

The first result of the practise was that each of the persons became clearly conscious of the fact that his own writing contained many irregular slopes. Attention to this matter grew so keen that it extended to the writing produced by others, and all the observers expressed surprise at the degree of irregularity that had, up to this time, escaped notice. There was a very general agreement that the recognition of this irregularity of slope was a definite experience resulting from an unusual and clearly conscious comparison of the forms of all letters looked at by the experimenters.

As soon as the irregularities were recognized, and the effort to correct these irregularities commenced, there was a general agreement as to the difficulty of finding any guiding slope to follow in actual writing. The effort to refer back to earlier letters in a given line, the effort to refer to letters in the line above, the effort to carry in memory a sort of standard angle with the horizontal line—all these devices are mentioned as methods of securing uniformity. There is not a single case among the early records of the ten adults in which reference of any kind is made to any form of movement. All the devices mentioned emphasize the visual guides as the ones consciously employed. Several noted the tendency to write more slowly and carefully, and one noted later that it cramped his hand to write regularly. All found it possible to improve the slope of the letters by constant attention. Several noted that there were days when the letters were very much less regular than on other days. Many times the days of irregular movements were described in terms which indicated that the physical condition of the writer was not good, but not infrequently the records merely remarked that there was no apparent reason.

Nothing could be more obvious from the records than the fact that the whole practise of these persons consisted in what we have called a non-rational effort to approach an end which was always presented to consciousness in terms of visual perception, and never presented in terms of the movements which were the real means by which the end must be reached. The *movements* were hardly more intelligently or directly guided than are those of a child. The whole attention was concentrated on the product.

After practise had been going on for four weeks with some evidences of improvement, but no definite notion on the part of the practisers as to how they might accelerate the improvement, they were all asked to write under observation a single word at the beginning of the line and then to pass over the middle of the paper to the extreme end of the line and there to write the same word again. The word "long" was used for this test, this being a suitable word to emphasize the slope both above and below the line.

Three distinct types of results showed themselves in this experiment. First, there were two cases in which the elbow and whole arm were carried across the page in such a way that the arm was, at the end of the line, in a position parallel to its first position. For these two subjects, the conscious control of the slope consisted, as throughout the practise, in a simple visual recognition of the slope of the letters produced. They could not even describe their movement when asked to do so. Secondly, there were three distinct cases in which the hand was adjusted by a movement of pronation, such as that described. But even in these cases the movement was present in such a completely automatic form that it attracted no attention to itself. Finally, the remaining five members of the group fall into a class intermediate to the first two classes mentioned. For these five experimenters, the movement was not purely automatic nor could it be described as wholly developed. When these writers reached the end of the line they found the hand in such a position that it was impossible to make a slope that satisfied their visual expectation without executing some kind of additional movement. The movements employed were of various kinds, but usually contained an element of pronation. The pronounced demand for a change in the position of the hand called attention to the hand itself. It is to be noted at once, however, that no one of the subjects paid attention to the hand any further than to try to get the fingers into an easy position. There was no disposition to make the hand the chief factor in attention. So long as the hand could not be used readily in producing the slope desired, there was a recognized demand that it be moved. The movement was of a tentative and non-rational kind, now in this direction, now in that. There was no distinct and clear recognition of the position aimed at, nor of the superiority of one kind of movement over any other. There was merely an effort to reach a certain end of production, and in order to reach this end, the hand had to be in an easy position, and it was moved until brought into this easy position. That attention to the hand was not of clearly recognized importance in developing the right form of action, appears in the fact that there was no uniformity in action even after some of the subjects had by chance hit upon the easy movement of pronation. They continued, time after time, to find it necessary to make tentative efforts in this direction and in that, until finally the proper movement was hit upon by what seemed in each case to be pure chance. No one of the subjects ever discovered the movement itself in any such way as to call attention to it as a fact of movement. In other words, the position of the hand was never clearly recognized in terms of its own movements. Consciousness on the part of these writers was always visual consciousness. Movements were not subjects of direct attention, and they were never held in consciousness in the form of memories of clearly recognized movements.

Here, then, is a splendid example of how, through one's own training, one may learn what are the difficulties in the educational process. Writing, which is essentially a coordinated movement, has to be developed through trial after trial, with consciousness directed, not upon the movement itself, but on the visual images which appear as results of the movement. What one is training is the movement; what one is thinking of is not movement at all, but visual images. When the movement becomes well enough trained so that one need not have any anxiety about its operating well, then attention is withdrawn in great measure from even the visual forms. Attention thus becomes free in the last stages of development to reach out into wider fields—that is, to leave even visual experience—and devote itself to the meanings of words and sentences.

The final result of the complete development of the writing habit is that the movement thus becomes wholly automatic. This automatic character of adult writing is one of its most interesting and significant characteristics. Because the habit is so thoroughly automatic, we do not recognize it in ordinary experience as a subject worthy of study. We come to think of it as we do of a hundred other automatic habits—as a natural endowment. Of course it is not a natural endowment. More than most of our highly developed habits, more than walking or talking, for example, writing has become automatic through individual practise.

Walking especially is a form of muscular coordination for which the nervous organization was largely provided in the brain of the infant when the infant was born. To be sure, it took some time after birth for the walking center to mature, but it was all provided for, and needed only to grow to its full maturity. But writing was provided for in the infant brain only in the general sense in which there are unorganized centers ready for development through individual practise. That this unorganized writing center becomes a fully developed center of muscular coordination, that we have in adult life a completely automatic habit of action in which attention is freed even from visual control of the movements, is an indication of how much individual practise can do to develop movement even when practise operates, as we know it does in this case, without attention to the movement itself.

It remains for us to become somewhat more fully acquainted with the meaning of the statement that writing is automatic. Let us begin with a description of the facts of experience. We sit down and think out the thought, and then the rest of the process goes on very easily, occupying a little time, to be sure, and requiring some little directing attention, but making no heavy drain upon consciousness. So slight, indeed, is the attention devoted to the writing process after the thought has been clearly worked out, that one finds himself making all sorts of curious slips. One finds himself writing *the* for *they,* as though the word having been once thought out, consciousness hurried on to the next word and did not notice in its haste that sufficient time was not allowed for the execution of the first order. Or the fact that consciousness is far beyond the laggard movement of writing appears in the mistaken ending which is added to a given word and is obviously borrowed from some word farther on in the sentence. I find illustrations of this in my own manuscript where I have written "in favoring" in the phrase "in favor of their learning," or where I have written "broal" in the phrase "broad and liberal." Again, one sees how little consciousness watches over the developed writing movement when some wholly undesired word is written instead of the one thought. Thus, one writes "is" for "if," "from" for "for," and less frequently makes such substitutions as the following, borrowed from a letter now on my desk, "shall" for "sound." Here the first letter of the word being well under way, the attention of the writer evidently left the movement to finish itself automatically. The writing habit is so thoroughly organized that for the most part it can be relied upon to do what is appropriate. These mistakes which show how far the movement may go wrong, give us a notion of how thoroughly we rely, in all cases, upon the organized movement to go on without watching.

Another way of realizing how thoroughly automatic the writing movement has become in adult life, is to contrast the easy flow of thought that one enjoys when all is well with the writing—as, for example, when one is using a good pen—with the utter impossibility of doing anything in the way of thinking when one is supplied with a poor pen or bad paper. The poor pen keeps consciousness so busy with the mere making of marks that there is no surplus attention to reach out into the realms of thought. Noble sentiments with a bad pen are at least difficult, one is probably justified in saying they are utterly impossible.

The statement that the writing movement requires very little attention to itself is an important description of the developed adult mode of writing. But to tell where attention is not concentrated, is a negative statement, and is never complete without its positive supplement. The positive supplementary statement has already been more than hinted at in our discussion, but is of sufficient importance to deserve special consideration. The attention freed from concentration upon any phase of the mere act of production, is turned to the thought to be expressed. Writing would not be a means of expression unless it were automatic enough to leave the mind free to arrange its ideas for expression. In adult life we are usually thinking about what we are expressing. In other words, the developed attention is turned away from the process of production, and in very large measure even from the product as it appears in the written lines, and is concentrated upon what is being expressed.

There are some cases, to be sure, in which writing

is not thus used solely as a means of expression. Then we notice at once a marked change in the character of our experience and in the direction of attention. For example, when one writes copy on the blackboard, he is sure to do something besides express ideas. He tries to make unusually regular lines and perfectly symmetrical letters. The thought which the word expresses is not uppermost in the mind. It is well to consider carefully the fact that such copy writing is not writing for expression, but is rather writing for beauty and regularity of form. Attention is brought back in such cases to the process of production, and the writing activity is not automatic.

Sometimes one withdraws attention from the process of production at a stage of development at which it is at least doubtful whether one ought to trust the process of movement to take care of itself. We have already indicated some such cases in our earlier discussions. Thus, the process of writing is usually not sufficiently developed in adult life to ensure regularity in the slope of writing. Most of us do not care to bother, however, with the labor of improving in this particular, and so it comes that long before the refined movement of pronation which we have described, is anything like completely developed, we withdraw attention from the process of getting uniform slopes and turn to the ideas which we are expressing. The first step, if one would improve the slope of his letters, is to go back to the stage of development in which attention is turned to the process of production. As we saw in the cases described, the first step toward improvement in slope is to attend to slope.

This study of adult writing marks out for us the problems which must be taken up when one attempts to investigate the development of writing in immature writers. There are two entirely distinct problems of development. One problem is to discover the character and degree of the muscular coordination involved at different stages of development, and the other problem is to discover the direction and object of attention. The one problem consists in the analysis of the movement into its factors, and in the intelligent understanding of the way in which these movement factors cooperate in the unitary and yet complex form of action under discussion. The other problem is the problem of the conscious states parallel to the physical movements.

And now our examination of the teacher's process of writing is complete, at least as far as we can carry it here. We find writing to be an automatic form of production in which all one's past development is expressed in one's own individual mode of coordination. Let us ask some of the questions that are so often asked in the discussion of writing. First, what is the most approved form of movement? Second, how shall one hold the pen, keeping in mind the fact that its angle to the paper must be changed as the hand moves across the paper? Third, how shall one hold the hand? Fourth, how shall one place the paper? Fifth, shall one make the letters round or long; and at what slope shall the letters stand? Sixth, what is the normal speed of writing? Seventh, what is the normal age at which automatic writing is attained? Do you not see that these questions can not be answered without very large consideration of the individual? You are not dealing, let me repeat it, merely with pens and paper when we take up these questions. You are not dealing primarily with forms and letters; you are dealing with some individual's muscular coordinations and with some individual's conscious processes of attention. I should rather see the writing teachers of this country intelligently interested in the development of this or that child; I should rather see them engaged in the careful study of the particular form of coordination that has been attained at any given stage of development; I should rather see them interested in the necessity of turning the attention of the individual child in this direction or in that—than to see them interested, as they now too often are, in all the systems of writing that can be invented. How often those who have given any attention to the writing taught in the schools have seen the same system successful in one class room and utterly unsuccessful in the next room. Why is this? The explanation is to be found in the difference between the teachers. Some teachers recognize even now that the child is the important center of interest during the writing lesson. Such teachers are on the right road. Let us follow their lead, striving only to extend our knowledge of the writing process beyond what is known at the present time.

The question is seriously asked again and again in these times: "Shall teachers be investigators?" And the wail of the overworked teacher is heard answering this question in the negative. I think that we have too often been misunderstanding what investigation means. We have been led to think that it means inquiring into matters outside of our practical work—that it means leaving untouched the matters that lie at our very hands. Of course you will be overburdened if you investigate some remote corner of the globe and then clumsily blunder with the processes of every-day school life. Will you not see that you should revise your notions of what investigation is? Will you not take up some investigation which fits your work? Make your investigation relevant, and then it will not overburden you. On the contrary, it will lighten your task.

What investigations are relevant, do you ask? I think there can be no difficulty in answering that. Study to understand the common forms of bodily and mental activity with which the school deals. Study yourselves and study the children. It will profit you more to know all about what you do when you write, and all about what your children are doing when they learn to write, than it will to know about some of the remoter phases of mental or physical life. The truth is that we are not quick to see the value of studying commonplace facts. We want something striking. We study children's preferences for colors, and children's secret languages, and what not, and we find their every-day commonplace activities with which we have to deal in our routine lives entirely escaping us. Or we try to answer some profound question about the nature of attention or memory, or about the forms of reasoning or the categories of thought. Give up all that for the time being. There are problems without number to be solved here at our very hands. They are the direct problems, the productive problems that we need to solve for the sake of our own activities. Let us try to solve them first, and then I am disposed to think that most of the others will disappear.

As we bring this chapter to a close, let us review briefly the ground we have covered. Writing is a complex movement. Its complexity is of the harmonious type which results from thoroughgoing cooperation of the various muscles. This cooperation is brought about through the development of a coordinating center in the nervous system. Individual coordinations exhibit certain typical differences which show that the whole problem of writing is one of individual coordination. The mental processes which parallel the development of muscular coordination may be described by pointing out that when coordination is complete the attention is freed from the producing process and may be devoted to the thoughts expressed. The direction in which attention is turned before writing becomes automatic is clearly indicated by observations which any one can easily make if he will try to develop some relatively undeveloped phase of his own writing—as, for example, the regularity of the slope of his letters. Such an effort to develop regularity of slope will show that attention in non-automatic writing is centered chiefly on the visual results, and on certain visual copies.

The acquaintance we have cultivated with the writing process as it is exhibited in ourselves will make it possible in our next chapter to take up a number of questions in regard to the development of the writing habit in others, especially in children. These studies of the development of the habit in others belong to our teacher-study as legitimate lines of supplementary investigation, and they will serve also to illustrate the unity in spirit which exists between our point of view of self-examination and the point of view of the true child-study, which is the study of growing faculties.

CHAPTER VII

RACIAL AND INDIVIDUAL DEVELOPMENT IN WRITING

A GOOD deal has been said and written about the parallelism between the development of the race and the development of the individual. Indeed, it has sometimes been argued that because there is such a parallelism, we may safely follow the history of the race in arranging the conditions with which to surround the developing child. This direct application of racial conditions to individual life is, however, out of harmony with the fundamental idea of adaptation as we have already studied it in our discussion of the meaning of development. The modern child has before him the problem of fitting himself to the modern, and future environment. He will never be placed in the same environment as was his savage ancestors, and it is a great mistake to drag him back to that primitive environment in the hope of adapting him in that way to the highly complex and highly developed conditions of life which really confront him.

I have made this prefatory statement in the hope of preparing your minds in a negative, as well as in a positive way for the discussion which we have now to take up, for we shall begin our discussion of the way in which the writing habit develops, with an outline of the way in which the race has developed the ability to write. Then we shall trace the parallelism between this general racial development and individual development. And I warn you again that the parallelism is not directly productive in the sense of giving us methods or devices that can be taken up in immediate pedagogical practise. For example, as we go back to the days when men wrote with pictures only, do not begin to think that the child of to-day would profit by a similar ordeal of picture-writing before he attains to symbol-writing. That is not the value of the parallel. The real value of the parallel lies in the fact that in the history of the race's struggle we have a long and complete record of how the human mind and the human hand have, under comparatively simple conditions, grown more and more skilful in this particular art. Having learned in this way something of the principles which underlie this art, something of its aims and purposes as revealed in its development under simple and diverse conditions, we can better attack the much more complex problem of the modern child learning to write under more complex and stable conditions. The development of this individual child will certainly not be the same as that of the race, for the child does not have to develop a system of writing. He has merely to learn what the race has prepared for him to use.

By way of positive statement, we may say that where the child differs from the race we shall look for differences in the conditions surrounding the two processes of development. Where, on the contrary, the motives and tendencies of development are dependent on characteristics of the mind or hand rather than upon variable external conditions, we shall gain from our study of racial development certain positive suggestions about the character of the child's development, in spite of the different ways in which these motives and tendencies actually manifest themselves in the two cases. Our study of the parallel can thus be made productive without our being misled into any effort to find direct applicability of racial history to the work of the school, or without our losing sight for a moment of the fundamental differences as well as the fundamental likenesses between racial and individual development.

The most primitive writing was of the kind which all of you have seen represented in our histories, where they describe the savage condition and early writing of the American Indians. A specimen of such writing is given in Fig. 21. Such writing always consists in a few rough pictures. There was evidently little ability to make fine, regular lines. The writer's muscles were not trained for delicate work. There was not even a clear and fully matured recognition of the form of the objects presented. No details were present, and the whole picture was a sort of rough approximation to the original. But rough and crude as these drawings were, they appealed to the savage's memory and imagination enough to communicate to him certain ideas. What could be more natural than that these lines and figures intended for the eyes, should reproduce that aspect of objects which appealed to the eyes, namely, the form? This primitive writing was, all through, a matter of visual interest and visual recognition. Its purpose was to communicate ideas as clearly and as accurately as possible by an appeal to the eye.

Starting from this primitive picture-writing, human development runs out in two different directions. In the first place, men began to take more and more interest in the reproduction of form. The details of the

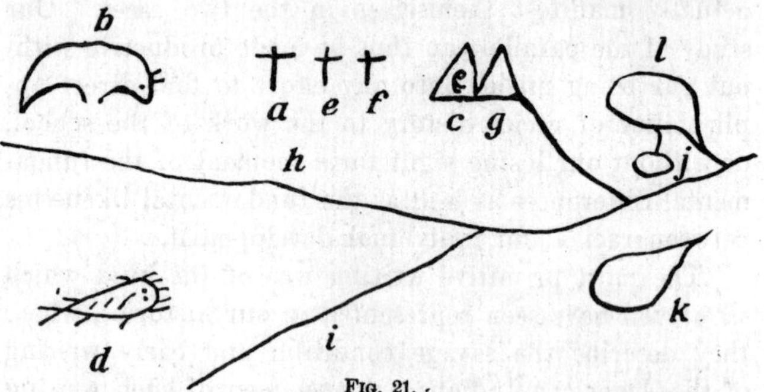

FIG. 21.

An Ojibwa love-letter, recorded and explained by Garrick Mallery in the Annual Report of the Bureau of Ethnology, 1888–'89, p. 363. The writer, a girl of the Bear totem (*b*), summons her lover, who belongs to the Mud Puppy totem (*d*), along the various trails indicated, to the lodge (*c*) from which the beckoning hand protrudes. The enclosed figures at *l*, *j*, and *k* are lakes. The crosses indicate that the girl and her companions are Christians. "The clear indications of locality," writes Mallery, "serve as well as if in a city a young woman had sent an invitation to her young man to call at a certain street and number."

original objects began to receive more attention and to be more accurately and fully incorporated into the reproductions. This refinement of form very soon began to go beyond the limits necessary for the communication of ideas, and an art developed whose chief interest is the higher and higher treatment of form. This art which deals with form appeared at first as drawing, later as sculpture and painting. In these various branches of what we call art in the narrower sense of the term, the direct appeal to the eye is continued and brought to its highest perfection.

The second line of development, which begins with primitive picture-writing, is the one in which we are interested in our present discussion. It is the line of development of writing proper. Here we must recognize a greater devotion than in art to the desire to communicate ideas. The form of the figures used in writing is of interest only in so far as form stands for some kind of meaning. The result of this chief interest in meaning rather than form is that the forms are reduced to their simplest terms. There is, indeed, a point beyond which the form can not be simplified without danger that it lose its power of communicating a distinct idea. Thus, if the savage wishes to make a distinction between horses and cattle, he must keep enough of the distinctive details to insure the communication of the right idea. He accomplishes his end in this particular case by retaining the horns as the distinctive mark of his drawing for cattle. But while form can not be lost sight of entirely, it is so unimportant that purely external causes may contribute to the corruption and simplification of the forms of the drawings. Thus, one such outside consideration is to be found in the fact that straight lines are easier to draw than curved lines in the kinds of materials frequently used for early written records. The result is that not only were forms much simplified in the early stages of writing, but they were simplified in Egypt and Greece and in many other primitive civilizations, so as to be more easily engraved on stone and metal or other inflexible materials.

Some excellent illustrations of corruptions in form are given to us by students of Chinese writing. Chinese writing, as you may know, is not like our own, made up of a few elements. It has a separate symbol for each word. The word for sun, for example, is a single symbol rather than a series of three letters as in our writing. The modern Chinese symbol for sun looks like a ladder with three rounds. At first sight this does not seem to have any relation so far as its form is concerned to the object for which it stands. But compare this modern symbol with another symbol of more ancient origin and the meaning is clear and the modification in form is immediately recognized as due to the general principle that straight lines are easier to draw with the brush-pen of the Chinese than are curved lines. The ancient form for the sun is a picture, consisting of a circle with a dot in the center. The dot of the ancient symbol is the middle round of the modern ladder-shaped symbol. The sides, and the top and bottom rounds of the modern figure, are the final rectilinear remains of the circumference of the ancient circle.

Fig. 22 reproduces a number of ancient and modern Chinese forms which bear out the same conclusions as those reached in the case of the first symbol for the sun.

Form-writing thus developed gradually into what might be called *convenient* or *simplified* form-writing. The convenient writing would not have been possible unless there had been the accompanying mental development away from the form to the meaning. This latter fact of greater and greater emphasis on meaning rather than form, makes the characters used in the writing *symbolic* in their use, and so we refer to such writing as symbolic writing. Finally, we must not lose sight of the fact that even in this symbolic stage, the

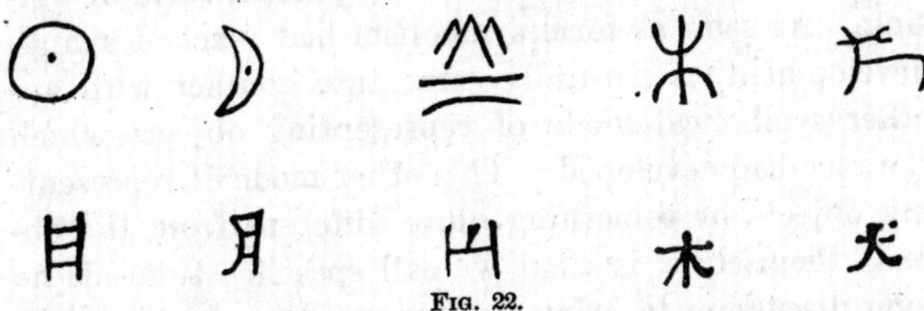

FIG. 22.

The upper line shows ancient forms of Chinese writing, the lower line shows the derived modern forms. The characters signify, reading from left to right: sun, moon, mountain, tree (or wood), dog.

imagination of the reader or writer is aroused directly through the eye. The visual symbol means a visual object, so that these written records constitute a series of purely visual experiences.

The symbolic attitude, or the attitude in which meanings are more attended to than forms, makes possible a wide range for development. Symbols freed from any direct references to objects of like form, came very soon to have two or three meanings, some very remote from the original signification. Thus, in Egypt the figure of the owl came to mean, not only the bird itself, but also, as with us, night, and still more indirectly, wisdom. Among our American Indians, the animal which the Indian chief painted on his totem pole came to stand for the man, and sometimes for the whole tribe. Symbolism of a highly developed type thus became common.

At this point there set in another line of development which was slowly worked out in Egypt and Phenicia, and which has had the greatest possible influence on the development of our present form of writing. As soon as form symbolism had reached a high development, it naturally came into contact with another symbolical mode of representing objects which the race had developed. This other mode of representing objects by something quite different from the objects themselves, is what we call speech. It needs no long discussion to bring to your minds a clear recognition of the fact that speech is a kind of symbolism. A given sound arouses in the imagination an idea which is quite remote from the sound itself. To make this step in the development of writing somewhat clearer, let us put it thus. Here is a given object. When the primitive man looked at that object he received a direct impression. If, now, after having received a direct impression, he wished to arouse in a companion a recollection of such a direct experience, he could do it in one of two ways, either by making a symbolic mark or by making a symbolic sound. The symbolic mark and the symbolic sound had at first no connection except as they both referred to the same object. But very soon the sound symbolism began to assert its superiority. The sound name of an object was so fully developed and so thoroughly familiar that it took precedence as the means of expressing thought. Men did not even stop to recall in full the direct impression made by the sight of the object. They began to do as we do, to think in words, and to let the objective appearances drop into the background. And just as soon as this happened, the written symbol was forced into relations with the sound symbol.

The first steps of this growing relation between sound and written symbols were of a type with which we are all quite familiar. You all know the kind of puzzle called a rebus, in which the first personal pronoun I, for example, is represented by a picture of the organ of sight, which has a name similar in sound. The verb "can" may likewise be represented in a rebus by that convenient tin article of household furniture with which we are familiar. We are thus well on the way to a sentence. "I can see a house," for example, would be easily completed in the same general way so far as the verb "see" is concerned by a picture or symbol of the ocean; and then all we need for the house is a true written symbol of the house itself.

Now this kind of rebus-writing actually appears in some of the old Egyptian records, to show us how sounds and written symbols began to be related. Thus, the Egyptians had a word, the name of one of their gods, which was pronounced *Hesiri*. They also had two distinct words, *hes* and *iri*, exactly like the two syllables of the name *Hesiri*, so far as the sounds were concerned, but in no way related in meaning to the name of this god. The two separate words, *hes* and *iri*, mean, respectively, a seat and an eye. When they wanted to write the name of the god, they did not draw his picture, but they evidently thought of his name, and then, thinking of the sounds only, they made this double pun that he was a seat-eye god. After that the representation of the god was easy, for they drew first the seat and then the eye and let it go at that. Another illustration from Egypt is the use of a basket to mean lord. This usage is perfectly clear as soon as we know that the word for basket and the word for lord were both pronounced *neb*.

Notice that the written symbol is, by this connection with the sound, given a wider range of usefulness than ever before. The picture of a basket, for example, came to stand, not only for the basket itself, and for the act of carrying, and for the idea of plenty, but it came to stand also, through the association with sound, for the word lord.

After this form of rebus-writing, the sound association went forward another step. Instead of using a symbol because of the total sound which it represented, the symbol began to stand for the first sound contained in its name. Thus, to invent an illustration using our own English words. Suppose one wanted to write the word monkey. This being a rather hard animal to draw, the writer would divide the word into two syllables, and would then look around for some object the first syllable of whose name was the same as the first syllable of monkey. *Mon* is the common syllable of the words money and monkey. Use the picture of a coin then to stand for the desired syllable mon, and our word monkey is half written. The last part of the word monkey can be easily represented in the simple rebus fashion by a key.

This way of breaking up words so as to extract the first syllable is a very clumsy device, to be sure. We can hardly understand how the race had ingenuity enough or patience enough to do it. But if you will think a moment you will see that the work of breaking words up into constituent sounds had to be done in some such gradual way as this. It is not an easy thing for the child of the present day to break up words with which he is familiar into their constituent sounds. Have you not heard a child saying over words which contain similar sounds with obvious delight at the similarity he has discovered? The pleasure which children get from such combinations as ding-dong, see-saw, is evidently due to the like sounds at the beginning of these syllables, and the interesting contrast in the later sounds. With such illustrations in mind, it is easy to understand how the old Phenicians gradually, by this comparison between initial syllables, discovered the fundamental sounds and produced a sound alphabet which was capable of expressing all the different possible phonetic variations in their language.

The illustration which we invented of monkey and money is paralleled by real historical facts in abundance. Thus in the ancient Egyptian language the name of the owl began with the sound which we represent to-day by the letter M. The Egyptians came to use the owl as a symbol for this M sound. And as little as one would guess it from the form of our letter M, this letter is the direct historical descendant of the Egyptian symbol of the owl. Fig. 23 will make it clear to you how the line of descent is traced. This series of figures also shows again the fact to which we have already called attention, namely, the fact that as interest in the form of the symbol grows less and less intense, the form will decay and become more and more simple and convenient. It will finally be reduced, as are all our letters, to comparatively simple groups of lines, not resembling even remotely the objects from which the figure was first derived.

Sometimes the historical evidence for this derivation of letters from the first syllable or sound of names, is preserved for us in the names of the letters them-

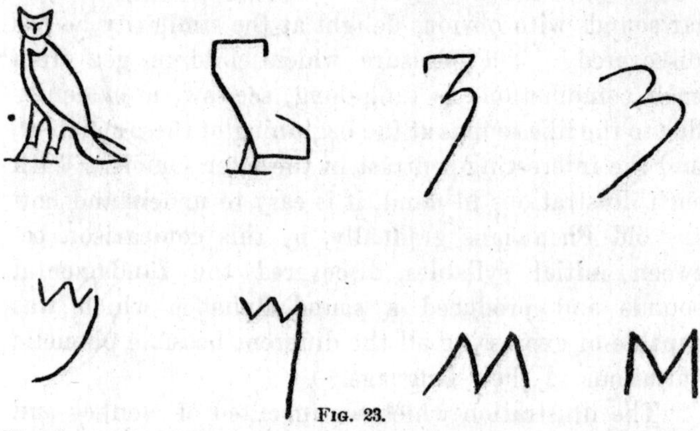

FIG. 23.

The figure shows the derivation of the letter M from the Egyptian hieroglyphic owl. The four forms in the upper part of the figure are Egyptian forms. The first on the left is the usual hieroglyphic picture of the owl, or, as it was called in the Egyptian language, *mulak*. The three remaining upper forms are found in the writings of the Egyptian priests. The first form on the left of the lower series is an ancient Semitic form. Then follow in order an ancient Greek form, and two later Greek forms. (From I. Taylor's The Alphabet, pp. 9 and 10.)

selves. Our own English letters now have names which correspond to the sounds of the letters and these simplified sound names are no longer indicative of the origin of the letters. For significant names we must go back to some of the more ancient alphabets where the letters retain their primitive names. Thus, in the Hebrew alphabet the first letter is aleph, and means ox; the second letter is beth, and means house; the third letter (like our English g) is gimel, and means camel; the fourth is daleth, and means door, and so on.

We have now traced the history of writing down to the point at which it begins to be a means of representing sounds rather than direct visual experiences. We should recognize clearly that the primitive attitude of mind was one of attention to form. That the gradual emancipation of attention from form and its transfer to meaning was complicated with the secondary line of development which grew out of the necessity of subjugating written symbolism to the more fully developed sound symbolism of speech. All this development was very ancient. The Greeks emerge from their early association with the Oriental world fully equipped with a sound alphabet, which was, doubtless, borrowed largely from the Phenicians. The Romans learned the same alphabet from their Italian ancestors and later modified it through their own use and through contact with the later Greek forms.

The forms of our own letters are derived in very direct lines of descent from the Roman forms, so that we may confine our attention to the Roman alphabet and the later European alphabets derived from the Roman.

The earliest Roman forms were used on monuments, and owe their form very largely to the hard materials on which they were traced. The letters were made up almost entirely of straight lines and sharp angles. They were all very nearly uniform in height, and were written without connections between the successive letters and without breaks between words. Fig. 24 gives an illustration of this earliest type of writing, as used even in some of the later Roman manuscripts. One needs only to look at the letters to recog-

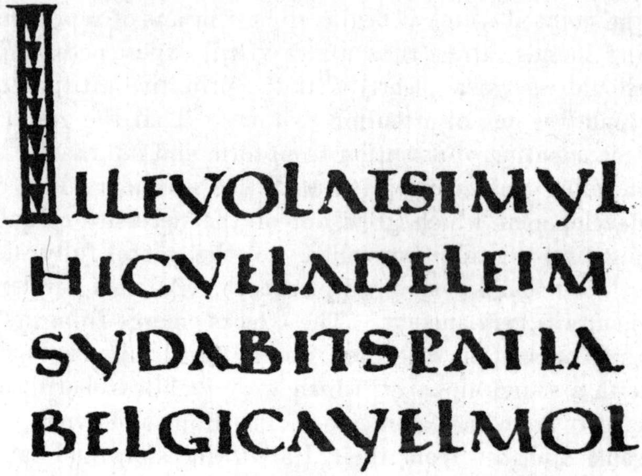

ILLEVOLATSIMVL
HICVELADELEIM
SVDABITSPATIA
BELGICAVELMOL

FIG. 24.

Roman capitals from a manuscript of Vergil's Georgics. The letters here reproduced show the first parts of four successive lines and are to be deciphered as follows:

Ille volat simul . . .
Hic vel ad Elei m . . .
Sudabit spatia . . .
Belgica vel mol . . .

(Copied from Arndt's *Tafeln.*)

nize at once that in the modern world many of these same Roman capitals are still doing service where straight, angular letters of great legibility are desirable and possible.

The capitals represent what we may call the maximum of legibility. It would be difficult to improve upon these forms if mere legibility were the only consideration in the formation of letters. But there are other considerations than mere legibility. The capitals are very clumsy letters to write. One could not write very rapidly when he had to make those sharp angles and separate letters.

The demand for a more rapid form of writing must have made itself felt very early. Indeed, we have evi-

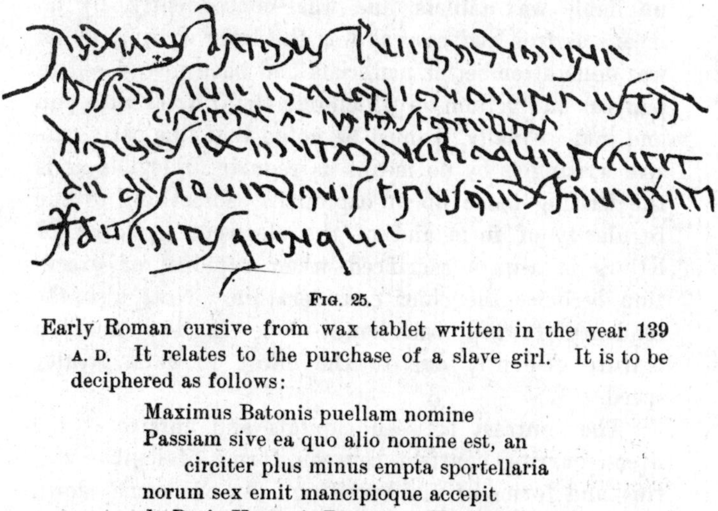

FIG. 25.

Early Roman cursive from wax tablet written in the year 139 A. D. It relates to the purchase of a slave girl. It is to be deciphered as follows:

Maximus Batonis puellam nomine
Passiam sive ea quo alio nomine est, an
circiter plus minus empta sportellaria
norum sex emit mancipioque accepit
de Dasio Verzonis Pirusta ex Kavieretí
* ducentis quinque.

(Copied from Arndt's *Tafeln.*)

dence from a few business records belonging to the beginning of the Christian era that even the early Romans had a rapid running hand which was used for ordinary business records. In Fig. 25 you see a specimen of this early Roman cursive, as it is called. This cursive differs from the capitals in a number of characteristics. The letters tend to run into each other. Indeed, in some cases in even the earliest cursive, there are connecting lines or ligatures between the letters. These ligatures are regular and pronounced characteristics of all the later forms of cursive. Their less frequent appearance in the early forms is due to the fact that this writing was done for the most part on very unpliable wax tablets, and was, consequently, by no means as free and easy as was the later writing which was done after better materials had been discovered in papyrus and vellum on which one could write with pen and ink. Finally, it must be noted that this early cursive writing is by no means as regular or legible as is the writing made up of capitals. Something of the regularity of form and of the clear-cut legibility of letters is always sacrificed when rapidity of execution becomes the chief consideration. Note also the tendency toward back-hand slope in the lines, a feature evidently due to the effort to gain greater speed.

The contrast between capitals and cursive is the ever-recurring contrast between forms of legible writing and forms of rapid writing. As one comes down through the later periods of the history of writing, he finds a succession of forms devised like the capitals for legibility and beauty, and on the other hand he finds other forms devised for rapid and easy writing. The tendency of the beautiful and very legible forms is to become more and more regular and difficult to make, and the tendency of the rapid forms is to become more and more difficult to read. Human nature does not seem to have changed much in these respects.

After the Roman capitals and the early cursive, there grew up a kind of compromise form which was more rapid and less angular than the capitals, and hence easier to write. It was used, however, only by the book-making scribes, for it was still too difficult for ordinary use. This form is reproduced in Fig. 26 and

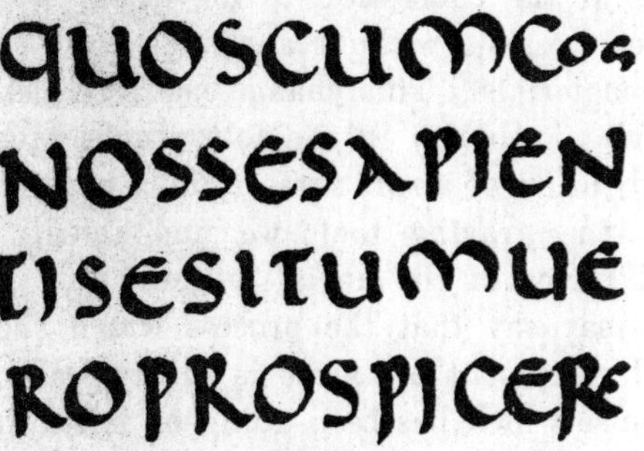

QUOSCUMCOG
NOSSESAPIEN
TISESITUMUE
ROPROSPICERE

FIG. 26.

Uncials from a manuscript of Cicero's De Republica. The manuscript was probably written in the third century. The lines are to be deciphered as follows:

quoscumque cog
nosse sapien
tis est tumue
ro prospicere

(Copied from Arndt's *Tafeln.*)

is the so-called uncial form. A typical letter in this form is the letter *e*, which is no longer angular as it was in the capitals, but is much more like our lower-case letter. The derivation of this round *e* from the square capital is sufficiently direct to be obvious. The motive for inventing this new form is also obvious. The round letter is much more economical in the number of movements which it requires. In the square capital, the upper and lower horizontal strokes and the one vertical stroke, all had to be made separately. In the round letter, one uninterrupted curved movement was substituted for the three separate movements just mentioned. The single curved movement is therefore to be looked upon as a concession to the demands of movement. But the concession to movement would never have been possible without a change from the earlier writing materials. This change has been described by an eminent authority in the following sentence: "To the substitution of a soft surface for a hard one, of the pen for the graving tool, we undoubtedly owe the rounded forms of the uncial letters." [1]

One may say that the process which shows itself in the development of this *e* is the typical process of compromise which has been going on since the Roman period even down to our own time. There is a constant and growing concession to the demand for easier movement on the one side, and a clear effort on the other side to preserve the legibility and beauty of the letter. The great variety of forms invented since that early date are nothing more nor less than the experiments of the race in legibility and beauty, and ease and fluency of writing.

During these experiments almost every conceivable form has been tried. The widest extremes have been reached and fortunately abandoned. The cursive grew so illegible in the thirteenth century, we are told, that

---

[1] E. M. Thompson, Ency. Brit., 9th ed., vol. xviii, p. 145.

Frederick II was obliged to prohibit its use. The tendencies toward elaboration among the careful and artistic writers went to such extremes that we are told of months spent on a single letter.

With the invention of printing there entered a factor which tended to put a stop to experimenting with forms. The makers of types began to select from among the various scripts used by the scribes of the time, and the alphabet began to settle into its final form. The German printers, for example, selected the forms we know as the Gothic letters. The world has decided that the German printers made a mistake, and most of the rest of us, and even some of the better German printers of to-day, are using the much simpler and more legible forms of the old Roman capitals and later uncials.

The invention of printing also fixed out English script. We borrowed the style of letter that had been made permanent by an Italian printer. Before we turn to that matter, however, let us glance at one or two forms of medieval script which will show us what we escaped. Fig. 27 reproduces one of the most elaborate and fantastic of the early scripts. It is without the virtues of beauty or legibility, and it was too elaborate to survive in a busy world. On the other hand, the specimen of Anglo-Saxon writing shown in Fig. 28 certainly is beautiful and legible; its cardinal, and fatal fault is its elaborate and unwieldy form.

We are indeed fortunate in the form of script which was finally adopted in England. We are fortunate as compared, for example, with the Germans, who are even to this day struggling with an elaborate and angular form of writing. And it is to Italy, as I said a moment ago, that we owe our script. In the days of Queen Elizabeth the educated Englishman went to Italy

FIG. 27.

A specimen of Merovingian cursive from the year 688 A. D. The part here reproduced is the end of the first line of the manuscript. The four lines which appear below the letters and extend into the writing, are the upper loops of some of the letters of the line just below the one here reproduced. The letters are to be deciphered as follows:

Ideoque vestra cognuscat industria quod nos

(Copied from Arndt's *Tafeln.*)

to gain the polish which comes from contact with an older civilization—much as we go to Europe—and from Italy he brought back a simple, beautiful, running script. This script was borrowed from the form of printed letters which we call italics. The very name italics shows you that the type was made in Italy. The story goes that one of the famous printers by the name of Manutius Aldus, who did his work early in the sixteenth century, copied the handwriting of the great scholar Petrarch, and that Pope Julius, in recognition of the beauty of his new type, granted Aldus exclusive right to use the same. This type of Aldus became our italics, and undoubtedly was one of the most influential factors in determining our modern form of script.

The general form of our letters was thus fixed after long periods of development. The race had to experiment a great deal in order to settle certain questions. But it has settled some matters definitely for us who inherit the benefits of all this experimentation. No one can tell us in these days that the chief function of handwriting is to be as legible as possible. We have a model of regularity and legibility in our printed capi-

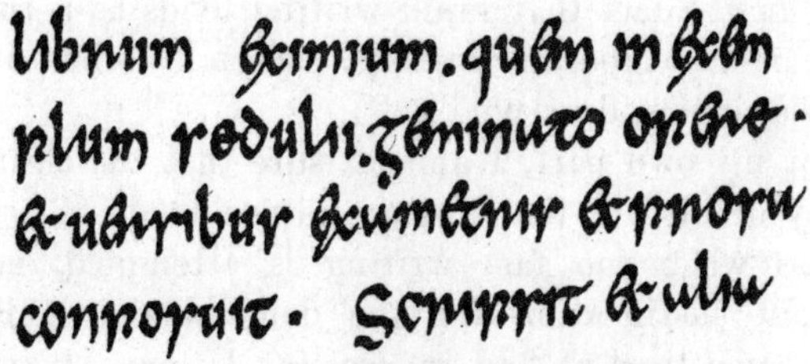

FIG. 28.

Anglo-Saxon forms from the eighth century. This is a manuscript of Beda's History. The lines are to be deciphered as follows:

librum eximium, quem in exem
plum Sedulii geminato opere,
et versibus exametris et prosa
conposuit. Scripsit et alia

(Copied from Arndt's *Tafeln.*)

tals, and we have preserved these forms in our printing just because they were very regular and very legible; but our fathers some hundreds of years ago gave up the employment of these capitals for the ordinary uses of every-day life and compromised with the legitimate demands for fluency and ease of execution.

It would seem as though the forms of many centuries might be appealed to in settling certain other questions. For example, all cursives have a certain running slope which grows too great when one writes very rapidly and carelessly, and which tends to disappear when one tries to write the most legible hand that can possibly be written. Perhaps it was an accident that Petrarch wrote with something of a slant. Perhaps it is an accident that most fluent writing of the type which imitates italics has a slant. Perhaps it is not an accident. Certainly history offers us a plain lesson in the fact that rapid writing tends as a rule to slant; more elaborate writing, especially when it becomes drawing, does not.

For my own part, I am not sure that the clear testimony of history that human nature tends to become careless when too fast writing is attempted, is not sufficient justification for the demand that children spend some time at first in *drawing* letters. I am not sure that the final slant of letters should not be allowed to appear after the drawing stage has passed. I am not sure, in short, that the compromise between the two tendencies toward legibility and rapidity does not have to be worked out in each individual.

I wish I might induce each one of you before I leave this brief historical sketch to interest yourselves in some study of these matters. There is a very good article under the title Paleography in the Encyclopedia Britannica which all of you could read, and any good library will have other material on the subject which will show you how much we depend for our present forms of writing on the labor of past generations. It is history of this type that will make us a little slower than we sometimes are in introducing sweeping innovations into our schools.

Of course, history can not solve all our doubts and difficulties. We must progress and improve, and progress means a better fitting of historical inheritances to present needs. With an alphabet evolved through long centuries on the one hand, and with the modern child on the other hand, the teacher's task is clear. What the study of history does not settle definitely, the study of present-day human nature will tend to make more plain. If we are in doubt as to whether children should draw or write at first, let us study the modern facts as revealed in modern men and children, and let us try to answer our question from such studies.

Our studies of adult habits of writing and of historical developments of letters have led us to a general point of view which we shall adopt in the rest of our study. An easy, fluent, well-coordinated movement, producing letters of a fair degree of legibility, is the end at which we aim. The movement must be highly developed enough in the end to be automatic, so that attention may be free to follow the thoughts expressed. And in looking toward this end, we must realize that the child has to pass through stages of immaturity at which the movement is not fluent, and attention is not free, at which the forms of letters must be studied, and at which the mind is absorbed in the process of writing rather than in comprehending meanings.

Certainly one can easily approach the practical problem of cultivating an easy, fluent movement in the child, from the negative side, by watching a child trying to write. If there is anything that can be definitely said of the child's efforts, it is that they are not fluent and easy. The child's movements are jerky and discontinuous. They are cramped, and excessive in the amount of energy which they require. They are uncertain, and seem to surprise the child as much as they do the teacher. In short, there is obvious lack of control and organization. We have already suggested that the adult can acquaint himself with the accompanying mental attitude which attends the child's efforts to write, by trying to perform the same task with his own untrained muscles. Under such conditions the adult's movements will also show lack of control and lack of organization.

All these excessive and unorganized movements of the child are the raw material, if we may use that term, out of which a fluent, easy movement must be developed. The child's movements and those of the adult when he tries to use unpractised muscles, are called diffuse movements. You will have no difficulty with that word, I am sure, for nothing is more obvious than that the untrained movements are too much spread out. The right muscle does not contract at the right time, and the whole irregular mass of activities lacks organization in just the way indicated by the word diffuse. And diffusion of movements can be understood when we recall our earlier discussion of the disturbing effects of sudden loud sounds on the regularity and control of movement. The real seat of diffusion is not in the muscles, but in the nervous system. When the muscles move diffusely this is sure evidence that the impulse in the nervous system has been spread out or diffused, rather than carried along definite fixed channels. And finally, this diffusion of impulses in the child's brain not being due to any sudden strength of the impulse, as it was in the cases of disturbance through sudden sounds, is explained by the fact that in the child the brain mass is itself unorganized and diffuse. The regular lines of connection necessary for coordination have not yet been laid down. An impulse is free to wander about and shoot out at this point or at the other, in a very irregular and uncoordinated fashion. The child's brain, therefore, needs organization to overcome this natural diffuse state; and the irregular movements with which he starts are, as we have said, the raw materials for development to work over.

I want to digress from our main discussion for a moment to call your attention to the fact that if it were not for this diffuse condition of the child's nervous system, there would be no hope of cultivating any individual habits of action. Suppose that all the possible lines of connection through the brain were inherited by the new-born infant ready for action. Then every form of movement would be fully provided for, and the infant would simply go ahead in a prescribed way without any possibilities of bringing forth in his own experience original forms of action. This is very nearly a true description of the condition of such an animal as the chick. The young chick just out of the shell, has a brain which is inherited in an almost completely organized condition. The young chick can, therefore, do whatever it is going to do in life fairly well from the very first; but it has no large possibilities of developing individual modes of action. Diffusion, as opposed to the chick's condition, means possibilities of organization. Absence of diffusion means completed development, and completed development always has a negative side. Where you have completed development you can not have possibilities of new and original individual habits.

With this word of digression to remind you that the child's diffuse nervous condition and diffuse movements are the necessary raw material for the development of a fluent individual form of writing movement, we proceed to discuss one or two of the details of this matter of diffusion.

One of the most noticeable facts about the child's diffuse movements is the fact that these movements are excessive, especially the movements of the finer muscles. Somewhere or other the false notion has crept into our pedagogy that the child's fine muscles do not develop until later than the large muscles. How can one believe such a false statement when he sees a young infant clutching with its little fingers and exhibiting in this grip one of its strongest movements? How can one believe this dogma when he sees the boys and girls in the first grade doing all the work that they do in writing with the fine finger muscles—literally overdoing this work in a very noticeable degree? The fact is, the finer muscles are in full operation very early in life. Indeed, they are the muscles which in diffuse movements are most apt to be called into action. It requires a less powerful excitation from the nervous centers to set the fine muscles into action. They contract at the slightest stimulation. These are the muscles which always grow tense first in later life when the brain becomes overexcited. In emotional excitement, for example, it is the fine muscles of the face and hand that are first affected. One's fingers are folded into his fist long before he strikes the angry blow; one's jaw is set long before he speaks the angry word. In short, diffusion always exaggerates first of all the movements of the fine muscles.

It is clear, however, from our earlier study of adult handwriting that the fingers alone can not do the work. The fingers become cramped—they must have an opportunity to straighten out. They must be carried forward by the arm in order to get across the page. These additional arm movements are made by the child, not as well-coordinated additions to the finger movements, but rather as separate and clumsy interruptions of the finger movement. The child writes with the fingers until they are so cramped that he can write no more. Then he stops the finger movement entirely and with a sigh he carries his hand across the page and settles down after this interruption to more writing with the fingers. While the finger writing goes on, the hand and arm are all the time, through the diffusion of the stimulation, kept tense and ready to move. Indeed, while we are noticing the fact that the fingers are the parts that are most affected by diffusion, do not let us fail to recognize the fact that a great many other muscles are sharing in the diffusion. Not only the writing arm is diffusely contracted, but the other arm also is having its part in the agony of effort. Have you not seen the left hand under the desk folded in a grip almost strong enough to drive the nails into the flesh? Have you not seen the left elbow drawn up against the side as if it would fain get over and help the right hand? This is all diffusion. So are also the facial contortions and the bodily movements and the movements of the legs. The bending of the head down to the paper, of which we complain so much, and which some people have falsely told us can be corrected by using this or that patent pen, or desk, or paper, is a natural consequence of the diffusion of the motor impulse throughout the whole body, and is also the natural bodily expression of intense visual attention.

In movement, as in every other sphere, nature attacks her problems of development by producing more than she needs and then picking out the best. Nature produces more flower-seeds in a single year than could grow on hundreds of times the amount of soil available on this earth, and then she lets the seeds struggle against each other until the best and strongest survive. And so it is with movement. Nature starts out with a diffuse brain as if she would say to the individual, "I will not place any restrictions upon you, but will let you have at first all the possible movements to select from." She stirs up the brain in all directions, and the diffuse movements begin to appear in abundance. There are movements of the head and arms and feet and trunk. Not all are necessary to the final form of action, and most will drop away as development goes on. But in the whole mass of movement the right ones must be there, and development means the selection of the right movements out of the total mass of diffuse movements. Only one limitation appears in all this provision of many movements. That is the limitation we have noted. No mechanism could be devised which would not, in the general stimulation of the muscles, affect the small muscles more than the large ones.

This limitation in nature's provision for free movement, is the first point at which the teacher's rational mode of developing the child must come in to supplement nature's provisions. The teacher should see to it that if diffusion tends to emphasize the small muscles, teaching should emphasize in due measure the large muscles. Thus, some teachers begin the teaching of writing by free use of the blackboard, because on the blackboard the larger movements have better opportunity to show themselves. Even if you try this, you will notice that through diffusion the fingers grasp the crayon too intensely, but yet the larger arm movement will be called into play, and that is well. Blackboard writing for a whole class, and during many years of school training, has many obvious objections, and so it is well to devise some other method of supplementing nature and of calling the large muscles into play. Large arm exercises are the most available devices for attaining this end.

I am well aware that these large arm exercises are by no means novelties in our teaching of writing. What we need, however, is to come to recognize them, not as mere incidental exercises to be taken now and then, but as the staple forms of early writing lessons. I am fully acquainted with the desire of children and even of parents, that the ability to produce actual writing should be cultivated as early as possible. I am also aware of the fact that teachers do not commonly see any immediate results from these large free exercises. Indeed, time and time again, I have seen neat, regular letters produced in copy-books by classes who never had any of these large arm circles or ovals. But our discussion up to this point has failed of its whole aim if you are not convinced that neat letters in a copy-book are not the ends of writing instruction. You are not succeeding in your duties as teachers if you are led by the desires of parents and children rather than by the larger considerations of final development. Look at the children who learn to write early, and who learn under a teacher who neglects the free exercises. I care not what their copy-books contain, look at their hands and arms. See them laboriously and in a cramped position carving out forms as the ancients used to before the beginning of the Christian era. Let us put an end to all this! Let us give up the notion of writing too soon, and let us train the arm with its larger coordinations, systematically and conscientiously, until its movements shall become through training coordinate in number and importance with the finger movements of which nature has furnished such a superabundance.

If we could have such frequent exercises in arm movements we could well afford to leave the ordinary writing exercises entirely out of our school programs for at least two years.

I do not wish to be understood as subscribing to the doctrine that is being offered to teachers by certain prominent educators, that writing should be left to grow up "incidentally" in connection with manual training and shop work. Writing seems to me to be too important a part of school training, too closely connected with reading, and too complex a form of activity to be neglected. Activities of such a complex type may grow up incidentally if conditions are not too loose, but then they will grow up in what we have called a non-rational way. Better far that we should devote the energy of the school to a rational cultivation of the right kind of movement. Let us have writing exercises, but let these exercises be planned to supplement nature, not to hurry nature, nor yet to leave the whole task to nature.

Another important step in supplementing nature, besides that which I have mentioned of having many free exercises of the large muscles before the school writing is taken up, is to recognize and act upon the principle that the writing teacher is not concerned merely with the hand that does the writing, but is responsible for a training of the body as well. During the effort to write, the child is wholly unconscious of the diffuse movements which keep the other arm and the face and the legs in motion. It is not enough to tell him to sit up straight from time to time, we must train him to sit up straight. The only way to get good position in writing is for the teacher to make just as much of a point of position as he makes of the work done on paper. Remember that it is the habit of the child that you are training, not the end of the pen. You can get good copy to show your superintendent even if you neglect position, but you can never train good writers.

The third principle I wish to lay down is one that involves some dangerous possibilities of misapplication. And yet in spite of these possibilities of misuse, I wish to emphasize this third principle as perhaps more important than any other. Briefly put it is this, every child should be allowed to sit and hold his pen and paper, and move his hand in the way best suited to develop his own individual mode of action. Every child is an individual problem to the teacher.

I said that this statement involves a good many possible dangers. In the hands of a careless or uninterested teacher, a class that is allowed individual liberty simply goes wrong at almost every point. Such a class does not have, however, what we should call individual liberty, it has rather license. The teacher who is careless and lets the children do as they please is by no means following the injunction to let the children do what is individually best for them.

I once saw a class in a school where the teachers were trying to develop the principle of individual training, and in that class about half the children were holding the pen between the first and middle fingers. Now, I shall by no means make the assertion that this position of the pen is bad. On the contrary, I have found that it is, in practical life, a very common position of the pen —certainly more common than the orthodox position which is described as pointing over the right ear. But, good or bad, the position of the pen in that class was wholly without justification. We found on some inquiry that the position in question had recently been imported into the class by a boy in one corner of the room, and that it had spread as a sort of fad. The children were many of them having difficulty with it, but it was the fashion, and hence was being accepted. I am not sure that children have not a right to introduce fads into the writing class. Certainly there has been much introducing of fads among their elders. But what I object to in this particular case is the interpretation which the teacher gave the principle of individual training. To leave the child to pick up whatever strikes his fancy is not individual training, it is educational anarchy. What that teacher needed to learn was the fact which I am trying to make clear in this statement to you. Individual training means a careful study of individual needs, and a suggestive, helpful guidance on the part of the teacher.

Helpful guidance should try to work out such a problem as that on which the children just mentioned were working, namely, the problem of holding the pen correctly. I often ask teachers whether they have ever worked out that problem of holding the pen. I will venture the generalization on the basis of a good deal of past experience in asking this question that if we could get a free expression of opinion on this topic, we should find that the directions given in the books are very seldom really accepted by teachers themselves, and even less frequently accepted by practical people. As a matter of adult writing, each of us holds his pen as he can best use it. Each of us has determined that position by a good deal of practise and non-rational adjustment. This lack of uniformity in actual practise is the outcome of a system of education which went forward according to an assumed rule of uniformity in training. How much time do you suppose you and I lost because we had to hold our pens in a position wholly unadapted to our needs? Are we any better off because there was a theoretical rule about pens preached to us every day? If not, what would have helped us?

Would it not have been better for the teacher to have given up preaching a purely theoretical formula about how the pen should be held, and to have helped us in developing our own way as rapidly and as well as possible? It is not an innovation in real life that I am asking you to consider. For in real life, the boy or girl does, sooner or later, develop his own position in spite of his teacher. What I am asking you to consider is the advisability of abandoning a false theory of impossible uniformity and of adopting the more rational method of helping the boy or girl in what he or she will do, and what he ought to do in any case. If this is an innovation in pedagogical theory and practise, then so much the worse for the theory and practise.

What I have said about the holding of the pen I should like to repeat about many of the other phases of writing. I should like to venture even on that most delicate of all topics, the topic of the form and slope of letters, far enough to say that I believe the day is coming when the pedagogical world will be at peace on this question, because it will be seen that writing is not a question of forms and slopes, but of individual habits. After a copy has been set long enough to make the young child recognize the fact that the race has a better alphabet than he could invent offhand, I believe that the copy has lost its chief significance. Let the child learn the essential features of this copy by drawing the letters ever so carefully at first, if that seems best, but do not be guilty of confounding writing with drawing. Those teachers who keep the boys and girls at the task of making beautiful copy when they ought to be writing, will have left us when we grow wise enough to let each child have his own slope, and it will be better for the schools.

One more suggestion and I am through with the part of our discussion which deals with movement. Every teacher should try to hasten the cooperation of arm movements and finger and hand movements by insisting on rapid writing as soon as the drawing period of the child's training is passed. This again requires a pedagogical insight that shall look beyond the dreadful scrawls which will be produced at first. It requires insight that sees that the true teaching of writing consists in securing beauty *and fluency,* not merely beauty of form. If beautiful copy is what you insist on having at first and always, then do not accept this suggestion. But if you can see that the child must somehow work out complete coordination of his movements, and if you can persuade yourself that there must be a period of faithful devotion to the development of this coordination under the guidance and helpful criticism of a wise teacher, then make it impossible for hand and arm to work apart, by demanding that the total speed be such as to make separate action less convenient than cooperation. If you wish to accept this suggestion in a conservative way, introduce in the very first years, an exercise of a few minutes in rapid writing at the end of a regular copying period. But in some form or other consider the advisability of cultivating fluency of these movements in school.

And now there is one more topic on which I have to touch very briefly. It is the topic of the child's attention during writing. In what direction is the child's attention turned? There can be no question about where it is not turned during the early years. It is not turned to the meaning of what he writes. I think another negative statement can be made on the basis of our earlier discussions with equal certainty. The child's attention is not turned to his movements. When we turn from these negative statements to show where the child's attention is turned, positive statement must be made in a somewhat more tentative way, for the child's attention seems to be divided between the copy and his own written letters. Probably his own letters are the factors which most naturally attract his attention. Every teacher has been drilled into the recognition of this division of the child's attention between copy and the child's own productions, by the effort which has to be expended in conforming to what is supposed to be the all-important and necessary duty of bringing the child back to the copy.

Let us consider the question of the advisability of concentrating so much attention on the copy. In the first place, the copy is unquestionably necessary at first. It is valuable in that it conveys to the child the experience of the race in regard to the advantageous form of any given letter. The copy is the social inheritance, and we say in effect to the child when we give him the copy, "imitate that as you imitate other social practises." The child strives to imitate. He comes very soon to get the fundamental lines well in mind. But now the difficulty is that he can not get regularity and fluency enough into his movement to reproduce these forms in a practical way. His muscles do not respond to his mental picture, and he gets poor products. We say to him again, this time in so many words, "look at your copy." He looks at his copy, and, without realizing fully the defect in his own work, and certainly without having the muscular control to do perfect work, he tries again to imitate.

Would it not be better to stop this mere reference to the copy in the hope of attaining non-rational imitation, and to substitute for the merely imitative attitude, a critical attitude on the part of the child toward his own work? Do you suppose a child would fail to recognize the fact, if you told him, that his own *l* was too flat, or his *o* too much opened at the top, quite as easily as he could see it by looking at his copy? To be sure, his copy would show him these things if he would examine it, but he does not ordinarily examine copy under our present method of instruction. It takes more training than he has to examine copy with a view to making a critical comparison with his own work. The copy shows certain forms to his eyes, but it does not discuss these matters with him as a living, intelligent teacher might. Thus, how easy it would be to get a boy to compare his own *u* with his own *n*, and he would learn quite as much in this way as by looking at copy. Show a boy the interesting things about his own writing, and you may make his improvement of his writing more interesting and intelligent.

Indeed, the strong tendency which shows itself in every individual's development is to accept his own forms sooner or later in spite of the copy. We ultimately grow tired of trying to recall the impossible, or at least impracticable regularity of copy, and we settle down to making forms which we consider adequate. If our teachers had only thought of this and had only helped us to cultivate proper ideals within our reasonable grasp, how much better writers we might be to-day! And now when we have come to occupy the positions of teachers, let us give up so much referring of our pupils to a dumb copy, and let us try to improve the boy's own style by individual criticisms.

During the first two years of actual writing, after the free-arm exercises, the copy may be retained as the standard of appeal. After the first year of actual writing, the copy need not, and should not, be made the chief guide. This first year is what I have referred to before as the drawing period of training in the forms of letters. After that first year, the form of the letters ought to be perfectly familiar. Then appeal to the child's own sense of symmetry and beauty, and concentrate training on the task of developing fluency. Allow the child some reasonable freedom in the construction of his letters, but criticize his writing with him. Compare his iregular letters with his own regular letters. Show him how to try again on the basis of his own past efforts. In short, substitute a living, rational teacher and a self-criticizing pupil for lifeless copy. The only value of copy after the form is mastered, consists in its repeated, but too often unheeded, exhortation to regularity and symmetry. After the fifth year there ought not to be any need of criticism. If there is, do not be afraid to use it, but certainly do not use it in the old and non-rational way of presenting mere copy.

The final problem of writing instruction carries us over into our next topic which deals with reading. When written characters begin to have meaning, the art of reading has generally been developed to a high degree. There is one condition necessary to fulfil in the development of the movement, before the advantages of the art of reading can be fully applied to one's own writing. That condition we have already discussed in our treatment of the question of the automatic character of writing. Reading can never be applied to writing until the attention becomes free in some degree to devote itself to meaning rather than to form. Just in the degree in which the child comes to be free from attention to copy and to the form of his own letters, just in that degree can he think of meanings. The art of seeing meanings in words is, however, a complex mental process, not connected merely with a mastery of the writing movements. We shall, therefore, treat the whole question of seeing meanings in the written words, more appropriately in our next discussion.

CHAPTER VIII

THE PROCESS OF READING

The methods of teaching reading have been very radically modified within the memory of our generation. The spelling-book with its long lists of unconnected words as the necessary introduction to reading, is no longer to be found in our schools. The method of deciphering new words letter by letter is no longer allowed. The monotonous formulas with which the first readers used to begin, are gone, with very little prospect of ever being heard from again. Instead, we have the modern nature-study reader with its phonetic alphabet. We have the reedited literary masterpiece from which even the primary grade pupil is supposed to derive high and worthy thoughts while he is gently led, without all the tumult of former days, into the intricacies of our unphonetic English orthography.

It is as if teachers had suddenly cast off the old notion that children can not grasp meanings in what they read, and had admitted the youngest child into the largest possible use of reading as a means of getting information. Where the old schoolmaster was satisfied to drill his pupils in the forms of reading, was satisfied to take almost any sort of reading material if he could only get the right pauses and the proper rising and falling inflections, we pass lightly over the formal considerations and seek to emphasize the import of what is read. We are everywhere seeking the shortest possible road to meanings. If a word can be recognized as a single whole without breaking it up into its letters, so much the better, we say, for it is the word as a whole that has meaning, not the letters that enter into the word. If a new word can be introduced in such a connection that its meaning shall be apparent without a formal definition, so much the better, we say, for it is the meaning in a practical form, not in a stilted definition, that we are aiming to cultivate. And so on in every detail of our modern reading, it is the meaning that we are striving to bring out.

All this is in the fullest accord with the spirit of our modern lives. There was once a time when reading was a kind of accomplishment. That was in the days when reading of Latin was quite as necessary a part of a gentleman's education as the reading of English. That was in the days when men did not read the newspaper every morning and did not have bulky correspondence to look over in their business. In those days a book or two a year, or even less, constituted the total reading of a family. The Bible, an almanac or two, Pilgrim's Progress, and a few other religious and medical works, made up the family library. But within a half century how all this has changed! One almost hesitates to count up the amount of reading done by even the ordinary man to-day. The common workman reads in these days. Of course he cares little for the short pauses at commas, and the long pauses at periods, and the other formal considerations. He wants the meaning of what he reads. And when his boy or girl goes to school, he wants that boy or girl to learn to read, not to learn to declaim. He sees, and we teachers see, that reading is not an end in itself, but rather a means to something higher.

So eager are we in the pursuit of meanings in our teaching of reading that we sometimes fail to realize that there are any mechanical and formal requirements that must be fulfilled before the child can attend to meanings. It is all the easier for us to overlook the earlier mechanical steps that lead up to the recognition of meaning, because in our developed adult lives reading has become, on its mechanical side, a purely automatic process. We do not realize that there is any process lying between our looking at a printed or written word and our recognition of the significance of that word. We do not see the process of development through which the individual passes in any such way as we see it in the case of writing, and so we not only do not realize the complexity of the process, but we do not realize that it is there at all.

Our first aim in this study of reading must therefore be to bring to consciousness what does not naturally present itself to adult consciousness—namely, the nature of the process which precedes and conditions our recognition of meanings.

In undertaking a complete study of the reading process, attention naturally turns, first of all, to the eyes which receive the impressions from the printed or written page. It has been possible, by means of photographs and by means of recording apparatus attached to the eyes of adults, to discover with a good deal of exactness just what the eyes do during reading.[1] They do not travel continuously along the line which is being read, but they move along in three or four steps from the beginning to the end of the line. That is, they move through distances which measure about an inch along the printed line, then they pause for a moment, and after the pause, move through another inch. After crossing the page in this series of steps, they come back in one long continuous sweeping movement to the beginning of the next line and then proceed again by steps across the page.

During each period of movement, the eyes see nothing. It is only during the pauses between movements that the eyes see. This has been demonstrated in a variety of ways by some of the ingenious scientific investigators who have studied the problem of how the eyes behave during reading. There is one very simple way of demonstrating these facts, to which Professor Dodge has called attention.[2] Take a looking-glass and try to see your own eyes move. They will never be seen moving. During actual movement, the eyes do not see anything. It is only when they stand still and fixate some point that conscious recognition is possible. It is evident, then, that the points where the eyes stop in their steps across the page are the points of interest to us in our study of reading. At such points the eyes see before and behind, taking in all the surround-

[1] Erdmann and Dodge, Psychologische Untersuchungen über das Lesen, 1898. Huey, Amer. Jour. of Psychology, 1900, p. 283.

[2] Psychological Review, vol. vii (1900), p. 456, and in earlier works there referred to.

ing letters at a single glance and then step on to the next point of fixation.

The number of points of fixation is of interest to us, for this number shows us what is the range of letters or words that can be taken in at a single glance. Make the observation for yourself sometime. Sit down in front of some one who is reading, and notice how the eyes move. Count the number of steps in passing across a line. You will find that the number of steps will differ from line to line and from individual to individual. It would be an interesting study if some one would make a table of the different ways in which different individuals move their eyes across a given line of print. Think, for example, of the difference between an adult and a child in this respect. A few observations that I have made, show that children move the eyes very slowly across the page, taking many more steps than do adults. How many such steps a child takes, one can sometimes see from the way in which the child uses the finger to point to the place. The finger is a kind of landmark to aid the eyes in their fixation, and it helps in keeping the path during the long journey through the jungle of letters where short, uncertain steps are in danger of going astray.

These facts of movement are of importance when we study the process of recognition of words. It is evident from the very movements that in adult life we do not treat the letters as separate objects of attention. We look at the letters in groups. This fact has been demonstrated in certain other experiments dealing with the time required to recognize words. It has been found [1] that the time required to recognize short words made up of four or five letters, is no greater than the time required to recognize a single letter standing by itself. The movement of the eye corresponds thus directly to the movement of the attention. Both the eye and the attention move across the line in steps or stages, not in continuous recognition of each successive letter.

We come thus upon a new confirmation of the principle which we laid down in the fifth chapter. You remember that we there called attention to the fact that the impressions made upon the eyes might be the same in the child's life and in the life of the adult, and that the movement made in response to these impressions might be very different. This movement, or fact of expression, stands, furthermore, as we there pointed out, in very much closer relation to the mental development of the individual than does the fact of impression. No better confirmation of all this could be found than that which we find in the like impressions from the printed page which come to the child and the adult, and the utterly unlike movements of the trained and untrained eyes as they move across the page. The stage of mental development attained in these two cases is indicated by the kind of movement, not by the kind of impression.

There is another group of movements connected with our adult recognition of words which serve to emphasize the principle so obvious from our study of the eye movements. This second group of movements con-

[1] Prof. J. McK. Cattell, Philosophische Studien, vol. iii, p. 485.

sists in certain involuntary tendencies to articulation which always accompany our reading.

You must have noticed, at some time or other, some adult who was moving his lips in inaudible whispers as he read with profound attention from the newspaper or from some written or printed page. If you have never noticed an adult doing this, you are certainly familiar enough with the tendency of children to do it to such an extent that the whisper becomes at times even audible. What that adult does with his lips, and what children often do so intensely, we all of us do in some degree with our vocal cords and other organs of articulation. Indeed, not only in reading, but even in thinking, we always tend to speak the word which we have in mind. So that we may lay it down as a general fact that recognition of a word, or thought about a word, is always accompanied by a tendency to articulate that word.

It is an interesting story of scientific investigation that lies back of the best demonstration which we have of this fact of involuntary whispering when we think of words. Two Danish scientists[1] became interested in some English investigations of what is known as telepathy. Telepathy is the name for the supposed process of thought transference. There are some people who believe that one mind can affect another at a distance, in such a way as to make the other mind think the thoughts of the first, and they call such influence of mind upon mind "telepathic influence." Two English

[1] Hansen and Lehmann, Ueber unwillkürliches Flüstern, Philosophische Studien, vol. xi, p. 471.

scientists made some experiments on telepathy. Their investigations consisted in a carefully recorded series of trials which aimed to determine whether one person who was sitting at the end of a long corridor and thinking intently of a certain number, could influence the thoughts of a second person at the other end of the hall, sufficiently to result in the second person's guessing the right number. The person who thought the number was, of course, to think to himself and in no way to communicate with the guesser at the other end of the hall. The English investigators, after a very carefully conducted series of such experiments, found that the guesser had succeeded in getting the right number a good many times, and they concluded that there must have been some sort of transfer of thought.

The Danish scientists who became interested in these experiments on telepathy were doubtful as to the conclusion that thought had been transferred. They said that perhaps it was some form of physical energy that had carried the communication from one person to the other. At any rate, they thought of a way of deciding whether or not it was physical energy. All forms of physical energy can be focused. You know, doubtless, how sound can be focused just as well as light. So the Danish investigators repeated the English experiments, with this modification—they put the thinker and the guesser at the foci of two focusing sound mirrors; and they found that the number of right guesses was decidedly increased. But where did the sound come from? The thinker had been perfectly sincere in the experiment, and had produced no sound so far as he knew. The rest of the demonstration is what interests us in our study. The thinker had been involuntarily whispering the number with every expiration of breath from his lungs. The more intensely he thought of the number, the more firmly his vocal cords and other organs of articulation became set for the name of the number of which he thought. The air breathed out with each expiration was enough to give slight sounds, and these slight whispers when focused, helped the guesser even more than they had helped him before being focused.

Every time we concentrate attention on a word, accordingly, whether it be in reading or in the mere effort to think of the word, we tend to make a movement of articulation. The investigations just reported are not the only ones which prove the truth of this assertion. Some years ago Professor Münsterberg[1] tried some experiments on the remembering of words. He found that if he prevented the person who was trying to learn certain words from making the appropriate articulation movements by requiring him to hum a tune, or to say ah, ah, ah, continually, the process of remembering was much interfered with. This experiment has been repeated by a number of investigators with many modifications, and it always gives the same results; showing that the normal accompaniment of attention to words is a movement of articulation.

These movements of articulation, like the movements of the eyes across the page, correspond, not to the single letters that make up the visual impression,

---

[1] Zeitschrift für Psychologie und Physiologie der Sinnesorgane, vol. i.

but rather to the words as wholes. Indeed, in their most highly developed form they may undergo a further reduction which we do not understand very fully, by which a single unitary movement may correspond to a whole group of words, rather than to even the single words.

These facts of active adjustment of the individual in his reading, are certainly the results of development. Progressive development turns in the direction of greater and greater complexity in both articulation and the recognition process. Given the letters in words and the words in sentences as the material for comprehension, the individual learns to take up these impressions and group them. This grouping of the elementary impressions into larger wholes is one of the most essential facts in the growth of recognition, and, as we have seen, it is always paralleled by some corresponding form of bodily activity.

So important for our consideration is this fusion of letters into words and of words into sentences that we must dwell upon it with some detail. We are fortunate in having a scientific record which will throw light on our discussion of this matter. The scientific record is not directly related to the common process of reading printed or written characters—it relates rather to the reading of the telegraphic language. It is somewhat easier to get a record of what one does in the process of acquiring ability to read telegraphic messages. In the first place, telegraphy is learned at a period in life when one can experiment more easily with the learner. One can measure results more easily, too, for the letters of the Morse alphabet require an appreciable time for transmission and reception, and the time furnishes a good means of measurement. We have very little data on the manner of developing the ordinary habit of reading print or writing. Children are very difficult to investigate in such matters, and the processes of reading are always difficult to measure. It is to be hoped that some day, through a careful study of the development of eye movements, we may have a direct record, throwing light on the character of the fusion of letters into words and words into phrases in ordinary reading. In the meantime, we shall get such light as we ean from the investigations of Bryan and Harter[1] on the development of ability to receive and send telegraphic messages.

The character of the investigations is not difficult to understand. Men who were learning to receive and send telegraphic letters, were tested at the end of each week of practise as to the number of letters they could send and receive per minute, and the results for a period of months were recorded in the curves reproduced in Figs. 29 and 30.

The curves in Fig. 29 represent the improvement of a single learner in a period of forty weeks. The upper curve is the sending curve; the lower is the curve for receiving. Notice two facts, first, that the learner shows more rapid improvement in sending than in receiving. The parallel to this fact in reading is that one must learn the active side of reading, especially the articulation side, before he learns to receive ideas from the printed page. We have seen how the art of

[1] Psychological Review, vol. vi (1899), p. 346.

writing was influenced in its development by the fact that men had a well-developed sound language before they began to write, we must never lose sight of the fact that our teaching of reading always follows the

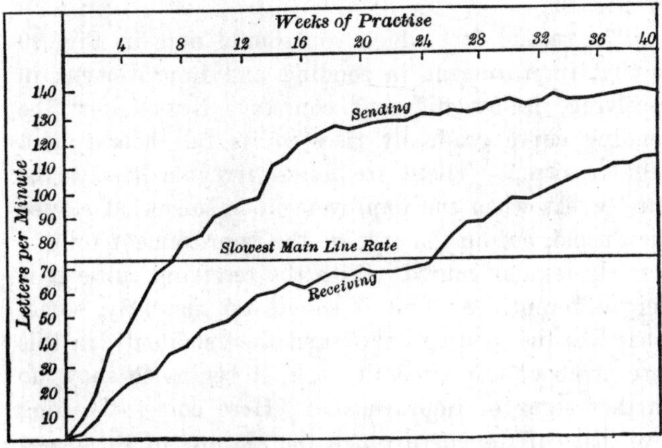

FIG. 29.

Sending and receiving rates of student Will J. Reynolds. Tested weekly by Noble Harter at Western Union telegraph office, Brookville, Ind.

acquirement of ability to speak. The recognition of a word as a whole is one of the important factors, as we have seen, in adult reading. The articulation, which is of words as wholes, is developed as an active fact, before the recognition of written words as wholes is possible. Indeed, one may insist in reading, as in writing, that before the attention is free to get meanings from written words there must be a full development of the activities, that is of the articulations and of eye movements. These must become automatic and must be disposed of fully in order to leave attention free for the higher process of fusion of words with thought. This lesson of the earlier development of the *active* processes is the first fact that comes to us from a study of Fig. 29.

The second fact which you should note in Fig. 29 is that improvement in sending and improvement in receiving, follow different courses. Notice how the sending curve gradually rises to its full height in a regular sweep. There are minor irregularities, to be sure, weeks when the improvement is somewhat slower than usual, but on the average the improvement follows a fairly regular course. With the receiving curve it is very different. At first it shoots up regularly, somewhat like the sending curve, and then suddenly, in this case at about the fifteenth week, it begins to show no further signs of improvement. Here comes the long level part of the curve which the authors of the investigation have called a plateau. This is one of those discouraging periods which you all recognize from your school experiences, when there is no marked improvement, just a standing still as it seems. But do not be discouraged by these plateaus, for as you see in our curve, there comes ultimately an end of the period of standing still and then there is another sudden rise. This plateau represents in education a necessary period of readjustment and assimilation. It is a period of preparation.

We must interest ourselves further in this difference between the sending and the receiving curve. It is not enough to say that the growth of ability to receive passes through a period of delay until certain steps of development can be fully prepared. We are interested in knowing definitely what these processes of development are. The investigators of the telegraphic language have given us a good deal of light on this problem by their later investigations recorded in Fig. 30.

Here they show in the upper curve the same kind of a receiving curve with its plateau, as that which we have

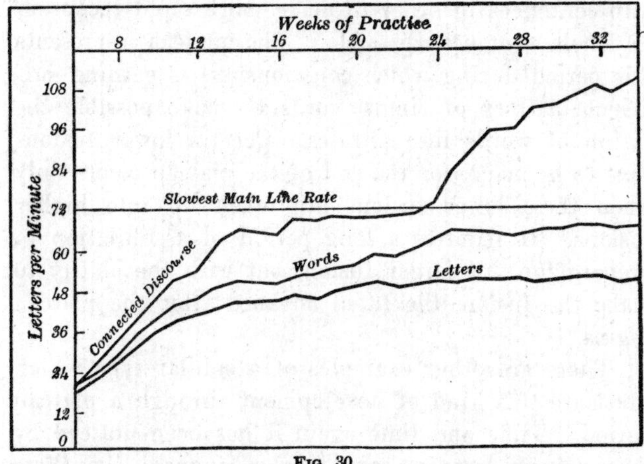

FIG. 30.

Receiving rates of student John Shaw, Brookville, Ind. Tests began with seventh week of practise.

already studied in Fig. 29. This upper curve in this figure shows what could be done under the ordinary conditions where the letters united to form words, the words in turn entering into sentences. The middle curve of Fig. 30 shows the rate of improvement in the reception of words which did not form sentences. This curve shows, accordingly, what happens when letters unite to form words, but the words are unrelated. Finally, the lowest curve shows the rate of receiving isolated letters which did not form words at all. The interesting and significant fact about these three curves when thus compared, is that they explain the meaning of the plateau. The plateau comes at the point in the curve where the power to receive the words as isolated factors has been fully developed. It remains for the learner to fuse the words into sentences in order to make more rapid reception of whole sentences possible. The plateau represents this period during which consciousness is gaining sufficient mastery of single words to make possible the fusion of words into phrases. Certain lower fusions have to be made, for the end of the plateau comes only when these lower fusions are taken up into higher fusions. It requires a long period of assimilation to prepare for this larger fusion, but with the ability to make the fusion, the rapid advance after the plateau begins.

There are other examples of a similar type which illustrate this kind of development through a plateau period. Time and time again it has been noticed by those who are learning some foreign language, that there is a most discouraging period when one does not seem to make any progress. You begin to learn your German, for example. You learn new words each day, and think you must soon have enough to be able to understand what is said to you. You find yourself even able to speak short sentences that you have worked out—but the time of understanding is not yet. You go on and on without seeming to advance a step, until suddenly you wake up some morning with a consciousness that you can understand whole sentences. You have passed the plateau.

These plateaus, or periods of preparation for higher fusions, are more numerous than our curve in Fig. 30 indicates. This particular plateau in the figure is, as we have said, the one which represents the growth of power to fuse words into significant sentences. It might be compared directly to a certain period in children's lives as they learn to read. All of you know that period when children read word by word. There is no expression or modulation, just a separate articulation of each word. If you ask the boys to do exhibition reading at this period in life, they exultantly shout out each word as if it were a triumphant success to get that word out, whatever becomes of the rest of the sentence. The next step in the reading instruction after this conquest of words, is to prepare for just such a step of fusion as that which is represented in our curve of telegraphic language, the fusion of words into sentences.

This one kind of fusion is, however, as we said a moment ago, not the only kind of fusion involved in the reading habit. There is the first fusion of all, when the child comes to connect a written letter or word with his spoken language. We do not think of this fusion of sound with written letters very often in our analysis of reading. Generally, children brought up in homes where reading is common, know something about the art before they come to school. They have already taken the first step. Something of the advantage that comes to our school work through these early fusions of written words with sounds can be understood when we think of that long period during which the race had to struggle with the problem of passing from pictorial writing to a sound alphabet. Or one can find present-day illustrations of the same fact by going to some institution for deaf-mutes where this connection between written words and movements of the organs of articulation has to be laboriously worked out. It would be a most enlightening experience for every teacher in our schools to see the methods of training deaf-mutes.

After the first general recognition of the fact that written letters may represent articulations, there is the process of fusion which combines letters into single words. This is a complicated problem. It deserves more careful study than it has ever received. Let us try, if we can, to understand something of the complexity of this process. Suppose, to begin with, that the child had to be taught to read Chinese. You will recall the fact mentioned in the last chapter, that the Chinese have a separate character for each word. The process of fusion in each case of a Chinese symbol consists, therefore, in uniting with a certain written figure a certain articulation. The articulation is all ready when the reading of the symbol begins, because of the child's knowledge of oral language. All that is necessary, therefore, is to fuse a known articulation with a written symbol. This requires some attention to the symbol to distinguish it from other symbols, and also requires some effort in bringing about the fusion.

The case that we have assumed is the case that parallels exactly what we do in our modern methods of teaching reading when we teach in the first years, words as single wholes. I think that this method of teaching has the largest possible justification in the fact that the child's articulations which are factors of these early fusions, correspond to words as wholes rather than to single letters or parts of words. The most natural fusion is always the one for which the child's past experience has partly prepared him.

It would be a relatively simple matter to follow this method of associating word articulations with word symbols, if it were not for the fact that we soon find it necessary to analyze both symbol and articulation into elements. The Chinese language is exceedingly clumsy because it has never made such an analysis. Our writing and reading is capable of the greatest possible range of recombinations because we have elementary forms as the material for our writing, and elementary sounds as the basis of our articulation. This use of elements in writing our language calls for a new phase of training which is never demanded of the Chinese child. We can get at the elements, after our first fusion of articulation wholes with word symbols, only by a process of analysis. Such analysis in our English writing and reading is made doubly difficult by the fact that the elements of articulation do not correspond in all cases to the elements of the printed word. We all of us realize this fact. Our alphabet and written symbols come with few modifications from the ancient Phenicians. The alphabet represented doubtless with some degree of accuracy the fundamental elements of both writing and articulation for the ancient language. But when we adopt this ancient, oriental alphabet, and try to fit it to our northern and modern language with its new sounds, we find difficulties innumerable. This is, however, what we have to do. We have to take written and articulated words and analyze them until we come to the elements of each.

This process of analysis was what the old spelling-book and letter method of teaching reading delighted in carrying out. Indeed, the old method began with the elements and after seeing to it that the child mastered the elements, the old method went about the building up of words in a synthetic way. I think we do better to follow the more natural order. Let the child synthesize or fuse written symbol and articulation first, and then let him analyze from the material in his own consciousness. The warning we need in our modern methods is that the analysis must not be omitted.

It is so easy when we have trained the child to attach the right articulation to a word symbol to believe that we have given him the same mastery over the word that the adult has. But we have not. The adult attaches the right articulation to a given group of letters because the combination of letters is thoroughly under his control as a combination of elements. It is a mere question of method of procedure whether you shall give this full mastery of the word through a placing of elements together as the old method did, or through an analysis of the whole into its elements as the newer methods should. The final stage in either case will be a mastery of both elements and combination. This is what must be had before development can be complete. The trouble with some of our teaching by words rather than letters, is that we sometimes believe that the mastery of elements can be left to take care of itself. It can not. We must teach our children how to break up articulations and written words into their elements. This is a necessary preparatory analysis before later and more complex forms of synthesis can be possible.

Now come back to the child who learns the fusion of a word symbol with a given articulation, as the Chinese child does. What shall be the next step? Again I believe that our modern method is right in that it begins the analysis with an analysis first of the articulation process which is under the child's control, rather than with an analysis of the inherited and wholly artificial written symbols. We ought to begin analysis with some sort of phonetic method. I do not know of any phonetic system that is free from objections. But we have had this idea too short a time to work it out fully. That we are on the right road is clear. Let us keep on. The combined experience of individual teachers is the only thing that can make the method perfect. Get the principle, and become a worker yourself in the field of constructive method-making.

The phonetic analysis is the starting-point of analysis, but analysis must not be governed entirely by phonetic considerations, for our problem is ultimately to come to a combination of phonetic elements and alphabetic elements. The perfect analytic method toward which we have to work is one that passes from purely phonetic divisions, and that very rapidly, to observation of the corresponding letter divisions. Good spelling results from an acquired habit of observing the elements of words. Good spelling is very easy if attention is trained in this direction early in life, it is difficult if attention gets a wrong bent. There can be no doubt that we tend in our modern methods to neglect analysis.

This neglect of analysis is one of the natural and most serious results of our modern desire to get at the higher forms of fusion as soon as possible. We are striving so constantly to grasp wholes in their totality that we fail to see that the wholes are made up of elements. Let us correct this fault. The older methods from their very nature avoided this, which is our most radical fault.

Enough has been said to show how complex and involved is the fusion of letters into words, and of words with appropriate articulations. But these preliminary fusions must take place before fully developed reading is possible. After these preliminary fusions, comes the stage of fusion illustrated in Fig. 30, the fusion of words into phrases and sentences. Connected with this last fusion and, indeed, probably as an essential phase of the process, is the completion of the fusion already begun in the earlier processes, namely the fusion of written or printed words with thoughts or meanings.

The complete recognition of the meaning of a word is one of the final stages of development. The recognition of the sounds connected with letters, the fusion of these elementary sounds into a single articulation are all preliminary processes. The attention can not be free to take up meaning easily and fully until these preliminary stages have been passed through. It was pointed out at the beginning of this chapter that our modern teaching of reading is in some danger of overlooking all these necessary preliminaries to the recognition of meanings. I hope that statement is clear by this time. The meaning which comes so easily in adult writing and in adult reading, is possible only because the preliminary processes have become automatic. Let us not forget the similarity between the more obvious organizing processes in writing and the less obvious, but no less necessary, organizing processes in reading.

And now as we attack the problem of the final fusion between meaning and written or printed form, we shall certainly not lose sight of the suggestions that grow out of our past discussions. The processes of fusion which we have discussed up to this time are not mere receptive processes, they are all intimately connected with certain forms of activity. When the eye moves in such a way as to indicate that words and phrases are taken in as single wholes, we can not fail to see the relation of the active individual to the process of fusion. And when the words of a sentence fuse with the thought which they express, surely there must be some active processes connected with this higher form of fusion.

I think we shall have no difficulty in recognizing the truth of this statement if we go back to our earlier discussion of the boy or girl who reads by pronouncing separate words, before those words are fused into sentences. Compare the active expressions of such an untrained reader with those of one who knows the thought of the whole sentence, and how different are the two! The fusion of the words into a significant sentence will be expressed by a single rising or falling inflection running through the whole group of words. The sentence thus becomes a single expression. It has elements, to be sure, but the elements are not held apart any more than are the elements of the fully developed movement in writing. They are fused into a single active utterance. This appears nowhere more clearly than in sentences that convey some emotional thought. Then, even the rate of articulation may change and help to express the emotional character of the thought. There may also be added to the emotional articulation of the words some other bodily expression such as a straining of the tension of arm muscles, as in anger. The hearing of some sentences or even the silent reading of them, may send the blood surging to the brain in a new and distinct response to the thought of the sentence as a whole. Such reactions as these are not reactions to the words, they are reactions to the thought. They appear at a stage of development in which there is being worked out a form of fusion higher than that which comes in the mere fusing of articulations and single words.

The emotional reactions which we have found entering so naturally into our discussion, are perhaps the most obvious reactions accompanying these higher fusions, but they are by no means the only forms. Take some simple sentence and try by an examination of your own mental process to see what enters into your understanding of its meaning. It makes no great difference for our discussion at this stage whether the words with which we start are read, or heard, or merely thought of. The preliminary fusions of written words with articulations are different from the preliminary fusions of words that are heard with the same articulations. But once let words that are heard, and words that are written, be brought up to the point where they can take on meanings, and the further process will be the same in either case. The taking on of meaning is a form of fusion which is alike for words written or spoken. And if you would understand this process of taking on meanings you must make, as I have said, a very careful analysis of the process in your mind, for a superficial analysis may lead you astray.

It has been a favorite formula in much of our science to say that the meaning of a word consists in a whole series of images of the object to which the word refers, this host of images hovering as it is supposed somewhere in memory. A sentence in like manner has been described as associated with a train of images also hovering in memory. But one is led to ask, why this train of images? Is that the end of recognition of meanings—just to have a series of pictures in the mind? Certainly not. Pictures when they are called up by words are merely the intermediate stages of a more complete process. Every recognition of meaning ultimately results in some appropriate total reaction. All our earlier discussions of action and its relation to mental life confirm this conclusion. This conclusion gives us the best and highest view of mental life, for under it we think of mental processes as contributing to our adaptation to our broader environment. In securing adaptation, there is no place for mere passive pictures in the mind. Pictures must lead to action, and pictures do lead to action. One can not see a picture of a hammer without feeling his fingers reaching for its handle. One can not look down a steep precipice without thinking either of the leap or of turning away to avoid a fall. Pictures are carriers of meaning. When they come into the mind they bring with them as their ultimate consequences some kind of reactions.

The ultimate value of words when fused with meanings, appears most clearly in the cases of thoroughly familiar words. In these cases the intermediate pictures are not needed. If they were ever present they have disappeared in the course of development. The familiar word passes at once into a reaction. Let me say to you, for example, "here are twelve dollars go and spend them," and I venture the guess that you did not think of my single words at all. You had only the haziest sort of a picture, if indeed you had any, of how the twelve dollars would look. The first thing you catch in consciousness as a result of my sentence is a feeling of yourself in some store *doing* what we were talking about your doing. If we had all the necessary apparatus attached to your muscles we should find them responding to the words that went into your ears with actual muscular contractions which faintly, but no less surely, tend to realize the command to "go and spend it."

Professor James will help us again in our effort to make this idea clear. He writes on page 27 of his Talks to Teachers as follows: "No truth, however abstract, is ever perceived, that will not probably at some time influence our earthly action. You must remember that, when I talk of action here, I mean action in the widest sense. I mean speech, I mean writing, I mean yeses and noes, and tendencies 'from' things and tendencies 'toward' things, and emotional determinations; and I mean them in the future as well as in the immediate present. As I talk here, and you listen, it might seem as if no action followed. You might call it a purely theoretic process, with no practical result. But it *must* have a practical result. It can not take place at all and leave your conduct unaffected. If not to-day, then on some far future day, you will answer some question differently by reason of what you are thinking now. Some of you will be led by my words into new veins of inquiry, into reading special books. These will develop your opinion, whether for or against. That opinion will in turn be expressed, will receive criticism from others in your environment, and will effect your standing in their eyes. We can not escape our destiny, which is practical; and even our most theoretic faculties contribute to its working out."

This development of all mental life toward practical activities is the most fundamental educational ideal which we have derived from the general doctrine of development. The place of reading in the development toward action will be obvious from a study of the way in which impression and resulting activity are related at different stages of development. The simplest case of activity, long before reading begins, is that in which impression passes at once into its appropriate reaction without even a word or thought intervening. This is the case illustrated when we start at a loud clap of thunder. Then come in order of their complexity, less direct forms of reaction in which we do not respond to the impression directly, but pass from impression to some suggested thought, some suggested image perhaps, and so on through this suggested thought or image to the appropriate reaction. This is the case when I hear a clock strike and think of my engagement and go to meet it. Indirect responses of this type come to be more and more elaborate in higher and higher development, and it is as an aid to such indirect reaction that language finds its great value. I see an object and think first of its name. The name suggests a further train of thought leading ultimately to action. The advantage of such a system of words is that some one else may often do the first stages of the reacting for me. The scientist sees the object and investigates it, and gives us the results of his developed recognition of meaning in words, and we can pass from words to the appropriate bodily response by following what he has put into words.

Words are of value only when they arouse something more than mere articulations; they must arouse ultimately reactions appropriate to their remoter meanings. So long as a word arouses an articulation as its only response it is an end in itself. It does not serve its highest purpose as a link in a chain of indirect reactions. This is nowhere better shown than in the fact that as words become more and more familiar the mere articulatory activity is more and more reduced. The most familiar words tend to pass directly into appropriate reactions. Take such a familiar word as "high" for example. One feels himself tending to roll his eyes upward when he hears or sees the word. The intermediate steps of reception of the impression, articulation, interpretation, have all faded into relative insignificance, and the final act comes without noticeable delay. This is an advanced form of development and shows that the fusion between word and meaning has reached its most advanced stage.

The line of thought which I have sought to bring out in this discussion of the relation of action and meanings is so rich in its suggestions to the teacher that it would require a whole volume to complete all the possible lines of application into which it leads us. Our whole system of modern education is getting at the fact that a real meaning involves direct contact with objects and direct manipulation of them. We try to give a child some reactions with which to build up these highest fusions with words, and we do well in doing this. Training which gives meaning to words is always practical training. Not narrow training in some single craft, but training in the broad recognition of our adaptive relations to the objects about us. And such training in the use of words is highly practical also in the possibilities which it brings to us of acquiring new indirect adaptations from our fellows.

The cultivation of this ability to receive adaptive suggestions indirectly is, let us repeat it, one of the highest stages of development. A very large part of the justification for the existence of our schools is to be sought in the necessity of bringing our children into full possession of language in order that they may borrow from the experiences of others and thus get knowledge indirectly.

The outline study of the process of reading which we have taken up, ought to suggest to you some of the yet unsolved problems. How are we to make the mechanical side of reading most complete without making articulation an end in itself? How are we to do our full duty in calling attention to the analytic work necessary for spelling and yet get at the synthetic processes as rapidly as possible? How are we to make language really productive as a means to adaptation? These are problems that we shall not solve satisfactorily until we understand the inner nature of the reading process.

It is with this group of problems then, that I leave you. Some hints we have had of their solution, but we need more study. More study on the part of individual teachers who see the meaning of the problems and then go forward to their solution.

CHAPTER IX

THE IDEA OF NUMBER

THE use of numbers is quite as ancient as the earliest forms of writing, and may have been even earlier. Our word calculate and all the words from the same root, are derived from an ancient Latin word meaning pebble. This carries us back in thought to an early period when, instead of making the simple marks which were very early used in keeping tally, primitive man laid aside a pebble for each unit as he counted, and the pebble was his tally-mark.

Or again, as we study the names used by primitive peoples for their numerals, we find them bearing unequivocal testimony to the fact that men counted on their fingers long before they tried to mark down the results of this counting. Thus, a student [1] of the Zuñi language tells us that the Zuñi word for one (töp'in te) means "take down to start with," that is, fold down the little finger; and the word for two (kwil-li) means "put down with," or put down the next one with the little finger. The Zuñis still count by starting with all the fingers stretched out and folding down one finger for each tally. They always begin with the little finger.

---

[1] Fr. H. Cushing, in Amer. Anthropologist, vol. v (1892).

Their names for three, and so on, are of the same character as the names given, and indicate the origin of their whole system of counting from the hand. One hardly needs to recall that the decimal system which we follow, is evidence of the influence of the ten fingers in developing our own system before there were even primitive means of keeping tally. As a matter of well-known fact, our decimal system is by no means the best system that could have been devised if men had been mathematicians from the first. A better system would have been one based on twelve. Indeed, we have this system in our measurements of time and in our measurements of circles, both of which were borrowed, not from the natural system of keeping tally on the hands, but from the Babylonian scientists.

But while men used number very early, they never succeeded in carrying numerical processes to any very high degree of perfection until in comparatively recent centuries. The Egyptians had a most clumsy arithmetic. We are told that in order to add fractions, the Egyptians were obliged to raise these fractions to the denominator sixty, instead of to some simple common denominator such as we use. Even the Greeks and Romans had a very unwieldy system of notation. We are all acquainted with the Roman numerals. They can never be set down in columns to be added; and multiplication is a bewildering process if one undertakes it with this system of notation.

Even while number processes were thus at a relatively low stage, and while number notation was still very undeveloped, certain forms of practical application grew up which have always been of great importance in connection with the use of numbers. These lines of application consisted in measurement. Land measurement was one of the earliest forms of measurement, and the measurement of values involved in primitive barter early needed the assistance of number. Indeed, so intimate has been the relation between number and its application in measurement that some recent writers [1] on the subject of number have urged upon us as teachers the importance of recognizing this relation as the fundamental basis for our teaching of arithmetic. We even have text-books prepared to illustrate how number may be taught through its applications to measurements.

It is interesting to note in connection with this recent urgency for a measurement-arithmetic that the greatest measurers and the greatest geometricians among the early nations, did not, as a matter of fact, have a very highly developed science of number. The period of Euclid, that master from whose work we still borrow in our school text-books on geometry, was not a period of profound knowledge of arithmetic.

For our arithmetic and for those sciences which deal with number, we have to wait until the dawning of the modern period. In the early beginnings of the Renaissance, that period of the revival of intellectual life in Europe, we borrowed from the Arabian scholars, probably from the Moors in Spain, the system of numerals which we call even to-day the Arabic numerals. With the arrival of these numerals the history of mathematical sciences enters upon a new

---

[1] McLellan and Dewey, The Psychology of Number.

period. And the interesting fact about the Arabic numerals is that their value consists, not in their more immediate applicability to measurement, but rather in the presence of certain characteristics which favor the development of easy processes of manipulating number relations. It was the expression of certain distinctly numerical relations which gave our modern arithmetic its start.

You are doubtless familiar with the essential superiority of the Arabic numerals over the Roman numerals. Every value has in the Roman numerals a separate symbol. In the Arabic numerals, we have a few symbols placed in different positions to express different number relations. The likeness of the Arabic symbols in various positions shows immediately that the possible processes or modes of treatment are the same whether the symbol is in unit's place or in thousand's place. The simplification of numerical processes which results is very great, so great indeed, that all our modern methods of manipulating number relations depend upon this essential fact. Thus, to take a concrete illustration, suppose we represent five hundred fifty five by Roman notation. It will be DLV, each five being represented by a symbol of its own. If one were going to multiply DVL by five it would not be obvious on the face of it that the numerical process is the same in the case of each of the three terms of the number. How obviously the process shows its character when, as in the Arabic notation we use 5 5 5. We see now that whether in hundred, or in ten, or in unit, place, the five means the same process of multiplication.

This suggestion from the history of arithmetic

that there are certain purely arithmetical relations, seems to me to be most fruitful for the teacher to follow out and I shall ask you to inquire more in detail into the nature of a simple arithmetical process. Let us begin, as we have all along been doing, with the developed consciousness of the teacher.

Take the simple process of addition, $7 + 5 = 12$. In some sense or other we place seven and five as identical with twelve. But after all, seven and five are recognized as not identical with twelve. If seven and five meant exactly the same thing as twelve, then there would be no motive for talking about them as in any sense distinct. So we see that our equation $7 + 5 = 12$, comes to be an expression of identity with a recognition of the fact that the two sides of the equation are not fully identical.

The kind of identity and difference which are here united will be obvious, I think, if we will recognize that twelve means one way of arranging a certain collection of objects, and seven and five mean another way of arranging these same objects. The identity consists in the fact that the objects dealt with all along are the same, and the difference appears in the mode of arranging the same objects. Let us try to express this equation $7 + 5 = 12$ in other terms. We may do so as follows: here are certain objects, we may arrange them in two unlike groups, or we may put them all together in one group. Or again, we may say, here are certain objects which are in two small unlike groups, let us put them into a single group when we shall have exactly the same objects, but a different arrangement. It makes no difference for our thought whether these processes of varying arrangement are actually carried out or not. The important consideration is that we shall think all the objects together in one case and in another case we shall think of them as not altogether, but in two separate groups.

This idea that number equations express different modes of grouping, can be carried also into the examination of any single number. Take five, what does it mean? It means that we have for some reason thought of one, and one, and one, and so on up to five, as belonging together. It makes no difference whether the things are actually together or not, we may think of them as together. Every time we count up a series of objects we put them together in a group. This appears in an interesting way if we inquire into the meaning of the word five as we use it in counting. We arrive at a certain object and say five. Our attention is chiefly on the object, but it is also in some measure on the objects which have gone before, for the word five refers, not only to this object at which we are now looking, but also to the whole group up to this point. Indeed, so strong is the group idea in the word five that we have in our modern language developed a word with which to designate more specifically the position of the object in the group. We call this derived word an ordinal numeral and we speak of the *fifth* object.

Follow out the line of discussion in any direction you please and you always come upon this same fundamental fact, that numbers express modes of grouping objects. Thus, take the process of subtraction as expressed in the equation $12-7=5$. The fundamental operation of grouping is here approached from a somewhat different point of view than that adopted in the equation of addition. This equation of subtraction calls attention to the fact that given a group of twelve objects, we may break the given group into two lesser groups, one of which is specified as seven. After seven are withdrawn from the larger group of twelve, a group of five still remains.

We all know how far this process of regrouping seen in subtraction may be carried out as a merely ideal process, in the fact that we ultimately come to apply the process of subtraction to cases where it involves us in curious complexities. Thus, suppose we have seven objects and some one demands of us that we give up a group of twelve. This is essentially a process of subtraction. 7—12 is the way in which the process is to be expressed. Now as a matter of actual transaction 7—12 is an absurd demand. As a matter of thought, on the other hand, it is quite reasonable. Given seven things with a demand that we produce twelve, we see at once that there is a deficit to be made up somewhere else. We ascertain the amount of the deficit which is five, and we indicate the amount by using the ordinary numeral 5, and we mark it as a deficit by giving it the sign which shows that it is to be withdrawn from somewhere else. The result of all this thought is that we say $7-12=-5$. This negative quantity expresses something that does not exist as a reality, but is demanded in thought. For our thought about processes it is a perfectly clear conclusion.

It will be seen that the processes of addition and

subtraction are, according to this explanation, nothing but different phases of the general process of grouping. Addition means building up larger groups from smaller. Subtraction means breaking up larger groups into smaller. Both addition and subtraction belong to the fundamental process of making up groups.

When we come to multiplication and division we have modifications of the process of grouping. The natural step to these processes of multiplication and division is not through multiplication, but through division. I believe that we shall come to recognize this some day in our school practise. Be that as it may, the kind of grouping present in both division and multiplication is to be defined by saying that the smaller groups involved in these processes are always equal to each other. Thus, when we subtract seven from twelve and get five, there is nothing about the two smaller groups seven and five, to lead us to compare them, except the general fact that they are unequal. But divide twelve into six and six, and the process proves to be an especially interesting case of subtraction. Here is a case of subtraction in which the two lesser groups are equal. Division is therefore a special case of subtraction. The character of the groups obtained by division into equal groups, leads to our development of a genuinely new mode of thought. When the groups are alike we begin to count the equal groups as single wholes, thus treating each group as a unit of higher order. Thus, when we say there are two sixes in twelve, we have said there are in twelve two units of higher order. If you ask what makes up each of these units of higher order, we answer six units of the lower order.

Division and multiplication thus come to be processes dealing with units of higher order.

There is another way of getting at this truth about division and multiplication. We all know how intimately the processes of multiplication and division are connected with the general fact that our whole system of notation is a decimal system. One can multiply by tens without any difficulty. Multiplying or dividing by ten is just like counting. Did you ever realize that this is due to the fact that ten is, in both counting and multiplying, a standard unit of higher order?

Think of the matter in this way. You are confronted with a large group of objects, say a hundred or more. The group is so large that you can not manage it well as a whole, and the individuals are so numerous that you can not treat them satisfactorily as individuals. What do you do? You do the most natural thing in the world, you break up the unwieldy whole into certain groups that can be managed. From the earliest times men have divided up armies, and cattle, and lands, on just this principle. Each smaller group is then treated as a unity of higher order. Thus, the small companies of the army were all given a responsible commander. He represented the unity of the whole group. Rations were given to him for the whole group. We have carried this same idea of dividing into companies into our counting. When we have a mass of objects we count one, two, and so on up to ten, and then we stop. We set aside that ten as a manageable group, as a unity of higher order, and then begin again.

The fact that ten is a unity of higher order, is expressed in the very fact that we label it with the same symbol as that which we use for the lower unities. We merely mark the higher order of the decimal group by giving to the digit when it expresses a unity of higher order a higher position.

When now, having arranged our great mass of objects into tens, we begin to count by tens, we do exactly what is done in every process of multiplication and division. We treat small equal groups as unities of higher order. That is what makes multiplying by tens so easy. The reason why multiplying by threes or fours or other numbers than ten is not so easy, is, that having adopted a standard group of ten for our whole notation, everything else has to be turned into terms of this standard notation. The ordinary multiplication is therefore, a double process; it is treating small equal groups as unities of a higher order, and then turning the results into terms of our standard decimal notation.

Without attempting to carry the discussion into any further detail, we may conclude that there is such a thing as the science of grouping. The objects which are grouped, are not centers of attention in this science, but rather the different ways in which the grouping may be carried out, no matter what the objects are. That two groups, one of seven and one of five may be made out of a single group of twelve, is a fundamental fact of the science of grouping. This is not a fact of nature-study or history or literature, it is a fact that deserves to have independent recognition. It is a fact of the science of number.

I have no patience with the efforts being made in so many departments of our education to swallow up such subjects as arithmetic into some other subject. By no means in the world can the fact that $7 + 5 = 12$, be taught except through a definite and well-ordered directing of the attention to a fact of grouping. It makes no difference how much you decorate the fact with outside frills, the fact will have to come out sharply and clearly as a fact of importance in its own right.

One of the sad results of our present-day efforts to evade arithmetic is that we get neither the other subjects we seek to reach nor the arithmetic. I once saw a teacher in one of the most widely known experimental schools in the country, illustrate very clearly the mistake here referred to. She was teaching a beginning class in social relations and was "incidentally" teaching number. For her own thinking the number expressions and processes were obviously the most important facts involved. So absorbed was she in number that she allowed a youthful storekeeper to sell a large well-bound book for ten cents and an unbound pamphlet for seventy-six cents. She then allowed the pupil who next in order of rotation became storekeeper, to buy back the ten-cent book at the ruinous price of sixty cents. In short, she forgot entirely the commercial relations; and the children, not being controlled by any deep-seated motives of either commerce or arithmetic, lost all the instruction that might have come from an intelligent pursuit of either of the relations alone.

Another difficulty with our teaching of arithmetic when we fail to recognize the fact that arithmetic is a science of grouping, is that we take up a whole series of subjects in arithmetic and think we have treated them adequately in arithmetic, when, as a matter of fact, they, as well as the science of grouping, ought to have independent treatment. For example, most of us learn the greater part of what we know about spatial relations, not from the spatial values themselves, but through the abstract numerical expressions of these values. The result is that we are deplorably deficient in ability to think in terms of real spatial relations. We can talk very glibly in number terms of ten feet and half a mile, but we do not think these values in spatial terms at all. Even smaller distances, such as eight inches and five centimeters, have little concrete meaning for the ordinary mind. Systems of form-study are fortunately being worked out to correct this defect in our educational system. But form-study is distinct and different in its motives from number work. The two must not be identified. Note that it is not for a moment asserted that the two kinds of study may not be advantageously combined at certain stages. But it is asserted that spatial relations are not identical with number relations and must not be confounded with them.

I agree heartily with Mr. Speer in his criticism of the blind mixture which we make of number and measuring. He writes in his Primary Arithmetic[1] as follows: "Place a measure in the hands of a pupil and set him to marking off spaces on this or that, and counting them before he is ready for such work, before anything has been done to induce the habit of looking from one magnitude to another, and you absorb him

[1] Page 9.

in a mechanical process which turns the thought from the relational element with which mathematics deals. He may write, 'the door is eight feet high,' when he has simply counted eight spaces. But he has made no mathematical comparison, observed no relation, done little which develops power to think."

I should be willing to subscribe to an extension of this criticism over most of the departments of our arithmetic. The great trouble in teaching percentage or fractions, or other departments of arithmetic, is that we are doing two things at once and commonly not doing either one fully. We are trying to teach certain practical relations of life such as business relations, and we are at the same time trying to teach number relations. We do not seem to realize that the number relations are not identical with the business relations. We do not seem to understand that a problem in interest, for example, involves a human relation which is not arithmetical at all. As a matter of fact, I doubt very much whether the majority of our children have the vaguest notion of what the meaning of interest on money really is. They always think of interest as a problem in number.

What I have said about the difference between number relations and spatial and business relations can be emphasized, I think, by calling attention to the fact that there are ways of dealing with spatial and business relations that do not involve any number. For suitable examples, we shall, of course, have to appeal to cases in which training has been of a different type from our own. Such examples are numerous, however. Take any savage who has not had a course in number, but has had a very thorough course in spatial relations. He can shoot his arrow or throw his spear with a nicety of spatial estimation that surpasses a hundredfold his ability to count. He knows at a glance whether an object can be reached sooner or later than another object. He knows how much higher the highest rock is than the one below. But he never translates any of his knowledge into number. His number relations lag far behind his spatial ideas. Now note that this does not show for a moment that spatial apprehension should always precede number expressions in individual development, it merely shows that spatial ideas have a reality and value which is peculiar to themselves. They are spatial quantities, not numerical quantities. The use of number in connection with these spatial quantities as we teach it in our schools, is not necessary, it is not universal, it is not a sufficient justification for the confusion of the two which usually takes place.

Again take the relations treated in that part of our arithmetic which usually deals with buying and selling. We are constantly buying things in practical life, that is, in technical language, we are securing goods of various kinds in exchange for the precious metals. In such transactions we use number calculations so constantly that we have come to look upon the buying process in our school treatment of it as entirely mathematical in character. But there is an important distinction to be made between the number expressions used in buying, and the end for which the number expressions are employed. The real relation involved is one of relative desirability of the goods in the eyes of the various parties to the transaction. That is, the real relation in commerce is illustrated in its simplest and purest form in the barter of the savage. He has one commodity and wants another, so he makes an exchange. Some day his descendants will use gold and silver and they will state their desires in terms of figures, but their essential act in buying will continue to be one of exchange.

This fact that the number idea is not identical with spatial ideas or with ideas of value, but is equally applicable to these different spheres of quantity, is what makes the number idea an abstraction. There is a good deal of vagueness in many minds about the meaning of the word *abstract*. We recognize in a general way that number is highly abstract, but do not know exactly what this highly abstract character consists in. Let us see if we can make the matter clear.

We have a certain group of objects lying before us; to be definite, let us assume that we have twelve coins. We may make a great many different kinds of real groups out of these twelve coins. For example, we can, if we wish, hold 5 in one hand and 7 in the other. Such a division of our twelve coins into two groups is a real division, or as we say, a concrete division. There is nothing abstract about such a process.

Now take the first step toward abstraction. Let the twelve coins lie together on the table, and with your eye draw a purely imaginary line through the group of twelve, dividing it into two groups, one of seven and one of five. Here the objects are concrete as before, but the division is a purely ideal division, real only for the thinking individual. This possibility of making purely ideal rearrangements of the objects about us is one of the first steps in the growing independence of our thought. We begin to realize the fact that there is a difference between objects and our mode of arranging them. We begin to see that we are the really important factors in the process of arranging. We can think of a certain arrangement whether it is actually carried out or not.

This fact that the mode of arrangement belongs to ourselves rather than to the objects may be made clearer in this way. Suppose I begin pointing to the various coins in my pile of twelve. I point first with my right index-finger and keep pointing with this finger until I have tallied off five of the coins. I can now turn about and point to the other seven with my left index-finger. I had a series of activities arranged in two distinct groups, one of five and one of seven, and the coins were in no way disturbed by the classification which I introduced by dividing them into right-hand coins and left-hand coins. The process of arrangement was my own. I tallied off the coins as I pleased. It may be that the coins were not mine or were quite beyond my power, but the arrangement was fully in my control. If I please I can at another time, point to nine with my right index-finger and to three with my left. Or I can point to all twelve with either right or left finger.

This is the first step in the process of abstraction, to realize that the mode of arranging objects is quite independent of any concrete redistribution of the objects themselves. There is no reason, for example, why we should not point with our left finger to all of the desks in the schoolroom and then point to all the window-panes with our right finger. And there is no reason, on the other hand, why we should not point to both desks and window-panes with the same hand. The notion that number depends on some kind of uniformity in objects is all false. Some writers tell us that only like things can be counted together. This is sheer nonsense. We can count anything we like together. We are the ones who do the counting. Counting is an individual process. We can control it without reference to outside difficulties of arrangement. When the process is developed in its higher forms, abstraction, or freedom from particular objects outside of ourselves, becomes complete.

I have used the illustration of pointing so as to get some definite and obvious form of personal activity. Of course, we can count without pointing, and we can distinguish groups without using the right and left sides. The division is easy enough when we are trained in counting, because we have different actions of the vocal cords for each individual object we count. We have already seen in our discussion of reading that word ideas always arouse certain activities in the vocal cords. This involuntary expression accompanying thought processes is nowhere more strikingly manifested than during counting. Each new object which we include in this or that group, is literally pointed out, not by a finger movement, but by a distinct response of the vocal cords. Thus, we see the truth that number arrangement is a process of individual activity, confirmed in a very literal sense. Even in its most abstract forms, number is related to individual activity.

We have said that the individual after acquiring this ability to use abstract number classifications may apply them as he likes. There is, however, one limitation to the free manipulation of his rearrangings, which we must notice. The individual is not at liberty to be inconsistent with himself. For example, I can not arrange a certain series of objects in my thought and call that series five to-day, and to-morrow call the same series eleven. To put the matter in another form, I can not point in a certain way to-day and in a totally different way to-morrow, and then treat the two cases of pointing as if they were the same. If I do I shall get into trouble. I shall find that inconsistency will be my undoing. The one thing that I must learn about this mode of arrangement which I cultivate is that it will be necessary for me to be consistent.

Some of the means by which the race has slowly worked out a series of helps to consistency are obvious. For example, suppose that instead of pointing time and time again with the index-finger—a form of movement which might easily lead to confusion and inconsistency—we point successively with thumb, index-finger, middle finger, and so on. Then we should be able to mark a given stage in the process of counting by the part of the hand that has been covered. This is exactly the sort of counting process which we see developed into written form in the Roman numerals. Again, when it comes to using activities of the vocal cords instead of finger movements, consistency is secured by developing a certain fixed order of vocal cord movements. The fixed order is learned and adhered to whatever the subjects of the arranging activity may be. The children of a developed race have the advantage of racial experience in this matter, for they find a fixed order of vocal cord movements all prepared in the racial series of names for numerals.

More important even than consistency in the counting of relatively simple groups, is the development of the power to be consistent in the combining of these groups in various ways. Suppose that we have a group of three and a group of four, we may rearrange these two groups in a variety of ways. But in all of the rearrangements we must be consistent with the first grouping into three and four. This may be expressed by saying that whatever we do with these two groups, we must always be able to come back to the original groups instantly and without contradicting ourselves. This necessity of always being able to return to the original form, leads us to study the rules of consistent arrangement. Anything that is consistent with a return to the original grouping is permissible in our handling of three and four. The study of what is permissible or consistent is the study of number relations. Do you not see that when I say 3 plus 4 equal 7, equal 5 plus 2, equal 6 plus 1, equal 4 plus 3, and so on, I am merely working out all the various consistent statements that can be made about three and four?

There is no difficulty in understanding now why the science of mathematics is so closely related to what we call logic. Logic is the science which studies the modes of consistent reasoning in all departments of thought, and mathematics deals with consistent modes of dealing with group relations. The reason why we have to have a science of number is that it takes much investigation in many directions to make sure that our modes of ideal regrouping are really consistent. It would be uneconomical for every individual to seek out all the different consistent forms of number arrangement, so the race has recorded what it knows about various modes of consistent reasoning, in the science of number relations, and the individual gets the benefit of all this accumulated experience.

Let us now ask ourselves, on the basis of our study of arithmetic as the science of groups, what the process is when we work out a practical problem by the aid of our mathematical principles. The practical problem presents to us certain facts arranged in certain relations with respect to each other. Our first step is to understand the given arrangement of the facts, and the second step is to express these relations in terms of our number system. This second step is not always easy, when the relations are complex, but upon its accuracy and completeness depend all the later steps of the operation. It is just at this point that there arises one of the great difficulties which our pupils have with the complex problems we give them in arithmetic. They frequently do not understand the nature of given relations and they do not know how to formulate the problem in terms of the number system. When such difficulties arise in the very first stages of an example, where is the remedy to be sought? In a more thorough comprehension of number relations pure and simple? Certainly not. If the pupil has difficulty in understanding the problem in its first stages, what he needs is some explanation of the real facts involved. He should understand the situation first in its ordinary terms. Then he should have some training in the means of expressing these real situations in terms of the purely numerical relations.

After the second step of intelligent statement of the problem in terms of number, the rest of the process falls within the domain of the science of number relations. We know through this science how to rearrange and manipulate the relations, always keeping ourselves consistent with the original facts. These manipulations do not affect the real facts one way or the other. They simply show us what would result if the relations were consistently rearranged. It does not make any difference what the facts are after they are once translated into the number expressions, from that time on we are interested only in the consistent rearrangement of the relations with which we started.

It is quite possible to start with relations that are entirely preposterous so far as the real world is concerned. One may start, for example, with ten houses costing fifty cents each. It makes no difference so far as the consistency of the process is concerned whether one can or can not reasonably make the assertion with which he starts. But from the point of view of intelligent education it is a mistake to misrepresent the real relations even where we might neglect them without danger to our science of number. The science of number as such may not suffer, but the pupil's notion of what an application is, certainly suffers. The number process may be the same when based on an absurd proposition as when based on a reasonable assumption, but there is always a loss in the character of any mental process when it contains an absurd element, even though that element is of secondary importance for the study of number relations.

The significance of this statement which we have just been making, that the best education can never be obtained by starting with absurd propositions, is wider than most of us imagine. Do you ever realize how absurd it is to tell a child to suppose that he has a thousand dollars in the bank? Most of us would have to think two or three times to rise to any very vivid realization of such a state of affairs in our own mature minds. To the child it is no real application of arithmetic to life to give him such a proposition. We mistake if we think that there is anything enlivening in such a proposition. As a matter of fact the mind simply passes as rapidly and as fully as possible over the absurd proposition and gets at the number process involved. The children soon get used to accepting absurdities without much thought about them, and our whole science of number gets to be a kind of vague mixture of more or less remote and senseless propositions and half-understood number rules. Through this maze the children are carried, wondering now and then that numbers seem to fit each other so well, and wondering somewhat less frequently that men in the arithmetics live such fanciful lives. But worst of all, losing all the time, what they should be gaining, an idea of the real utility of their science.

It is not to be wondered at that we feel sometimes the inadequacy of our number work. It is not to be wondered at that business men and practical men condemn our methods in the school. The trouble with us is that we have no clear notion of what we are doing, or of the end at which we are aiming.

And now I suppose you are prepared to ask how all this discussion is to be turned into practical school work. I am tempted to make short work of your question by saying that it is your business and not mine to turn this into practical school work. I believe I should be justified in disposing of the matter in that way. Indeed, I can think of nothing which would be more opposed to the whole spirit of my discussion, than for me to formulate for you a fixed system of arithmetic teaching. Arithmetical knowledge does not consist in a series of rules or examples. It consists rather in a growing comprehension of the consistent methods of treating number relations, whenever and wherever these number relations appear. If that sort of knowledge is to be taught to children, there must be a living teacher who can help the child with his special difficulties. The child's difficulties do not appear in accordance with any fixed system that was ever written. The teacher who does nothing but follow some set system is not going to succeed in helping children where they need help most, and when they need it most.

There is another reason why I shall not take it upon myself to lay down any new system of arithmetic teaching. If the analysis of the number idea which we have been working out is valid, if it agrees with your own study of the mature number ideas which you find in your own minds, then the principles of teaching to which we shall be lead by this analysis are applicable to all the existing systems of teaching arithmetic. When you find a man who has to change the whole system of education in order to fit some of his ideas, beware of that man. No man can impeach a nation. No man can impeach our schools. They are the products of centuries of development, they represent something vastly broader than the individual. There is something worth retaining in every system of teaching that has been followed in the schools. And so now we may say that whatever system of arithmetic you teach, you can teach it more intelligently and with better results, if you will make yourselves intelligently familiar with the fundamental nature of the number idea. Indeed, we may boldly venture the assertion that it is only through such a clear understanding of the nature of the number idea that you can teach arithmetic in any other than a blind non-rational fashion.

Such practical suggestions as I have to make, therefore, are intended to fit the system which you teach, whatever that system may be. The first suggestion is that in teaching arithmetic you should never lose sight of the main purpose which is to give instruction in number relations. Do not let this chief purpose become obscured through your interest in the illustrative examples which you may have occasion to use. Do not fail to keep in mind the fact that the examples are examples, and not the chief subjects of attention.

You have heard some of those tedious talkers who begin to give you an account of something and are distracted from the line of their narrative by a hint which comes up in the course of their talk. They lose the point of the story and they lose the advantage of the secondary line of discussion as well. The same thing is true of the sort of false correlation which we sometimes see practised in arithmetic. The lesson starts out bravely as a lesson in arithmetic, but it gets confused by its own illustrations, and at the end of the period it is neither arithmetic or anything else.

The only true principle of correlation is to have one main line of interest at a given time and cluster examples about that main line, never for a moment allowing the chief consideration to be lost sight of. At some stages of school work the only way in which it is possible to maintain such a clearly defined line of thought and work is to give relatively little in the way of distracting illustrative thought to be mastered. In the early grades of school it is not well in a single day of school work to approach the same object from too many points of view. Let the children have a fair opportunity to become acquainted with one aspect of a situation before you thrust another upon them. If it is an example in arithmetic, the objects should be simple, and should be chosen for their availability to illustrate as simply as possible the facts of number relation.

We shall never economize time in our school programs if we fail to recognize this fundamental principle of arrangement, that certain lines of instruction have at times the right of way. It is only by arranging arithmetic with reference to the demands of arithmetic, that we shall ever get over that subject completely. How long do you suppose one would have to wait before all the possible number relations came up "incidentally" in connection with a course in manual training? Almost indefinitely. If we want our arithmetic to be in any sense of the word complete, we shall have to force examples into the course at times for no purpose other than to give a complete view of number relations. The teacher who does not recognize the right of arithmetic to be taught as the main line of consideration, and to be taught at times in a forced way, is simply turning back from the rationalized order of school training to the purely accidental order of the natural environment.

Of course a child can get training by the purely incidental method, but it is like the training of the savage. Such training is never complete. The training of the street gamin is also of this type and it is never complete. Within the limits of their natural experience, savage and street gamin may be ever so acute, but their unsystematic training has never prepared them in an all-round way for a full, broad grasp of any subject. A full, broad grasp can come only from taking up sooner or later a systematic, rather than the purely natural, order of study. Our arithmetic of to-day is suffering in some quarters from a giving up of the idea of completeness. We are too often satisfied to deal with those number relations which appear incidentally rather than with all the number relations in their completeness.

There is, of course, a sort of seeking after immediate completeness which is absurd. The old Grube method which aimed to treat every possible phase of a single number before passing on to the next, was mistaken in its devotion to such immediate completeness. Completeness does not mean that the child shall go through a subject at one sitting, or in the absolutely logical order. Let the order be flexible so far as it can be, but let the teacher be ever aware of the need of making this flexible order ultimately complete. If the teacher will hold the situation clearly in mind and will resolutely set out to make the work in arithmetic lead to completeness of training in number relations, the path to that completeness may be varied by this or that reasonable bending. The warning which we need these days is not to get out of sight of the main line of training. Do not forget that there is a body of number relations and that these are worth teaching.

The second suggestion which I have to make is one which I realize is out of harmony with some of the seemingly general tendencies of the times. But I shall nevertheless venture the suggestion, and you shall judge of its soundness. If it be true that the race has found it advantageous to establish certain fixed orders of counting; and if it be true that the race has spent a great deal of time in discovering certain series of consistent relations; and if it be true that the children need to have these series of established relations firmly fixed in mind—then there is nothing which we as teachers can do to make a royal road to all these possessions which the race offers the child. The child must exert himself to acquire these fixed orders and these discovered consistencies. The child must be drilled into line and must learn to march according to the rules of the army. If he is not drilled, he may learn how to straggle along by himself, but he will never get the full advantage of his social inheritance. All this means that some of the facts of the science of number have to be made automatic by diligent and long-continued practise. We shall have to give up our bright dream that the hard ways of school life can be made easy. These ways may be made less difficult perhaps by judicious preparation and by careful subdivisions of the task to be completed. But the work of learning consistent number relations as they appear in the multiplication table, for example, can never be escaped.

The third suggestion which I have to make is that the teacher will never find a better opportunity to cultivate the power of abstraction or to study the development of that power than in the teaching of arithmetic. Like all abstract thought, arithmetical thought must be based upon concrete experiences. We can not expect the children to acquire the control of highly abstract modes of thought suddenly. There must be a gradual detaching of the process of thought from the particular objects to which the thought is applied. We have been working at this problem in the past without recognizing always just what we were doing. Our method has been to apply a given process of number manipulation first to one concrete situation and then to another, depending on the child's mind to arrive ultimately at a kind of general mode of thought. We have too seldom directed the attention of our pupils to the processes themselves. This can be done, however, very successfully, even at an early age. Thus, one can lay a group of blocks before children in even the first year and ask them to think how they could divide them into groups without actually making the division. Then one can go a step further and ask the children to close their eyes and think how they would divide the blocks. To be sure, this is not a very high degree of abstraction, but it is abstraction begun. I think the true value of the Speer method is not in what Mr. Speer calls the ratio idea, so much as in the fact that the children have to think divisions into the blocks where there are in reality no divisions. Whenever you teach a child to think a division where there is no division, you have taken a step in the direction of cultivating his power of abstraction.

The training in abstraction must not stop at these early stages. A form of number manipulation which is sufficiently freed from the objects to be transferred to the fingers, is not yet fully developed, as we all know from our recognition of the evils of the counting-on-the-fingers method. Nor is abstraction complete when every problem of number relations has to be thought out in terms of any concrete objects other than the fingers, as for example, blocks. The watchful teacher who uses the Speer method, knows that the time comes when the next step in abstraction means the freeing of the children from even the blocks. The number processes must stand out by themselves. This is what accounts for the pause in the development of children trained by any of the concrete methods. They come to a certain stage of development where abstraction is necessary for further progress and then the inevitable mental struggle has to be made to pass on to the higher processes.

If some teacher would make it his special study to find out how children can be assisted in cultivating the power of abstraction, he would perform a great service for the science and practise of education. There have been a good many theories of abstract thought in psychology and none of them seem very helpful to the teacher, and about all that we do now in a practical way seems to consist in keeping children at various examples and in waiting for the abstraction to work itself out. Perhaps we may learn some day how to call the attention of the children more to the process itself. For example, I think even in such advanced problems as interest, we might advantageously take a little time to show the children that the fundamental combination of processes is the same whether the base and rate be given, or the base and interest. At the more elementary stages of the study, we should similarly make a distinction between the concrete factors and the fundamental relations. One method is that which I described a moment ago of thinking out divisions without actually making them. But in any case, abstraction is not easy for the children, and we must make some effort to help them in carrying it out. Let us see if we can not gather some new observations on this subject so that we may do more than throw the children blindly on their own resources in this difficult matter.

We must close this discussion of arithmetic with these general suggestions. They are all of one type. They all center about the fundamental pedagogical principle which it has been our aim to illustrate in each of our discussions. That fundamental pedagogical principle is that the teacher should first understand the inner nature of his own mental processes and seek in his own understanding of these processes the methods of teaching. It is futile to study children unless we undertake the kind of study which the biologists call comparative study. Comparative study consists in taking various specimens illustrating different stages of development, and comparing them so as to find out their likenesses and unlikenesses. This discovery of the likenesses and unlikenesses, gives the only true basis for an understanding of the process of development. A study of child life without an application of the comparative method is a veritable groping in the dark. It has no sure footing and it has no definite outcome. It has no sure footing, for we do not know whether or not external expressions of the child mean what our external expressions mean. It has no definite outcome, for our study of children can never be undertaken with a view to keeping children at their present level. We want to elevate and develop them. And before we can answer the question of what we want to elevate them into and develop them into, we must study the higher as well as the lower stages of mental development.

There is a passage in Wundt's Outlines of Psychology which I shall quote to you in closing, for it states the case with all clearness and with the high authority of one who is undoubtedly one of the leaders of scientific thought in our day. Wundt writes:[1] "For these reasons it is an error to hold, as is sometimes held, that the mental life of adults can never be fully understood except through the analysis of the child's mind. The exact opposite is the true position to take. Since in the investigation of children and of savages, only objective symptoms are in general available, any psychological interpretation of these symptoms is possible only on the basis of mature adult introspection which has been carried out under experimental conditions. For the

---

[1] Outlines of Psychology, second English edition, p. 330.

same reasons, it is only the results of observations of children and savages which have been subjected to a similar psychological analysis, which furnish any proper basis for conclusions in regard to the nature of mental development in general."

CHAPTER X

SOME LIMITATIONS OF OUR NATURE

IN this last chapter I shall bring together several miscellaneous topics which should be included in our teacher-study, and shall also review briefly the ground which has been covered in the earlier chapters. Our present task is to gather up the loose ends and main lines of our thought so that we may secure a general grasp of the nature of teacher-study and may carry away some clearer recognition, I hope, of the importance of continuing this study in every-day class-room work.

For want of a better title for these miscellaneous topics I have called them all, discussions of the limitations of our nature. That may sound like a rather discouraging subject with which to close what has aimed to be throughout an optimistic view of school life; and it would be a discouraging subject if there were not means of bridging over these limitations. I believe there are such means, and that is why I shall call your attention to these particular limitations. If there are other limitations of which any of us are conscious and for which no means of correction are in view, let us consider them in secret. In public we shall think only of these limitations which can be overcome.

The first limitations of the teacher's nature which

are important for our consideration are those which grow out of the fact that we, and all our ancestors, were originally made to live outdoors where the air is free, and the ranges of vision are long, and the light is strong and well distributed and shaded by the soft colors of nature. We are not in our natural environment when we find ourselves shut up in small closed spaces which are insufficiently ventilated and lighted, and where we are set about accomplishing confining tasks.

Take for example, the means which nature has given us of testing the air we breathe. We call it the sense of smell. This sense of smell is nature's sentinel at the portal of our lungs. Any foul gas which should not pass this portal is challenged by the sentinel and a general alarm is sent to headquarters. But the poor sentinel finds himself quite unable to cope with the hard tasks set for him in the schoolroom. Have you never come into a badly ventilated schoolroom from the fresh air of outdoors and noticed at once the warnings given by your sense of smell? But stay in that room a few minutes and the protests grow fainter and fainter and finally you breathe the foul air without any consciousness of its impurity. If you had been in the room from the early morning, and the air had gradually grown impure, it would have been quite impossible for you to notice the gradual process of deterioration. Nature's sentinel at the portals of the lungs is a very imperfect guide in the artificial rooms in which we live. If we lived in the open air where changes are of no importance unless they are sudden and marked, it might be different. But nature can not make a man suited for the outdoor conditions of life and yet have him suited to artificial indoor life as well. What is to be done in such a case? Obviously, there is only one course to follow. Recognize the limitation of one's nature and prepare to meet it. If you can not depend on your sense of smell to tell you when a room is filled with impure air, then adopt some other safeguard quite as artificial as the room itself—get a ventilating system.

The trouble with most of us is that we are not convinced of the limitations of our natures. It seems to be useless to produce statistics. That has been done time and time again and has proved beyond the shadow of a doubt that the ordinary teacher, in any schoolroom not provided with adequate means of ventilation, is breathing impure air and is allowing the children to breathe impure air. I think the most convincing argument which could be brought to bear on most teachers would be to have them go outdoors for a short recess each day in the winter just before school is out, and let them come back with their natural air-testers in condition to act for a short time in an artificial environment, and let them in this way get an individual realization of the air they had been breathing all day.

Or turn to another illustration and note how nature was limited in the production of a natural thermometer. Suppose you felt the cold of a winter day as keenly all the time you were outdoors as you do when you first go out of a warm room. The cold of a winter walk would be simply excruciating. As a matter of fact, nature has arranged our temperature sense in such a way that we soon get adapted within wide limits to the surrounding air, and do not feel cold and warmth except when there is a sudden or extreme increase or decrease of the surrounding temperature. You do not feel cold on a spring day when the temperature is 60°, nor hot on a summer day when the air is 80°. The skin has adapted itself to the surrounding air. The scientist expresses this fact by saying that the skin has a fluctuating or adaptive zero. This skin zero goes up or down within wide limits with the atmosphere, and we do not notice anything but sudden change above or below the skin zero. The practical application of all this you know. The teacher forgets about the temperature, and his sense of temperature does not warn him, and the temperature gets up above 80°. The result is that everybody gets restless, and work does not seem to be easy—all because nature could not make us into good thermometers and at the same time fit us to be comfortable in the various temperatures in which we have to live at various times.

Take still another limitation of our natures. Nature did not give us any sense at all with which to recognize changes in the amount of moisture in the air. Most of us never know, except in extreme cases, anything about humidity. We know it is humid when everything is damp, and matches will not light; and we know it is dry in rooms where furniture warps and cracks; but we do not know about the lesser changes, and we do not recognize any of the changes directly through our senses. And yet there is many a day when the throats and mucous linings of our pupils are suffering from the parching of the dry air of the schoolroom. Nature expected when she made animals and men to live out of doors that the ordinary atmosphere would have at least enough humidity to keep the mucous membranes from drying up. Nature never provided the proper senses to go with steam-heating plants or furnaces.

When it comes to the sense of vision what havoc we have made with nature's plans! Many of us are reaping the rewards in the artificial supplements to nature which we wear to indicate the effects of indoor life on eyes. Nature ought to have attached some sort of a fatigue-recorder to eyes. As it is, we use our eyes under the most adverse conditions. We concentrate the eyes on fine print. We try to see in dark corners for which only owl's eyes are made in nature's scheme. We sit facing the strongest light in the room. We do almost everything imaginable, just because nature never attached this fatigue-register to our eyes. We get a headache in the end, but even that is not labeled so that we may know where it came from. We squeeze our eyes literally out of shape, but the eye is the one thing the shape of which we can not see, and so we do not know it is deformed until the oculist tells us.

Finally, if we overwork with our eyes, we who teach seldom get enough exercise with the rest of our muscles. The muscles should have been provided with an exercise-gage if nature had been fitting men to do most of their work at desks. But here again nature prepared the simpler methods of knowledge to fit the simpler stages of life, and left us to work out the more complex problems of our more complex life with higher forms of knowledge.

I hardly need to dwell longer on these lines of consideration. If you will not see that a higher form of knowledge is demanded of you than that which comes to you through your senses, then further argument will not convince you. And as to the means of meeting all these limitations, you are referred to the very excellent treatises now in existence on personal hygiene and school hygiene. We can not go into the details of this study now. The study of one's own nature gives many hints as to realms of desirable knowledge beyond, and one of the natural sequents of our teacher-study is, as I hope you see, a perusal of hygiene. Do not think you can get on without this enlargement of your world of knowledge. You will never do your full duty as a teacher until you learn to surround your pupils with healthful conditions of air and heat and light, and nature did not provide you with the necessary senses to accomplish all this without study.

Let us turn now to a second line of thought which has been discussed here and there throughout this course. What can the teacher with all his and her regular duties, hope to do in the way of actual study of the problems appropriate to the profession of teaching? Generally, teachers have been urged in answer to this question to take up some line of child-study.

Child-study has been something of a disappointment to the world at large. There are a few enthusiasts who seem to be satisfied with the results, but in general the results have to be recognized as rather meager. I think one can understand the limitations of much of our child-study. In the first place there has not been enough preliminary teacher-study. It has been the aim of this whole book to convince you of that and so I shall not dwell on this necessary preliminary to child-study any longer. The limitations of child-study to which I wish to call your attention now are those which appear in the very problems which have been attacked and in the methods which have been employed. If we could get a new view of the productive problems and methods of this study, I believe much might yet be done for child-study.

One of the general problems which has been very prominent in the minds of those who have undertaken the study of children has been the problem of ascertaining the time when certain traits of character and certain instinctive forms of action first show themselves in the child's life. Such a study of the time facts of mental development can be undertaken only in one of two ways. Either the history of a single child is carefully followed, and then the result will not be a general formula applicable to other children, or a large number of cases are brought together in what is known as an average time for a whole class of children. This average time is, however, just as inapplicable to the single child as the history of the single child was inapplicable to the whole class. Indeed, it is a familiar principle of all statistical inquiry that average results hold true only for masses, not for individuals. Thus, when we say that the average life of man is thirty-three years, this has no meaning whatsoever for the individual. It means only that while some individuals die young and others die at an old age, the general average of all lies between the extremes. Note that we are not denying that for certain broad general purposes there is value in statistical inquiry, but we are stating that the value of such inquiries is not in their immediate utility for the teacher who deals with small numbers of children and who should, in an ideal educational system, deal with these children as individuals.

Our criticism of child-study is not, however, directed merely against the method, it is directed also against the choice of the problem. It makes very little difference after all at what moment a certain event occurs. If you want to understand the inner character of an event you must go about the study of the conditions which lie back of the event. Science is interested in the time of an event only in so far as the time helps to locate and define the underlying conditions. Law courts sometimes inquire into the time of events, but they want the time, not for itself, but for the purpose of discovering through the location in time what the causes were which produced the fact.

The only legitimate reason for inquiring what a certain child does at a certain time, or for inquiring at what time the child shows a certain trait, is that we want to make use of this time fact in order to understand the real inner nature of the child's development. But we shall get at this problem of the inner development of the child's nature much more directly and completely if we neglect very largely the mere time facts and attack the main problem of the analysis of the child's mental nature. One can see the evil results of neglecting the analysis and seeking dates and times only. The time investigation usually gets at nothing but superficial expressions. Furthermore, it is a matter of practical observation that a child will, when ripe for a new step in his progressive life, frequently fail to show this fact by any external sign. If we are attending merely to the time problem and its superficial determinants, we shall make a twofold mistake. In the first place, we shall get our time wrong because we shall not see the inner trait in question when it first really began to exist. And in the second place, we shall be hindered in doing the most advantageous thing for the child by the absorption of our interest in the earlier or later appearance of a mental condition which we should very often not wait for but actively engage in producing. A careful examination of the disagreements that appear in the results of various studies of children, can leave little doubt that most statistical averages of children's habits contain a large number of cases in which the external manifestation of characteristics has been delayed for a period, thus rendering the average time too late for the real demands of natural education, and consequently vitiating the results entirely and rendering them wholly worthless to the teacher.

The really important question for the teacher is this: What are the conditions that must be fulfilled before the mind is prepared for a new step in development? Or to make the matter concrete, suppose one is about to teach fractions, the question is not, "When is the child going to exhibit a natural interest in fractions?" It is rather, "What are the mental conditions which will make it natural for interest to arise?" The time when a phenomenon takes place is significant only in so far as the appearance of that phenomenon shows that certain conditions have already been fulfilled. What we must know are the conditions. If we know the conditions and can control them, we can then produce the phenomenon at such a time as we may deem appropriate. And I take it that it is in very large measure the business of educational endeavor to produce certain processes of mental development at a rate which is more rapid and in a way which is more economical than that in which the same result would have been accomplished without supervision.

Such a knowledge of the conditions of the child's development can best be gained through concentration of attention on some single definite phase of mental development and through a close analysis of the succession of conditions actually appearing in such development. Study the way in which your children progress in writing or arithmetic, or whatever you please. Do not take up all these subjects in the same year, but divide the work, and concentrate each year on one particular cycle of growth and study it carefully and fully.

This is the sort of child-study which I hope may issue from our review of teacher-study. Let the dates of nascent periods go. Never mind at what age abstract thought begins. Do not even devote yourselves to a determination of the date when the pupils of your grade pass from the state of "savagery" into that of "barbarism." The dates will take care of themselves if you know how to recognize and manage the conditions of mental life at those periods.

A third line of thought which I wish to touch upon briefly concerns our relations as workers in the broad field of education. We have taken up these chapters from different points of view—you from the point of view of practical school life, I from the point of view of the university student of science. There are some of you I know, for I meet such people in every company of teachers, who look with some degree of misgiving on the universities and the work they are trying to do by way of studying education. And I am very sure that there are a great many university men who doubt seriously the propriety of our taking up this close relationship with the schools.

The fact is, universities and public schools have been separated by a wide breach ever since there began to be universities and common schools in our occidental civilization. The universities, as you know, came first, and represented at the time of their origin, as they have down to a very recent date, the spirit of exclusiveness and specialization. The universities were attended by the ruling class, and the priestly class, and later by all those connected with the so-called learned professions, but they were not attended by the common folk. The influences that emanated from the great centers of learning in Europe reached the people only in the most indirect way.

The result of this exclusiveness was twofold. In the first place, the universities, removed from the activities of common life, cultivated a form of study and a form of training that was highly artificial. There came to be a conventional university spirit which in its worst forms was, and is, arrogantly boastful of its remoteness from the people. And while the universities were thus withdrawing more and more into the narrow circles of their own exclusiveness, the effect upon the common man was the cultivation of a feeling of disrespect for an institution that did not deal more directly with the common, practical affairs of life. And even to-day it is not difficult to find business men, and men in many other walks of life, who sneer at the university.

When the common school began its long struggle for establishment and recognition, it was, in its very birth, and because of the attitude of the universities, an institution at variance with the universities. The common school came to embody the ideals of the common man, it fitted his needs and prepared for his workaday life. University men regarded the people's school as so fundamentally different from the university that in the older civilizations of Europe even to-day we have the spectacle of two distinct systems of education: one for the boys who expect to attend the universities and through the universities to enter upon the professions, the other system adapted so far as may be to the non-university class—one might almost say the antiuniversity class—the common folk.

The antithesis between university and common school has unfortunately been seen in our own land which boasts so often of its freedom from caste distinctions. To be sure, we have done more than any other nation to remove this antithesis, but we have it yet. The institution of our American educational system which more than any other has shown the effect of this struggle between the spirit of exclusiveness on the one hand, and the spirit of practical helpfulness to the common people on the other, is our American high school.

The history of our high schools is a most remarkable educational record. The old Latin schools of colonial times were distinctly preparatory schools for the highly specialized universities of that day. The common people did not attend either Latin schools or universities. But the pressure from the common schools was very great, and soon there began to arise in distinction to the Latin schools, academies and general high schools which were equipped to give the common people more advanced training than they could receive in the common schools, but in a spirit and form differing from that exhibited in the Latin schools. The public high school of to-day is a compromise between the university preparatory school, or Latin school, and the academy or general high school. Its influence has been great in remodeling our university life and in remodeling also the life of our common schools. The breach between the plain man and the proud academic scholar has not been healed by this high school, standing as it does between them and reaching out toward both, but certainly the difference is less than it used to be, and compromises are easier to make, and revisions of educational creeds more frequent, because of the influence of this high school in which we are all interested.

But while the high school has done much toward establishing unity where there was before division, yet the careful student sees all too clearly that unity and harmony are not yet at hand. The traditions of centuries are yet alive. New forms of subdivision threaten our system. The high school is not practical enough, says the plain man once more, and he endows a technical school. The university is too abstract, let us have engineering departments, and schools of agriculture and schools of forestry. And the academic man in his turn shrugs his shoulders at the new professors of "corn-planting and wood-chopping," and breathes out the wail, "It is learning's decline! Let us withdraw once more into our academic exclusiveness!"

All this lack of harmony finds most emphatic expression in the views held by school men on the matter of the training and securing of teachers. Who among us has not heard the criticisms launched against university graduates, who, fresh from the flights of academic experience, have sometimes shown themselves deplorably incompetent to walk along the practical paths of school life? And, on the other hand, who among us has not noted with approval the plea of this or that great educator for the better training of teachers, and for the more frequent attendance of our common school-teachers on the courses offered by the university?

We all of us know perfectly well that in the presence of such a fundamental lack of harmony there is no use of one party trying to put the other out of court. The facts are that our educational system is not a unit and never can be a unit as it now exists. I shall not seek to gain the ends of harmony by asking you to give up altogether your belief that there is something wrong with the university, nor shall I tell you falsely that the university is coming to accept your modes of thought and teaching as its own. What I have to say is by no means as final as that, and yet it is, I believe, more hopeful for the future of American education than either of those propositions would be.

What is true, is that the universities are rapidly taking up the work of making a thorough study of all phases of education. The universities see, no less clearly than the teachers in the schools, that our American system is not a unit, and they have finally been frank enough and clear-headed enough to say that the whole problem shall be opened for full examination and revision. In this task of canvassing the whole situation, the universities ask the schools of other grades and interests to join. No intelligent word on educational problems escapes the careful students of education in our American universities to-day. Indeed, very many of our universities have gone further. They have undertaken to organize within themselves practical departments for the special study of education. All over the country are growing up departments of education, or teachers' colleges, within the universities.

I can speak only with somewhat less assurance of the spirit on your side. But I am profoundly in error if I do not observe the same tendency among the more progressive leaders in the schools. Certain it is that the modern normal school is taking up its task in a much broader and more comprehensive way than did the normal school of a few years ago. Certain it is that the books which teachers read in these days are not so much as they used to be mere collections of devices. The indications show clearly enough that teachers are studying *education*, not merely their own grade work, and not merely formal methods.

All this is more hopeful for the future than any lazy agreement between the schools and the universities could possibly be. If the lack of unity in our American system has set us all thinking, then lack of harmony has not been by any means an unmixed evil, and lack of harmony will not last very long after the study and thinking begin on all sides.

What I have said in regard to universities and schools in general, I shall now take the liberty of repeating in regard to our relations to each other. I would not seek to tell you in any dictatorial fashion how to teach your classes. I offer to you university-made studies on education. I want to insist that you recognize the fact that study carried on in a university may include material gathered from every source from which educational facts can be gathered. I wish you to understand especially that we study your kind of education in the universities. I have made bold to ask you to follow the processes by which some of us work out our views about the schools, and then I leave this material with you. I am quite willing to have you subject it to criticism. I am quite willing to have you improve upon it. As I understand it, that is the way in which we are to work out the salvation of American education, by contributing each the kind of material he has at hand. The main exhortation I would leave with you is, study education. I shall be glad, of course, if you can accept some of my lesser exhortations. But I shall not insist so much on those.

I shall, however, do my duty by my minor exhortations as well as by my main proposition. I shall add a brief summary of each of the chapters so that you may see the conclusions clearly after all the details have been removed.

I. Teacher-Study, its Scope and Aims

In periods of change in educational methods, teachers often find it difficult to adjust themselves to the new order.

Teachers need to study their own education at such times. Their own capacities and their own difficulties are quite as important to understand as are the needs of their pupils.

A study of the teacher's education will also throw much light on the character of the mental development of pupils.

Some very good illustrations of the teacher's present state of mental development may be borrowed from the study of ordinary perception of space.

Length as we see it, depends on the character of the surroundings and on the individual's mental standards, both of which may vary. Illusions are figures which are so new and so complex that we interpret their lines in a way different from that in which we should interpret the same lines if they appeared in simpler figures. Practise with such complex illusory figures makes it possible to overcome entirely the illusion. Thus, it is shown by direct experiment that practise may modify one's way of seeing lengths.

Direction and size are recognized in the same way as length.

If one can find new possibilities of self-study in such a simple case as this, the further pursuit of teacher-study certainly promises to bring to light material worthy of examination.

II. How Experiences are Consolidated into Interpretations of Meaning

The images that strike the eyes, and the sounds that come into the ears, are not attended to for their own sakes, but are interpreted in such a way as to concentrate attention on their broader meanings.

Developed mental life of all forms, is constantly dealing with meanings. Sometimes the meanings attached to experiences are right, sometimes they are wrong. When wrong the distinction between experience and interpretation becomes very obvious.

Education consists very largely in training in the recognition of the true meanings of experiences.

Meanings arise from experience, but they are not due to mere memory, that is, mere retention of experiences in their original forms. Meanings are consolidated experiences—experiences stripped of their unnecessary and non-essential factors and reduced to their lowest terms. Meanings can be learned only by working over and sifting experiences for oneself. Consolidation of experience may sometimes go so far as to leave behind no possibility of revision or enlargement. This is to be avoided by a judicious combination of memory, or retention, with consolidation.

III. The Origin of Some of our Educational Ideals

The absence of immediate results makes the teacher's work largely dependent on ideals. Ideals are sometimes blindly borrowed from tradition or from wholly outside sources. The teacher's ideals are to be regarded as consolidated social experiences. They represent the fixed, and often unreasoned, forms of educational thought.

For example, it is very difficult to account rationally for many of our accepted traditions of school order and instruction.

The reform of traditions can be effected economically and advantageously only by a careful examination, first, of the grounds of present practises, and secondly, of the true foundations of rational practises.

The changes in our course of study demand most urgently such rational consideration. Nature-study, for example, and especially manual training, can not be rejected because of any lack of agreement with earlier traditions of school life. Perhaps it is the traditions which should be rejected. This is clearly the case with our traditional attitude toward bodily movement. All our modern science shows that earlier ideals were at fault in their sharp separation of mental and bodily activity. Bodily activities parallel mental life at every point. It is necessary for us to modify our ideas of activity so as to include certain inner activities and certain constant external activities which often escape attention.

IV. The New Ideals of Development

The gradually disappearing traditions of the past are making place for the new ideals of development.

Development is most fully understood in connection with the bodily life of animals and man. Individual variations from the parental type are the first steps toward development. Advantageous variations are favored by natural selection. The variations thus selected are transmitted from generation to generation. This process of development ends in the adaptation of a species or individual to the environment.

Social habits are transmitted, not through structures, but through imitation.

At the beginning of development an individual is neither good nor bad, he is simple unadapted to his environment. Development begins thus with possibilities of either good or bad. Our whole notion of the child's moral character is coming to be determined by this view.

Mental development consists in a change of a very fundamental type in the character of mental activity.

Development is usually non-rational, that is, not guided by any consciousness of the ends to be attained. Such non-rational development in the child should be guided by a teacher who is conscious of the course and ends of the child's progressive changes. The teacher thus becomes the rationalizing factor in the pupil's mental development.

V. Individuality, Adaptation, and Expression

Development would not be possible if all individuals were alike; there must be variation. The highest form of individuality, the type to be cultivated in the school, is not attained by making all children alike, but by fostering advantageous variations and cultivating different individuals along the lines most appropriate to their various capacities.

Not refinement of functions, but the fitting of functions to the environment, is the end of development. It is possible to be over-refined in certain directions. In working out the ideal of adaptation, the term environment must be broadly interpreted. It should include more than merely scholastic subjects, or technical interests. Especially must the environment of the child in the schools be extended so as to include the broad social life accessible only through indirect modes of knowledge.

The modern ideal of training is that it can be attained only through activity, not through mere receptivity. In the acquirement of knowledge, the senses are active; attention and feeling are conditioned by activity; memory and the formation of ideas are dependent on practical interests.

The activities of the child have not, up to this time, been sufficiently investigated—thus a broad field of productive study opens up to the individual teacher.

VI. The Teacher's Writing Habit

Writing is, first of all, an organized movement. The various fingers that hold and move the pen, and also the hand, and the arm, all contribute to this movement, but they do it in such a way as to cooperate with each other in a single well-coordinated act.

The index-finger is most active in downward strokes, the thumb, and in less degree the middle finger, guiding. In upward strokes, it is the thumb that does most of the work, the two fingers guiding. Such coordinated action is the result of organization in the nervous centers. This organization is a result of gradual growth and not of arbitrary willing.

Individual differences in nervous organization show themselves in the different forms of writing, and may be demonstrated by means of experiments showing the different parts played by fingers and hand in different individual cases. Even in the same individual, the coordination may be modified by changing conditions.

An effort to develop greater regularity in the slope of one's writing brings out the fact that there is a phase of movement—a slight pronation—especially important in securing regularity of slope. This is not a subject of direct attention as a movement, but is developed through a blind series of trials and failures during which attention is directed chiefly to the written lines. This brings us to the general question of the direction of attention. In developed automatic writing, it is on the thought. In undeveloped writing, it is on the written forms.

VII. Racial and Individual Development of Writing

Racial development does not furnish any direct suggestions as to the proper sequence of work in the school, for the child must be adapted to a wholly different environment from that which the race faced. Racial development, however, shows the aim of development and some of its difficulties, in such a way as to give indirect suggestions advantageous to the teacher.

The race began with picture-writing. This gradually gave way to writing which imitated sound language. Ultimately, a sound alphabet was developed. The present forms of letters are due to a series of developments in which the character of the writing material, the demands for rapid, easy movement, and the demands for legibility, beauty, and expression, have all been operative.

The child's movements are at first uncoordinated, uncertain, and discontinuous. This is due to the fact that the nervous system is unorganized, and impulses are diffusely discharged. The diffuseness appears, not only in the irregularities of hand movement, but also in the movements of head and body which accompany writing. Diffuseness is the first stage of all development of movement.

Practical suggestions. Large free exercises should precede writing. Organize all the movements of all parts of the body. Give play to individual coordinations very early, and aim at the development of these coordinations as the chief end of the training. Make the child critical of his own writing.

The problem of the meaning attached to written words brings us to the next topic, Reading.

VIII. The Process of Reading

Modern methods of teaching reading aim to cultivate the ability to recognize meaning as rapidly as possible. This leads sometimes to a failure to recognize the stages of the reading processes preliminary to recognition of meanings. And such failure to recognize the process, is all the more dangerous because in adult life the process is automatic and therefore not a subject of attention.

The process of reading is a very active process in that it requires active adjustments of the eye and active response in the organs of articulation.

The process of reading is complex in that it requires

a recognition of the elements of words and their fusion into single wholes. This kind of mental synthesis undoubtedly comes to include, in the highest stages, not merely single words, but whole phrases.

The synthesis of elements into single wholes as we have it in the recognition of words, gives us a clue to the process of synthesis by which words and meanings are combined into unitary wholes. The active element in such a case as the latter must always include factors other than the mere articulation movement. Emotional reactions are obvious in the rate and intensity of articulation itself and in accompanying phenomena. Other reactions of a less obvious kind also appear.

Meaning can be grasped only in terms of individual reaction. This is the lesson of practical, rather than purely theoretical, verbal training.

IX. The Idea of Number

A study of the development of the number idea shows that in its elementary form it was very ancient. In its fully developed form it depended on the relatively late discovery of certain special modes of numerical expression and manipulation.

What, then, is the specific characteristic which makes the number idea distinct from all other forms of thought? Number is an expression of grouping, and number processes are processes of regrouping. Thus, 7 plus 5 equals 12, means that given two small groups, one of seven, the other of five, we may group them together in a single large group of 12. Other processes are of like character.

The number idea is distinct from any of its concrete

applications, so that when a problem in application is presented, it calls for three distinct kinds of thought. First, a recognition of the real relations; secondly, their translation into group ideas, and finally, the manipulation of the groups according to mathematical laws.

Number is abstract. It is a mode of arrangement which may be thought of as applied to any objects whatsoever. Number processes are limited only by the demand that they be consistent with each other. The science of mathematics deals with the consistent modes of grouping objects.

Applied arithmetic should be reasonable in its examples. Never lose sight of the purely mathematical relations. Make your instruction cover these relations completely, and fix these relations thoroughly through drill. Develop the abstraction after starting with the concrete objects. The abstraction is the essential phase of the development.

X. Some Limitations of our Nature

Nature never provided us with senses suited to securing direct knowledge of the artificial indoor environment in which we live. We must use a higher form of knowledge. We must know about proper hygienic conditions through special study.

We can not understand or direct children properly by merely noting the time when they exhibit certain characteristics. We must study the conditions that lie back of the stages of development in which we are interested. This determines the proper lines of study and investigation in child-study.

Our American educational system is not well organized. There are signs of improvement. The most promising indications are to be found in the cooperation of universities and common schools in the study of education.